SOFT FURNISHINGS

SEWING HOME DECOR

NICHOLAS BARNARD

CREATIVE
HOME
ARTS
—CLUB—

CREATIVE
HOME
ARTS
—CLUB—

A DORLING KINDERSLEY BOOK

Project Editor Lee Stacy
Art Editor Gurinder Purewall
Managing Editor Krystyna Mayer
Managing Art Editor
Derek Coombes
DTP Designer Cressida Joyce
Production Controller
Rosalind Priestley
US Editors
Ray Rogers, Barbara Minton

Cover Design, Text, and Production
Julie Cisler, Tom Carpenter,
Michele Teigen

Photography by Tim Ridley
Soft furnishings demonstrations
by Alison Kingsbury

Published in the United States
by DK Publishing, Inc.
375 Hudson Street, New York,
New York 10014

First American Edition 1994
Revised and expanded 2000 by
Walton and Pringle

This edition published for the Creative
Home Arts Club by Dorling Kindersley
in 2003

A CIP record for this book is available
from the Library of Congress

ISBN 1-5815-9192-6

Color reproduced in Singapore
by Colourscan

Printed and bound in China
by Toppan.

CONTENTS

INTRODUCTION

GOOD DECORATING – IDEAS AS WELL AS THEIR IMPLEMENTATION

– CAN TRANSFORM YOUR HOME AND MAKE IT SOMEPLACE

SPECIAL. OF COURSE, FINDING GREAT IDEAS, AND THEN MAKING

THEM HAPPEN, IS ANOTHER STORY. THAT'S WHERE THIS BOOK

COMES IN. SOFT FURNISHINGS (CURTAINS, DRAPERIES, SHADES,

PILLOWS, CUSHIONS, TABLE LINENS, LAMPSHADES, UPHOLSTERY, AND BED ACCESSORIES)

HELP CREATE YOUR HOME'S MOOD AND PERSONALITY. SO HERE ARE DECORATING IDEAS

YOU'LL LOVE, ALONG WITH THE STEP-BY-STEP PHOTOGRAPHS AND INSTRUCTIONS YOU

NEED TO SEW EACH ITEM PERFECTLY. YOU DON'T HAVE TO BE A

DECORATING OR SEWING PRO TO BENEFIT FROM THIS BOOK. ALL

THE IDEAS AND INSTRUCTIONS ARE RIGHT HERE. ALL YOU ADD

IS A LITTLE ENERGY TO BRING EVERYTHING TO LIFE.

TYPES OF FABRIC

YOUR CHOICE OF A FABRIC DEPENDS both on its use and on how it will affect a room's character. Although the range of natural fibers for textiles is essentially limited to wool, silk, linen, cotton, and jute fabrics are available in more textures, colors, and patterns than ever before. This is because manufacturers are able to blend fibers together, and with synthetic materials, to make fabrics that are easier to care for, stronger, and more shrink resistant than fabrics made from only one type of natural fiber. When choosing fabrics, bear in mind the soft furnishing project for which it is intended and whether the fabric is recommended for light or heavy wear.

LINING FABRICS
When you make a window dressing, you may wish to use lining fabric to protect the main fabric from harsh sunlight, add insulation, or provide a neat finish to the draping. Cotton sateen is suitable for lining. Blackout lining will shut out all light. Muslin is a coarse cotton used for inner covers.

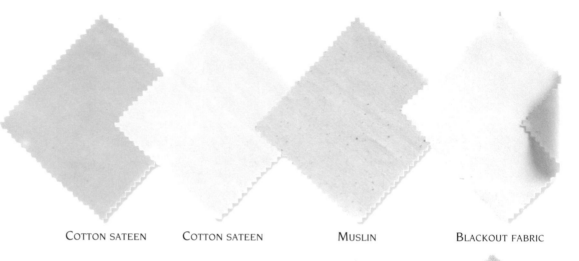

COTTON SATEEN   COTTON SATEEN   MUSLIN   BLACKOUT FABRIC

SHEER FABRICS
These thin and lightweight fabrics are often used as translucent window dressings or decorative edgings. They include nets, lace, batiste, voile, and English embroidery. They gather more easily than thicker materials of a heavier weight, and many are inexpensive. Sheer fabrics are available in a wide range of plain colors, printed patterns, and mixed weaves, and can be difficult to work with.

WHITE BATISTE PRINT   NATURAL BATISTE PRINT   NATURAL COTTON MIXED WEAVE

LIGHTWEIGHT FABRICS
Lightweight fabrics are made from cotton, silk, and synthetic fibers. Like sheers, they are often translucent and can usually be gathered in quantity. If you use silk for a curtain or shade, consider lining it – silk can be damaged if exposed to sunlight for a prolonged period.

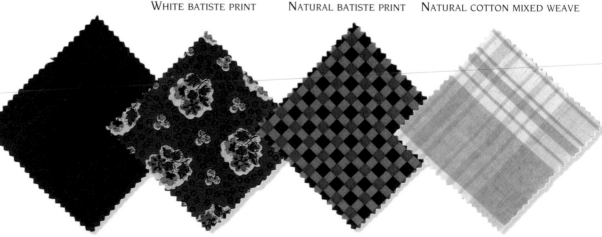

SILK   COTTON FLORAL PRINT   COTTON CHECK PRINT   WOVEN COTTON CHECK

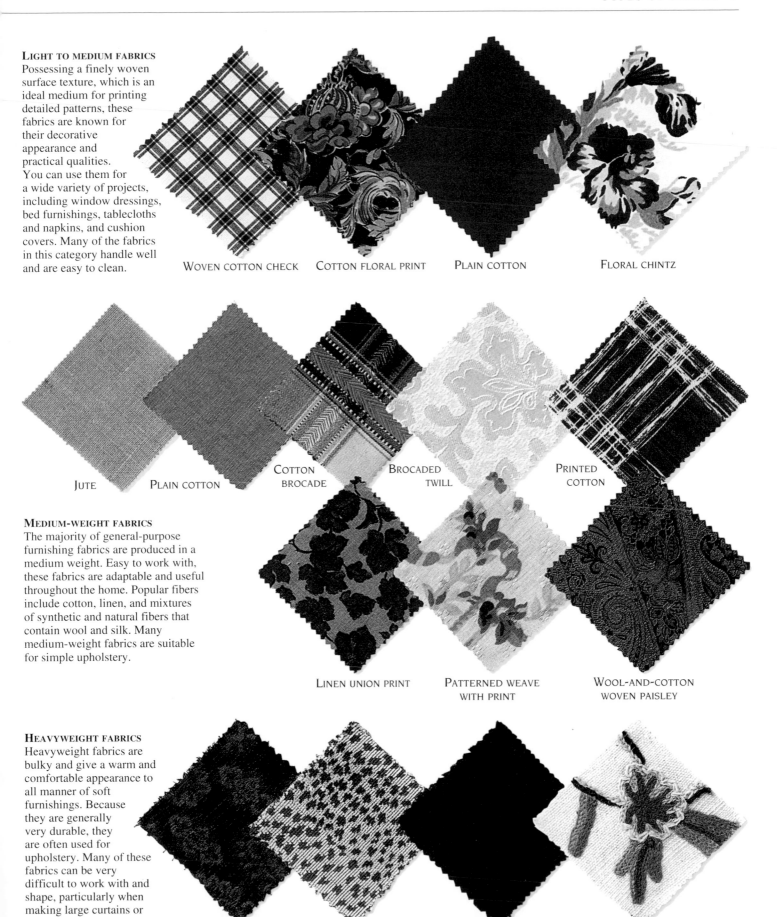

LIGHT TO MEDIUM FABRICS
Possessing a finely woven surface texture, which is an ideal medium for printing detailed patterns, these fabrics are known for their decorative appearance and practical qualities. You can use them for a wide variety of projects, including window dressings, bed furnishings, tablecloths and napkins, and cushion covers. Many of the fabrics in this category handle well and are easy to clean.

WOVEN COTTON CHECK   COTTON FLORAL PRINT   PLAIN COTTON   FLORAL CHINTZ

JUTE   PLAIN COTTON   COTTON BROCADE   BROCADED TWILL   PRINTED COTTON

MEDIUM-WEIGHT FABRICS
The majority of general-purpose furnishing fabrics are produced in a medium weight. Easy to work with, these fabrics are adaptable and useful throughout the home. Popular fibers include cotton, linen, and mixtures of synthetic and natural fibers that contain wool and silk. Many medium-weight fabrics are suitable for simple upholstery.

LINEN UNION PRINT   PATTERNED WEAVE WITH PRINT   WOOL-AND-COTTON WOVEN PAISLEY

HEAVYWEIGHT FABRICS
Heavyweight fabrics are bulky and give a warm and comfortable appearance to all manner of soft furnishings. Because they are generally very durable, they are often used for upholstery. Many of these fabrics can be very difficult to work with and shape, particularly when making large curtains or loose covers.

CHENILLE   LOOPED-AND-CUT PILE   COTTON-LINEN VELVET   CREWEL WOOL ON COTTON

BASIC SEWING KIT

TO ACHIEVE A PROFESSIONAL FINISH for your soft furnishings, proper equipment and a clean, neat work surface are essential. Keep your sewing equipment separate from your other household tools, and use it only for sewing tasks. Having a work surface large enough for the task is vital – when making extremely long curtains, the floor may be the only suitable surface on which to work. Bear in mind comfort when establishing a work area. Sit on a chair with firm support, and position the table high enough to avoid backache. Work in a well-lit room, particularly when there is limited daylight available.

CUTTING TOOLS

Fabric must always be cut accurately to ensure perfect hanging and fitting. Select scissors that are sharp, durable, and comfortable to use. Avoid using fabric scissors for household chores, since they will quickly become blunted. Use dressmaker's scissors for cutting out patterns and fabric, embroidery scissors for cutting detailed work, and pinking shears for neatening raw edges.

EMBROIDERY SCISSORS

DRESSMAKER'S SCISSORS

PINKING SHEARS

IRON AND IRONING BOARD

An iron should be used not only at the finish but throughout the process, for tasks such as flattening seams and hems. Select an iron with a steam feature, if possible: it is not the weight of the iron but the moisture and heat that flattens the fabric. An ironing board should be height adjustable and possess a padded cover that is easy to keep clean.

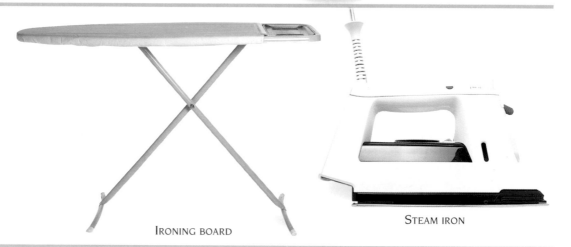

IRONING BOARD

STEAM IRON

SEWING MACHINE

In most cases, a sewing machine is faster and easier than sewing by hand. Modern sewing machines are simple to operate and provide an extensive range of useful options, including straight stitch, zigzag stitch, and reverse settings. Most machines are available with sewing attachments like a zipper foot, which is used for such tasks as securing a zipper to a seam. Keep spare bobbins nearby, and wind the thread on before you begin to work.

BOBBINS

SEWING MACHINE

ZIPPER-FOOT
ATTACHMENT

STRAIGHT STITCH-
FOOT ATTACHMENT

TWIN AND
SINGLE NEEDLES

BUTTONHOLE GUIDE

SEWING EQUIPMENT

Use plain, stainless steel pins or, for greater visibility on the fabric, pins with colored glass heads. For safety and easy access, keep pins in a box or in a pincushion. A wide range of sewing needles is available for fabrics of different thicknesses. A threader facilitates threading a needle. Select thread according to the project, and to the color, type, and weight of the fabric. Tacking thread is available in a range of colors and is easier to break than other threads.

PINCUSHION

HAND-SEWING
NEEDLES

STRAIGHT
PINS

SEWING THREADS

TACKING THREAD

THREADER

MEASURING AND MARKING EQUIPMENT

Accurate measuring and marking are essential for sewing. A stretch-resistant cloth tape measure enables you to work easily around curves and corners. Mark fabric with a clearly visible color that is easy to remove – use tailor's chalk or a vanishing-ink pen for this purpose. Do not press fabric before vanishing ink has disappeared completely. Many soft furnishings require the fabric to be cut at perfect right angles; a large, transparent try square is ideal for helping you to mark right angles accurately.

LARGE
TRY SQUARE

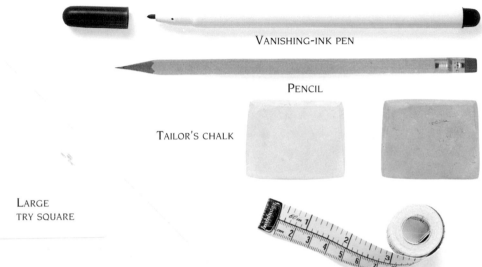

VANISHING-INK PEN

PENCIL

TAILOR'S CHALK

CLOTH TAPE MEASURE

MISCELLANEOUS

A bodkin is a blunt, thick needle with a long eye, used for threading cord, ribbon, or elastic through heavy fabric or casings. Unpick seams quickly and easily using a seam ripper. Clothespins are helpful when you need to temporarily secure fabric to stiff objects such as buckram or a lampshade frame. You can use brown paper, tracing paper, or graph paper for making a pattern or template.

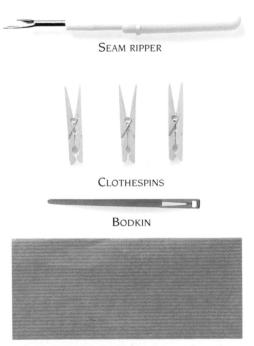

SEAM RIPPER

CLOTHESPINS

BODKIN

PAPER FOR PATTERN MAKING

UPHOLSTERY TOOLS

Few special tools are required when making most cushion covers or simple upholstery. For attaching buttons or tufts to a cushion cover, you will need a long upholstery needle – these are available in a range of sizes. To fit a fabric cover to a simply shaped piece of furniture such as a footstool, use upholstery skewers to stretch and hold the material firmly in place before securing. These upholstery tools should be used only on thick fabric – do not use skewers or upholstery needles on sheer fabric, because they will tear the material.

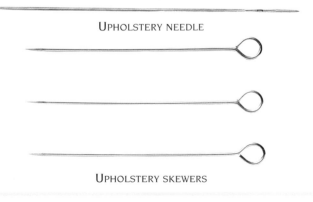

UPHOLSTERY NEEDLE

UPHOLSTERY SKEWERS

BASIC SEWING TECHNIQUES

EQUIPPED WITH GOOD MATERIALS, HAND-STITCHING ON FABRICS

AND MATERIALS CAN BE A RELAXING, SATISFYING HOBBY,

PRODUCING SOME HIGHLY DECORATIVE AND ORIGINAL DESIGNS.

WHERE PROJECTS REQUIRE REGULAR SEAMS, BUTTONHOLES, AND

ZIPPERS, THERE IS NOTHING TO BEAT THE SPEED AND PRECISION OF

A SEWING MACHINE. EVEN BASIC MODELS WILL SIMPLIFY ROUTINE

SEWING JOBS, WHILE THE NEWEST MACHINES, FEATURING

COMPUTER-CHIP TECHNOLOGY, MAKE IT AMAZINGLY EASY

TO CREATE A WIDE RANGE OF EMBROIDERED PATTERNS

AND MONOGRAMMED INITIALS.

CONTEMPORARY CREWEL WORK
Stylized flower and foliage motifs in violet and
lime crewel-work stitching stand out against a
ground of crisp white linen to give a modern
twist to this traditional decorative technique.

HAND SEWING

ALTHOUGH SEWING MACHINES can produce almost every variety of stitch, there are always times when you need to sew by hand. Sometimes a hand-sewn effect is desired, and hand sewing can also complement machine sewing – tacking, for instance, is the best way of aligning and holding together layers of fabric for machine stitching. Needle marks and stitches can be hidden by careful preparation: before undertaking any hand sewing, select the finest needles possible and a thread of suitable color and weight. Right-handed people should work from right to left, left-handed people from left to right.

PINNING AND TACKING

Pinning and tacking is used to hold fabric pieces together before sewing. Pin perpendicular to stitching. Use tacking thread in contrasting color. Remove tacking after sewing.

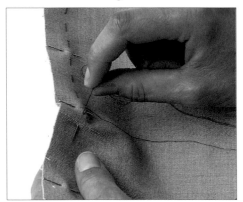

JOINING FABRICS
Pin the fabric pieces together. Secure the end of the thread either by stitching over it or by tying a knot in it. Make all the tacking stitches about ⅜ in (1 cm) long, or alternate stitches ⅝ in (1.5 cm) long at the front with stitches 3/16 in (5 mm) long at the back.

SLIPSTITCHING

The slipstitch is used for hems or where a seam must be sewn from the right side of the fabric: for example, to close the opening through which something was turned right side out.

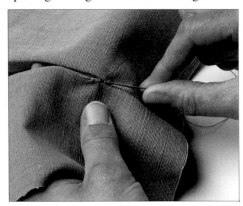

CLOSING A GAP
Secure the thread and take the needle across the opening. Make a stitch 1/16 in (2 mm) long in the seam-line fold. Bring the thread back across the opening and make a similar stitch in the first side. Continue this process to the end, and fasten off in the seam.

TAILOR'S TACKS

Tailor's tacks are used to mark fabrics that need to be joined accurately, or to transfer a pattern mark to one layer of fabric or two identical pieces. Make tailor's tacks with doubled thread in a contrasting color to the fabric. When a number of different marks are needed on one section of fabric, use a different color for each to help you to distinguish them.

1 STARTING OFF Make a stitch about ⅜ in (1 cm) long through the fabric. Pull the thread through, leaving a ⅝ in (1.5 cm) length of thread on the surface. Insert the needle into the first hole of the stitch again.

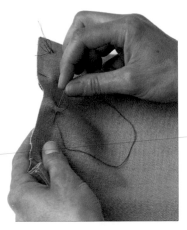

2 FORMING A LOOP Make a second stitch through the same holes. Pull the thread through, but leave a loop of tacking thread large enough to fit around your index finger standing out from the fabric.

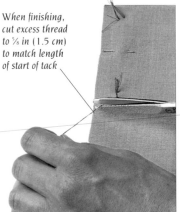

When finishing, cut excess thread to ⅝ in (1.5 cm) to match length of start of tack

3 FINISHING OFF A few stitches make a loop of many threads on the fabric. Finish the tack with the needle at the front of the fabric, and cut the thread to leave an end of ⅝ in (1.5 cm), matching the start of the tack.

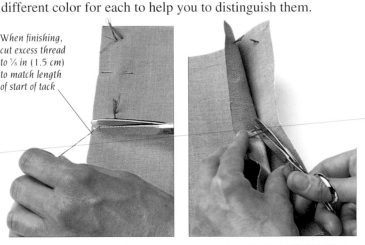

4 SNIPPING THE THREADS If the tacks are marking two layers of fabric, ease the layers apart and snip the threads as above. If they are made through a pattern lying on the fabric, cut the loop to remove the pattern.

LADDER STITCH

The ladder stitch is ideal for joining two pieces of patterned fabric, ensuring that the pattern matches exactly across the seam prior to a more permanent sewing. Essentially, it is tacking the fabric sections together from the right, or patterned, side. Although the ladder stitch may result in a certain waste of fabric, it is an essential technique for achieving a neat and professional finish when joining pieces of patterned fabric. You will need an iron for this task.

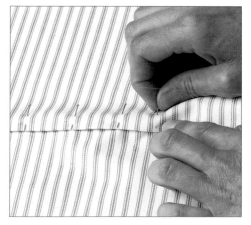

1 ALIGNING PIECES Lay the fabric right side up, overlapping the edges. Fold the edge of the top piece under by ¾ in (2 cm), or more for a heavy fabric. Press the fold, align the pattern, and pin the pieces.

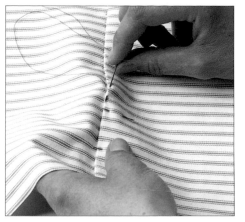

2 STARTING SEAM Thread a needle with tacking thread, and secure the end of the thread on the seam line. Make a stitch ⅜ in (1 cm) long inside the seam-line fold in the top piece of fabric.

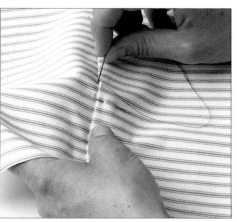

3 FORMING LADDER Make a stitch ⅜ in (1 cm) long in the bottom piece of fabric. Make ladderlike stitches to the seam end and fasten off. Fold the fabrics right sides together, sew, and remove ladder stitches.

BLANKET STITCH

The blanket stitch is used mainly for neatening raw edges of fabric, but it can also be used decoratively. Use a thick thread for decorative blanket stitch, especially if the thread is the same color as the cloth, so that the texture of the edging is clearly evident. Closely worked blanket stitch is used to secure the edges of buttonholes: proper buttonhole thread, which is fine but very strong, should be used for this.

1 MAKING STITCH Make the blanket stitches about ⅜ in (1 cm) in from the raw edge for heavy fabrics, ³⁄₁₆ in (5 mm) for light fabrics, and ⅛ in (3 mm) for buttonholes. Catch the thread behind the needle.

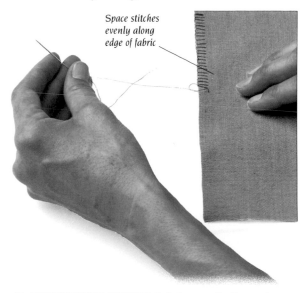

Space stitches evenly along edge of fabric

2 TIGHTENING STITCH Pull the needle through. The caught loop of thread runs along the edge of the fabric before turning into the stitch away from the edge. Tighten gently to avoid puckering the edge of the fabric, and repeat the stitch all along the edge. Space the stitches widely on heavy fabrics, closer on light fabrics, and right next to each other for buttonholes.

BACKSTITCH

This stitch is used for strong, permanent seams, particularly in awkward places such as tight corners, where a machine is difficult to use. It can also be used to sew in zippers, if a machine cannot be used. A backstitch every so often in a hem ensures that even if the hem catches and rips, only a short length will come undone and need resewing.

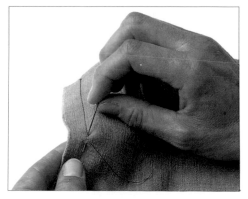

THE STITCH
From the front, make a stitch ⅜ in (1 cm) long. Push the needle to the back of the fabric ³⁄₁₆ in (5 mm) back along this stitch, and bring it to the front ³⁄₁₆ in (5 mm) beyond the stitch. Repeat sewing each stitch into the end of the previous one. At the front, the stitches should be ³⁄₁₆ in (5 mm) long; at the back, they should be ⅜ in (1 cm) long and overlap.

SEAMS

WHEN MAKING ANY SOFT FURNISHING, it is necessary to use a number of specific hand- and machine-sewing techniques to create a durable and neatly finished article. The choice of a suitable seam for joining the pieces of fabric, from a variety that includes French, overlocked, plain, and flat fell seams, is most important. Consider the task ahead before selecting the most suitable method for the purpose and appearance of the seam.

BASIC SEAMING

The plain seam is the most simple and versatile means of joining together two lengths of fabric. Always pin and tack the lengths of fabric together along the seam line before sewing. Neat corners and curves are achieved by cutting and clipping: at a corner, cut away a triangle of fabric; along a curve, cut a serrated edge or snip into the seam allowance.

PLAIN FLAT SEAM

Pin and tack, then position the fabric under the machine needle and clamp it in place with the presser foot. Secure the thread in the seam by sewing forward and backward along the seam line for ⅜ in (1 cm) several times. Sew along the seam as required, and finish by stitching back and forth on the seam line again. Remove the tacking stitches and press the seam open. When using a new stitch or type of fabric, sew a short length of test seam on a scrap first, to check that the machine settings are correct.

CLIPPING CORNERS

At corners, cut across the seam allowance after sewing the seam. Leave about ¼ in (6 mm) between the seam and the cut edge of the fabric, or the seam allowance may fray away when the piece is turned right-side out.

CLIPPING CURVES

Clip a convex seam into a serrated edge, as above, to reduce its bulk and prevent distortion. Snip into the seam allowance of a concave seam to ease the fabric and prevent pulling. Be careful not to cut too close to the seam.

NEATENING RAW EDGES

The raw edges of pieces of fabric should be finished to prevent them from fraying – this is called neatening. It is particularly important on furnishings that will have to endure hard wear. You can neaten a raw edge in one of several ways – by oversewing or overlocking it, by sewing a zigzag stitch along it, by applying bias binding to it, or simply by serrating it with pinking shears.

Probably the easiest and the most commonly used neatening technique is zigzag sewing with a machine. Bias binding ensures that no raw edges are visible. Overlocking also hides raw edges, but you must allow extra fabric for this. When the reverse of a fabric and, therefore, any seams will be visible, it may be worth using a self-neatening seam *(see opposite)*.

MACHINE ZIGZAG

Set the machine to the zigzag stitch and clamp the raw edge under the needle. Secure the thread, stitch along the fabric as close to the edge as possible, and fasten off.

OVERSEWING BY HAND

Make evenly spaced stitches from the back to the front of the fabric, bringing the thread over the raw edge. Do not pull the stitches too tight, or the fabric will pucker.

BIAS BINDING

Unfold one edge of the binding and align it with the raw edge. Pin, tack, and sew on the binding fold. Fold the binding over the edge, and sew through all the layers.

OVERLOCKING

Make seam allowances 1–1¼ in (2.5–3 cm) deep. Trim one to ³⁄₁₆ in (5 mm) after sewing, and fold the wide edge over it, tucking the raw edge under. Pin, then stitch along the fold.

PINKING

Pinking shears cut a serrated edge. Pinking is a quick and easy way to neaten a raw edge, but it is not hard wearing and is therefore best used only on internal seams.

FRENCH SEAM

This is a strong, self-neatening seam that does not show any additional stitching line from the right side of the fabric. It can, however, be used only on straight edges, and you must allow ⅝ in (1.5 cm) for the seam allowances. A French seam is ideal to use if both sides of the fabric will be visible, as is the case when sewing with sheer fabric.

1 FIRST SEAM Pin and tack the pieces of fabric wrong sides together. Machine sew a plain seam *(see opposite)* ³⁄₁₆ in (5 mm) from the edge. Take the fabric from the machine and remove the tacking stitches.

2 TRIMMING SEAMS Carefully trim both of the seam allowances to ⅛ in (3 mm) with a pair of sharp scissors. Turn the pieces of fabric right sides together, fold along the seam line, and press.

3 SECOND SEAM Tack the layers of fabric right sides together close to the folded edge. Sew a second seam ⅜ in (1 cm) from the first (which is now the folded edge), enclosing the raw edges.

4 FINISHED SEAM Remove the tacking stitches and unfold the fabric right side up. The neat seam will be visible, with no stitching evident. Press the seam allowance flat to one side of the seam.

FLAT FELL SEAM

The flat fell seam is extremely useful where both strength and a flat finish are required, which is often the case with upholstery. The stitching will, however, be visible on the right side of the fabric with this seam.

1 SEWING SEAM Sew the pieces of fabric right sides together, ⅝ in (1.5 cm) from the aligned edges. Trim one allowance to ³⁄₁₆ in (5 mm).

2 FOLDING SEAM Fold the wide allowance over the narrow one. Lay both to one side, the raw edge underneath, and tack.

3 SECOND SEAM Sew along the tacking from the right side and press the seam flat. One row of stitches will show.

TOPSTITCHING

This is a simple technique that can be used to emphasize a line such as a seam. A thick, contrasting thread or a long stitch can be used to give more emphasis. Pin, tack, and sew a plain seam, remove the tacking stitches, and press the seam open. Run a line of stitching along either side of the seam from the right side.

QUILTING

Quilting not only provides an extra thickness of insulation, it also gives a decorative finish. Wadding can simply be stitched between the layers of fabric, as here, and the edges bound.

Alternatively, you can tack the wadding to the wrong side of one piece and put the pieces right sides together. Seam on three sides, turn right sides out, and slipstitch *(see page 12)* the fourth edge.

1 MARKING PATTERN Decide on the pattern. Diagonals are simple and prominent, but you might quilt around designs on a fabric. Mark the quilting lines on the fabric with a suitable marker.

2 ASSEMBLING LAYERS Cut the wadding, the backing fabric, and the main fabric to the same size, and sandwich the wadding between the layers of fabric. Pin and tack the layers together.

3 SEWING QUILTING Run lines of tacking across the fabric to hold the wadding firmly in place. Sew along the quilting lines. Remove the tacking and trim wadding out of the seam allowances. Bind the edges.

USING FABRIC

BEFORE YOU BEGIN A SOFT FURNISHING TECHNIQUE, there are a few basic rules that
you need to bear in mind about handling and estimating amounts of fabric. Cutting out fabric
and joining panels are skills that are essential for almost every sewing project. When using
patterned fabric, you must match the design motifs between joins in panels, and between pieces
of fabric that will be positioned side by side, as in the case of curtains. Before you cut out the
fabric, assess the final appearance of the pattern by placing it against the object that it will
cover and adjusting it until the design motif is positioned to your satisfaction.

PLACING THE PATTERN

When you intend to make a soft furnishing using a patterned
fabric, first consider the placement of the pattern in relation to
the item you are decorating, such as a window or piece of
furniture. You should match the pattern across any seams in
the fabric, as well as over panels of fabric. Use a tape
measure to determine the size of the pattern repeat on
a fabric. It is important to bear in mind the size of the
pattern repeat when calculating the amount of fabric.

MEASURING PATTERN REPEAT

Manufacturers indicate the size of
the pattern repeat on the selvage,
or on a ticket attached to the bolt.
To establish the dimension of
the pattern yourself, measure the
distance between identical motifs.

MATCHING ACROSS PANELS

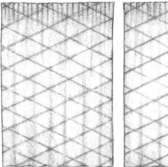

When making a pair of furnishings to hang
side by side, such as curtains, consider how the
pattern matches across the drops. Make sure
the pattern will match edge to edge when the
curtains are closed. Cut out one curtain, then
match the second to the first (see page 41).

PARTIAL REPEATS

When dressing a window with a curtain or shade, it may be
impossible to avoid having a partial pattern repeat at the top
or bottom. For a short curtain (left), place the partial pattern
above the heading and the full pattern at the bottom hem.
A full-length curtain should have a full pattern at the
heading (right) and a partial pattern along the bottom hem.

CUTTING OUT FABRIC

Cutting out fabric is not difficult as long as you are careful and use a sharp pair of scissors.
The most effective and comfortable method of cutting out fabric is to lay it out on a smooth,
flat surface. You may need to use a clean floor as a work surface when cutting out a large
piece of fabric. To cut out fabric accurately, you will need the basic sewing kit.

NOTCHING FABRIC

You may need to join
lengths of fabric from the
bottom edge to the top edge.
To identify the direction of
the lengths, and to continue
any pile or shading from
length to length, cut notches
at the top edges.

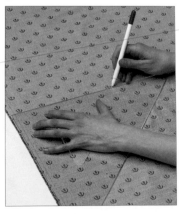

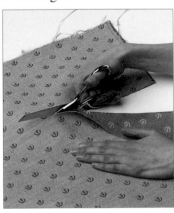

1 **MARKING FABRIC** Fabric
should be cut on the grain –
along the weft threads and
across the warp threads. Lay a
try square at right angles to the
selvage, and mark the cutting
line using a vanishing-ink pen.

2 **CUTTING FABRIC** Using a
pair of dressmaker's scissors,
cut steadily along the marked
line. Some loosely woven fabrics
can be cut following the gap
made by pulling out a single
thread (see page 41).

JOINING PLAIN FABRICS

For most soft furnishing techniques, you will need to join panels of fabric to form a single large piece. Most techniques require joins to be made with plain flat seams *(see page 14)*.

When greater strength or flatness is desired, however, use flat fell seams or French seams *(see page 15)*. To join panels, you will need matching thread and the basic sewing kit.

1 **TACKING PANELS** After the fabric has been cut to size, lay out the panels right sides together, and match their raw edges. Pin and tack the panels together, making a seam ⅝ in (1.5 cm) from the edges.

2 **SEWING SEAM** Remove the pins before machine sewing along the tacked line. Remove the tacking stitches after you have finished sewing.

3 **FLATTENING SEAM** Press the seam allowance flat to smooth the finished join.

JOINING PATTERNED FABRICS

When you are using patterned fabric, you will need to match the pattern repeat across seams. Before cutting out the fabric, decide where you want the pattern to lie when the soft furnishing is complete. Cut out the first piece, then cut the second piece by matching the pattern with reference to the first. Join panels after all of the required pieces of fabric have been cut out. To align the pattern repeat when joining fabric, you will need matching thread and the basic sewing kit.

1 **MATCHING PATTERN** Along the edge of one panel, press a ⅝ in (1.5 cm) seam allowance to the wrong side. Turn the panel over and place the pressed edge on top of the raw edge of the other panel, right sides up. Match the pattern over the panels. Keeping the edges together, fold the pressed panel onto the other panel, right sides facing. Pin the panels together along the fold line.

2 **STITCHING PANELS** Open out the panels, and make sure the pattern remains aligned. Ladder stitch *(see page 13)* along the fold line to temporarily secure the panels together. Fold the panels right sides together again, and sew a plain flat seam *(see page 14)* along the fold line. Remove the ladder stitches.

PLACING JOINS

The placement of joined panels of fabric on or across large pieces of furniture or windows is as important as the positioning of pattern repeats. Place the fabric against the furniture or window, and decide what looks most appropriate for each type of furnishing and fabric. Across a window, place the fabric joins to the sides. For bed and table furnishings, center a complete fabric panel down the middle of the length of the furniture.

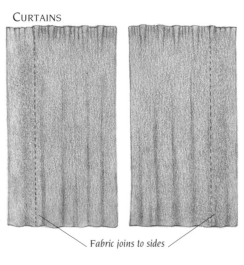

CURTAINS

Fabric joins to sides

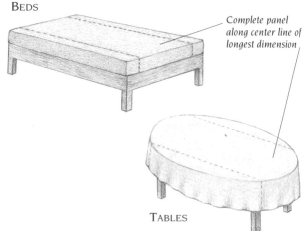

BEDS

Complete panel along center line of longest dimension

TABLES

HEMS AND MITERING

FINISHING A HOMEMADE FURNISHING with suitable hems and correct mitering is an important part of achieving a neat and professional look. The careful preparation and execution of hems is as vital as choosing the right fabric or the best type of seam to use. When deciding on a hem, it is important to select the appropriate depth for the fabric and the scale of the furnishing: deep for large items and heavy fabrics, shallower for lighter fabrics and smaller pieces. Mitering is a vital skill to master, because it is the only effective way of achieving a professionally neat corner on deep hems.

HEMS

Hems can vary from ³⁄₁₆ in (5 mm) to 6 in (15 cm) in depth. If it is not important to hide the sewing, you can sew the hem by machine. Use a straight or zigzag stitch, or (if the machine has the option) a blind hem stitch. For inconspicuous stitching, it is best to hem by hand. Use a thread slightly darker than the fabric: hemming stitches catch the light more than the fabric.

HERRINGBONE STITCH, SINGLE HEM

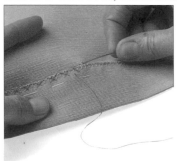

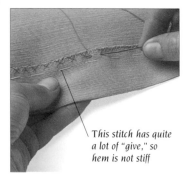

This stitch has quite a lot of "give," so hem is not stiff

1 **STITCHING FABRIC** This method is used for heavy fabrics and on lined curtains. Neaten the edge by oversewing or with a zigzag stitch. Turn the hem up to the required depth, pin, and tack. Secure the thread, and catch up a few threads of the main fabric against the direction in which you will sew.

2 **STITCHING HEM** Pull the needle through. Crossing the thread over the first stitch, push it into the hem farther along. Make a stitch through the hem turning – again, working in the opposite direction to the seam. Repeat this procedure along the hem, with each stitch crossing over the last.

DOUBLE HEM WITH CONCEALED STITCHING

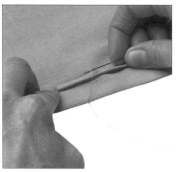

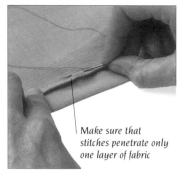

Make sure that stitches penetrate only one layer of fabric

1 **STITCHING FABRIC** This method is suitable for finer fabrics. Turn up the hem to the required depth, press, and turn up by same amount again. Pin and tack a little way from the top. Fold back the top of the hem by ³⁄₁₆ in (5 mm). Secure the thread, and catch up one or two threads from the main fabric.

2 **STITCHING HEM** Sew a small stitch through one layer only of the folded back top of the hem. Continue this way, stitching alternately through the hem and the main fabric. When the hem is finished, fold the top part of the hem flat and press it: the stitching will be concealed within the hem.

TWICE-TURNED AND SLIPSTITCHED HEM

This hem uses less fabric than a double hem

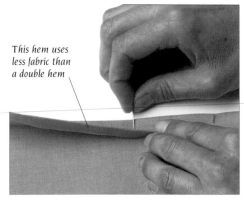

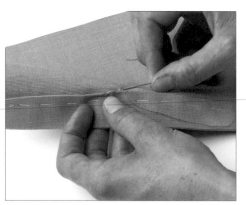

1 **PINNING HEM** Use this method for hiding raw edges on medium-weight and lightweight fabrics. Turn the raw edge up by ³⁄₈–³⁄₄ in (1–2 cm) and press. Turn the edge up again to the required depth, pin, and tack.

2 **STITCHING HEM** Slipstitch the hem by alternately catching up a few threads from the main body of the fabric and making a stitch of ³⁄₈ in (1 cm) in the hem fold. Continue along the length of the hem.

MACHINE-STITCHED HEM

This is a quick way to hem if the stitching need not be hidden – for example, on curtain linings. Turn the hem up to the required depth, as for a double or twice-turned hem, pin, and tack. Machine sew close to the top of the hem.

MITERING CORNERS

Mitering hem turnings at corners ensures a neat and tidy finish, no matter how bulky the fabric. It must be done before the rest of the hems are sewn. Mitering is an important technique and is particularly useful when making curtains. It is not difficult, but the method does vary according to both the type of hem used and the depth of the turnings. Folding the corners to make a miter can be an awkward task with some particularly thick and difficult-to-handle fabrics. Cutting excess fabric out of the corner miters will reduce the quantity of layered fabric and help to make a neater finish.

SINGLE HEM MITER

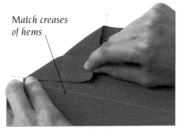
Match creases of hems

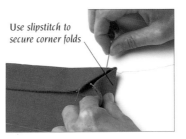
Use slipstitch to secure corner folds

1 MARKING CORNER Neaten the raw edges. Fold the hems to the required depth, one over the other, and press. Mark the points where they cross with a pin in each turning.

2 FOLDING CORNER Unfold the hem turnings. Make a fold across the corner from one pin to the other – the creases from the hem turnings should align. Press the fold.

3 STITCHING MITER Refold both of the hems over the diagonally folded corner to give a neat miter. Slipstitch the corner folds together, and sew the hems as required.

DOUBLE HEM MITER

Fold hems twice. Mark where the one on top falls on the other with a pin. Repeat with the other hem on top. Unfold the second hem folds, fold from pin to pin, press, refold hems, and slipstitch miter.

TWICE-TURNED MITER

1 FOLDING EDGES Lay the fabric wrong side up. Fold the edges to be hemmed to the wrong side by ³⁄₈ in (1 cm) and press the turnings. Fold them up to their required finished depths and press again.

2 FOLDING CORNER Unfold the second turnings and fold across the corner diagonally. Align the second turning creases on the folded corner with the same creases running along the edges. Press flat.

3 COMPLETING MITER Refold the hems along the fold lines of the second turning, with the corner folded inside the hems. Slipstitch the mitered corner and sew the rest of the hems.

CUTTING A SINGLE-HEM MITER

1 FOLDING CORNERS Follow steps 1 and 2 for the single-hem miter. Unfold the fold across the corner, and refold the whole piece of fabric on a diagonal into the corner, with the right sides together and the adjacent sides aligning.

2 CUTTING ACROSS The crease left by the fold across the corner is now folded double on itself. Sew along it, and trim away the excess corner fabric beyond the seam, leaving a seam allowance of ¼ in (6 mm). Press the seam open.

3 TURNING OUT Unfold the fabric and turn the mitered corner right side out. Carefully push out the corner with the end of a pair of scissors: use scissors with rounded, not sharp, tips. Sew the rest of the hems as required.

CUTTING AN UNEVEN MITER

1 TRIMMING Follow steps 1 and 2 for the twice-turned miter. Open the corner. Fold the piece on a diagonal, right sides together, through the crossing of second turning creases, not into corner. Sew across the corner, and trim excess fabric.

2 COMPLETING CORNER Press the seam open, turn the mitered corner right side out, and refold the hems. Carefully push out the mitered corner with the rounded tips of a pair of scissors. Sew the rest of the hems as required.

TRIMMINGS

A VARIETY OF EASY-TO-APPLY edgings can be used for decoration. Trimmings are not structurally important, but when used with imagination, binding, piping, or a frilled or pleated edging can add a smart and individual finish to curtains, pillows, bed linen, or shades. In addition to these hand-finished edgings, there is also a host of ready-made trimmings available, such as braids, fringes, lace, ribbons, and cords, that can be stitched onto or into a seam or hem to provide extra color and texture.

BINDING AND PIPING

These edgings add both decoration and strength to soft furnishings. Binding is made from strips of fabric that are cut on the bias – a line diagonal to the grain, or weave – and will not pucker on curves. Ready-cut bias binding can be bought in a variety of weights and colors, but it is easy to cut strips from most kinds of fabric. Piped edging is made by covering a length of piping cord with strips of bias binding. Piping cord is sold in a range of diameters, suitable for different furnishings and weights of fabric. Always preshrink piping cord and bias strip by washing them.

BIAS STRIPS

Snip off corners of pressed seam to reduce bulk

1 FINDING THE BIAS Check that the edges of the fabric are cut along the grain. Fold the fabric diagonally, so that one straight raw edge lies parallel to the adjacent edge. This fold is the bias line. Press in place.

2 MARKING STRIPS Calculate the length and the width of binding needed – allow extra for joins. Rule measured lines parallel to the bias crease, marking with vanishing ink or tailor's chalk, and cut the strips.

3 JOINING STRIPS Join strips by placing them right sides together at right angles to each other. The raw edges and the straight grains should align. Pin, tack if necessary, and sew ³⁄₁₆ in (5 mm) from the raw edges.

4 TRIMMING JOINS Open the seam and press it flat. You now have a bias strip with two corners sticking out at the seam. Snip off these corners. Join pieces as necessary to make up the required length of strip.

CONTINUOUS BIAS STRIP

 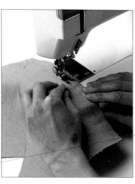   

1 FINDING THE BIAS This is a useful way of making a long length of bias binding. Take a rectangle of fabric with straight edges, and fold one short side down diagonally to meet the adjacent edge. Press in place and cut along the bias-line crease.

2 SEWING PIECES Lay the triangle on the other piece, right sides together and short straight edges aligned, so that when sewn they will form a diamond. Sew the pieces together, using a plain seam with a ¼ in (6 mm) allowance, and press the seam open.

3 MARKING STRIPS Lay the fabric right side up. Mark lines parallel to the bias across the whole of the fabric, spaced to the desired width for the finished strip. Use a straight edge and either vanishing ink or tailor's chalk to mark the lines on the fabric.

4 FORMING A TUBE Fold the fabric right sides together, aligning the marked edges. Align the ends of the marked lines, offsetting them by one: they will form a spiral. Pin along these edges to form a tube: the seam will spiral. Turn the tube right side out.

5 CUTTING A STRIP Check that the bias lines on the pinned edges meet. Turn the tube inside out again, tack, and sew a plain flat seam ¼ in (6 mm) from the edge. Press the seam flat. Starting at one end, cut along the marked line in a continuous spiral.

COVERING PIPING CORD

1 **MEASURING CORD** Choose a cord and wash to preshrink. Measure around it and add 1¼ in (3 cm) for seam allowances: this is the width of bias strip that is required. Cut a strip to this width and the required length.

2 **COVERING CORD** Lay the cord along the center of the wrong side of the bias strip. Fold the strip over the cord, and pin and tack. Sew close to the cord, using a zipper attachment if you use a machine.

APPLYING PIPING

1 **PINNING PIPING** Cut and cover the required length of piping cord, adding 4 in (10 cm) for joining lengths if necessary. Lay the piping on the right side of one piece of fabric, with the raw edges aligning. Pin in place, snipping the seam allowance at corners, and tack.

2 **SEWING IN** Lay the second piece of fabric on top of the piece with the piping attached, right sides together and raw edges aligning. The piping will be sandwiched between them. Tack and sew through all the layers close to the cord, using the zipper attachment.

JOINING PIPING STRAIGHT ACROSS

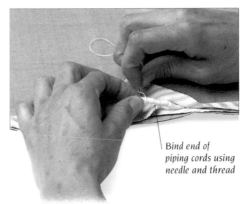

Bind end of piping cords using needle and thread

1 **THINNING CORD** Sew the piping to the right side of one piece of fabric. Allow a 1 in (2.5 cm) overlap, and leave 2 in (5 cm) of each end free. Open a few stitches on each end to reveal the cord. Unravel the ends, and cut half the strands from each.

2 **BINDING CORD** Twist the ends of the cord together and bind with thread. With the piping ends flat and wrong side up, fold one end to the wrong side by ¼ in (6 mm). Lay the other end of the binding on top of it and trim the overlap to ⅝ in (1.5 cm).

3 **SEWING JOIN** Fold the overlapping ends of the binding around the cord. Sew along the seam line, over the join, securing the piping to the fabric. Slipstitch the join in the binding. To disguise a join, make it at a seam or in a central position on a panel.

JOINING PIPING DIAGONALLY

Use this method to give least conspicuous join possible in piping

1 **MATCHING UP** This is the neatest way to join piping. Sew piping to the right side of one fabric piece, with a 4 in (10 cm) overlap free and with seam unpicked. Fold back the corner plus ¼ in (6 mm) of one end of the bias strip diagonally, on its straight grain, and press.

2 **PINNING BIAS STRIP** Lay the other end of the bias strip on top of the folded end. Make sure that the straight grain of the two ends matches, and that both ends lie flat. Carefully pin the two pieces of bias strip together along the fold in the bottom end.

3 **JOINING ENDS** Tack and sew along the pinned fold line, and trim off the excess fabric from the ends of the bias strips. Press the finished seam flat. Unravel the ends of the piping cord, cut strands away from each to thin them, and twist them together.

4 **FINISHING JOIN** Stitch and bind the two ends of the piping cord together securely with a needle and thread. Fold the diagonally stitched bias strip over the bound piping cord ends. Tack the joined piping to the main fabric, using a zipper attachment if machine sewing.

FRILLS AND PLEATS

Frills are most often used on bed linen and throw pillows. Use single frills for a delicate effect, double frills for a robust finish or for furnishings with different fabrics on each side. Frills need from one and a half to three times their finished length in fabric: gather heavy fabrics gently, light ones more tightly. Pleats, which need two and a half to three times their finished length in fabric, give a formal look. Use tailor's tacks *(see page 12)* to align pieces, and allow extra fabric at corners.

SINGLE FRILL

Cut a strip of fabric to the width and length required, allowing extra fabric for the seam you choose for joins. Hem the bottom edge by hand or machine, as shown here. Neaten the top edge of the fabric and gather it using one of the methods shown here.

DOUBLE FRILL

Double thickness of fabric gives this frill body

Cut a strip of fabric to the length required and to double the finished depth plus 1¼ in (3 cm). Join lengths as necessary and press the seams flat. Fold the strip in half lengthwise, wrong sides together, and press. Gather the fabric through both edges.

HAND GATHERING

Use small stitches for fine or close gathering

1 GATHERING STITCH Use this method for medium- to heavyweight fabrics and double frills. Using a strong thread, tie a knot in the end that will not pull through the fabric. On the seam line, make stitches as if tacking, adjusting the length to suit.

2 GATHERING FABRIC When you reach the end, hold the free end of the thread firmly. Ease the fabric toward the knotted end to the correct length and fullness, and knot the free end. Even the gathers out and pin and tack in place.

MACHINE GATHERING FOR LIGHTWEIGHT FABRICS

1 LONG STITCHING Set the machine to the longest stitch. Slightly increase the top tension to make the gathers easy to pull up. Sew ⅜–⅝ in (1–1.5 cm) from the edge, leaving the end free.

2 GATHERING FABRIC Run a second row of stitches close to the first. Pull up the free ends of the threads, making sure that the secured ends stay in place. Knot the gathering threads.

MACHINE ZIGZAG FOR HEAVYWEIGHT FABRICS

1 SECURING THREAD Cut a piece of strong thread or fine twine to the length of the fabric band, and lay it on the band about ⅝ in (1.5 cm) from the raw edge. Carefully zigzag over it.

2 MAKING GATHERS Stitch over one end of the strong thread several times, and gather the fabric by holding the free end and easing the fabric along toward the secured end.

SINGLE- OR DOUBLE-LAYERED KNIFE PLEATS

Pin each pleat close to its edge

1 MAKING A SAMPLE Decide on the size of pleat, make a strip of four or five pleats, and pin and press it. Make the pleats deep enough to give a firm edge, but do not overlap them, except at corners. Measure the length of the sample section.

2 CALCULATING LENGTHS Unpin and measure the strip. Divide the length of edging you need by the length of the pleated strip. Multiply this by the length of the sample piece when unpleated. The result is the length of fabric needed.

3 MARKING PLEATS Make up the edging, joining with plain or flat fell seams as required. Mark up the wrong side with lines for folding as you join the lengths, ensuring that joins will be hidden in the folded back section of a pleat.

4 STITCHING PLEATS Fold the pleats on the lines and pin them. When all the pleats are pinned, tack along the seam line about ⅝ in (1.5 cm) from the top edge. Press the strip. Sew along the seam line and remove the tacking stitches.

BOX PLEATS

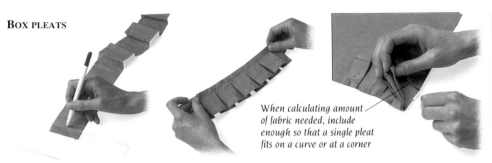

When calculating amount of fabric needed, include enough so that a single pleat fits on a curve or at a corner

1 MARKING UP Box pleats take three times the final length in fabric, so multiply the length to be edged by three for the fabric needed. Mark lines for pleating on the wrong side of the strip.

2 MAKING UP Fold and pin the fabric on the marked lines to form the box pleats. To secure the pleats, tack along the seam line, and press and sew the pleated strip.

3 TURNING CORNERS At a corner, fold the pleated strip, and attach as necessary. The corner fold should run down the middle of a pleat. Finished box pleats make a very formal decoration.

BOWS

A bow can either be used as a simple trimming or act as a fastener. Cut a strip of fabric to the length and double the finished width required, adding ¾ in (2 cm) each way for seam allowances. Fold the strip in half lengthwise. Pin, tack, and sew ⅜ in (1 cm) from the raw edge. Leave a gap in the center of the seam on the long edge to allow for turning right side out, and sew across the ends diagonally. Snip the seam allowances at the corners, turn right side out, and press. Slipstitch the opening closed and tie in a bow.

READY-MADE TRIMMINGS

Fringes, colorful ribbons and cords, and delicate lace can be found in department and sewing stores. Allow for seams, corners, and neatening, and check that trimmings are preshrunk and colorfast if they are washed. If a trimming needs two rows of machine sewing, sew the same way both times, to prevent puckering.

FRINGING IN A SEAM

1 APPLYING FRINGE If there is a line of "stay" stitches on the fringe edge, leave them in. Lay the fringe face down on the right side of the fabric, with the part you will sew through on the seam line. Pin and tack in place, butting the ends at any joins.

2 STITCHING IN Lay the second panel of fabric right side down on top of the first piece and the fringe, aligning the edges. Pin and tack through all three layers along the seam line. Sew along the tacking line and remove the tacking. Turn right side out.

3 FINISHING SEAM If necessary, remove the manufacturer's stay stitches from the fringe by unfastening them at one end and gently pulling them out. Fringes can also be sewn on the edge of a fabric, or over the stitches of a hem, on the right side.

LACE

1 FOLDING CORNERS If lace is sewn into or onto an edge, it must be mitered at corners. Fold it back on itself, right sides together, and press. Fold one end back diagonally, and press.

2 SEWING ACROSS Fold the top end flat on the other again. Pin, tack, and sew along the diagonal fold. Remove the tacks and trim the excess lace. Press, and neaten the edges.

RIBBON

1 TACKING Always mark the position and tack ribbon first. Needles mark some satin ribbon, so tack this at the edges. At corners, fold narrow ribbon, and miter bulky ribbon as for lace.

2 JOINING ENDS At corners, diagonally fold one end under and sew it on top of the other. On a straight length, fold one end under by ⅜ in (1 cm), lay it over the other, and slipstitch.

FASTENINGS

A COVER THAT HAS TO BE REMOVED from time to time for cleaning needs a suitable fastening. Fabrics for removable covers range from sturdy materials suitable for a sofa to fine cottons and delicate textiles used for bed linen and cushions, so take care to match the fastening to the type of soft furnishing. For a heavy-duty closure, use a zipper or sturdy hooks and eyes. More lightweight, decorative fasteners include fabric ties and buttons. Hide snaps and Velcro tabs or strips within a seam. When a cover needs only infrequent cleaning, consider slipstitching one seam, opening it when necessary.

VELCRO

Velcro is also known as "touch-and-close" fastening. Two strips of material, one covered with tiny hooks, the other with small loops, adhere to each other when brought together.

Although easy to apply and use, it is too stiff for light- or medium-weight materials. Continuous lengths of several widths and colors and tabs of various sizes are available.

VELCRO SPOTS

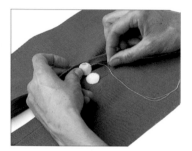

1 **FIRST SIDE** The seam allowance must be wider than the tab. Mark sites for the tabs and pin half a tab to one allowance. Hand sew in place.

2 **SECOND SIDE** On the opposite allowance, align the second half of the tab with the first. Pin and sew in place. Space tabs 2–4 in (5–10 cm) apart.

VELCRO TAPE

1 **FIRST STRIP** Use a tape slightly narrower than the seam allowance. Place one half on the allowance and pin, tack, and sew it in place.

2 **SECOND STRIP** Pin the other half of the tape on the opposite allowance. Check the alignment and adjust if necessary. Tack and sew in place.

SNAPS

Snaps are available in both metal and plastic, and in a limited variety of colors and sizes. They are sold either loose, to be stitched on individually, or mounted to a tape, which is more convenient for long openings. Although they are a simple

means of fastening two edges together, snaps are not very sturdy and will pop open under any moderate strain. They are suitable for bed linen and throw pillows, where they can be unobtrusively mounted for a neat finish.

SEW-ON SNAPS

1 **THE SOCKET** Mark positions ¼ in (6 mm) from the edge with pins every 2–4 in (5–10 cm). Place the socket of a snap on the seam underlap, and work a few stitches through each hole.

2 **ALIGNING HALVES** Place the ball half of the snap on the overlapping fabric in the position marked by the pin. Check its alignment with the socket half, and sew in position.

SNAP STRIP

1 **FIRST STRIP** The seam allowance must be wider than the strip. Turn under the raw edges on the ends of the strip, position it on the seam allowance, and pin in place.

2 **ALIGNING STRIPS** To align the two strips accurately, lay the second one on the first and close the snaps. Pin the second strip in place, working from the back, and turn under the raw ends.

3 **SEWING ON STRIPS** Open the snaps and tack and sew both edges of the strips. Work in the same direction each time to prevent puckering, and use the zipper attachment on a sewing machine.

HOOKS AND EYES

Hand-sewn metal hooks and eyes are a simple fastening for edge-to-edge or overlapping fabric pieces. These easy-to-hide fasteners are available in a number of different sizes, and are sold either loose or mounted on a plastic strip. They are strong enough to take quite considerable strain, making them particularly suitable for furniture covers.

INDIVIDUAL HOOKS AND EYES

1 **THE EYES** Mark positions for the fasteners with pins every 2–4 in (5–10 cm). Hold the eye in place, and sew five or six times through each metal loop.

2 **THE HOOKS** Check the hooks' alignment. Stitch over the hook neck and through the loops. If the seam allowances gape, slipstitch the edges.

HOOK-AND-EYE STRIP

1 **FIRST SIDE** The seam allowance must be wider than the strip. Neaten the raw edges of the strips. Place the eye strip on the allowance and pin, tack, and sew in place. Use a zipper attachment if necessary.

2 **SECOND STRIP** Fasten the hooks and eyes to align the strips. Pin the hooked strip from the back, undo the hooks, and tack. Sewing through both layers of fabric will leave visible stitching. If sewing through one layer only, slipstitch the seam allowance to prevent gaping.

TIES

Fabric ties make an unusual change from ready-made fasteners. Flat fabric ties are easily made up and attached and make a decorative fastener for lightweight furnishings such as bed linen and throw pillows. Rouleau strips are narrow tubes made up from bias strips, which can be tied or mounted as loops along an opening as an alternative to buttonholes.

FLAT TIES

Cut across inner corners diagonally to reduce fabric bulk

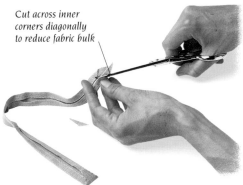

1 **CUTTING ENDS** Cut the length and twice the width of the tie, plus ⅜ in (1 cm) all around. Fold the edges of the long sides to the wrong side by ⅜ in (1 cm) and press. Cut across the corners diagonally and fold the ends down to wrong side. Press.

2 **SEWING** Fold fabric in half lengthwise, wrong sides together. Pin, tack, and sew all sides, about 1/16 in (2 mm) from edge. Make up the other tie. Pin one end of each tie to each side of the opening, sew in place, and tie into a bow or knot.

ROULEAU STRIPS

Needle and thread will help to ease fabric through tube

1 **SEWING A TUBE** Fold the required length of bias strip, using a strip 1–1¼ in (2.5–3 cm) wide, in half lengthwise, right sides together; press and sew ¼ in (6 mm) from the edge.

2 **ATTACHING THREAD** Thread a large, blunt needle with strong thread or fine twine. Secure the thread to one end of the rouleau and push the needle into the opening of the tube.

3 **TURNING TUBE** Work the needle and thread along the tube and out at the other end. The end of the rouleau will follow: take hold of it and pull the tube right side out.

4 **FINISHING STRIP** Snip the thread from the tube, and tuck the raw edges of the rouleau back to the inside. Oversew the ends neatly with small stitches to finish off.

BUTTONS

Although they are associated with clothing, many buttons are eminently suitable for soft furnishings. They are made from plastic, wood, leather, and shell, or may be fabric-covered.

Buttons can be both functional and decorative. They are not very strong, so use them where they will not receive a great deal of strain: bed linen and throw pillows are ideal.

BUTTONS WITH SHANKS

1 **MARKING UP** Mark up for buttons and buttonholes, and make holes. Check the button position through the hole, and secure a thread.

2 **STITCHING ON** Sew on the button, making stitches through the hole in the shank. Make 12 to 14 such stitches before fastening off.

BUTTONS WITH HOLES

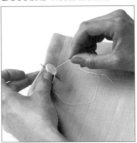

Sew parallel stitches over a pin under the button. Take out the pin. Wind the thread around the slack to form a shank. Fasten off on wrong side.

COVERING BUTTONS

1 **FITTING FABRIC** Cut fabric to cover the button and overlap. Lay button face down on the wrong side, and fold the fabric over the teeth.

2 **SECURING** Snap the back of the button into place. These buttons are sold in a variety of types and sizes. Read the instructions; they vary.

BUTTONHOLES

Position buttonholes and buttons very carefully to prevent openings from gaping. To give a buttonhole strength, make the fastening edge from a double thickness of material and

use the buttonhole stitch. Many sewing machines have a special attachment for sewing buttonholes. For an unusual finish, you can use rouleau loops instead of buttonholes.

MACHINE-SEWN BUTTONHOLES

1 **MARKING UP** Mark the center of the buttonhole and align the button with the mark. Mark the width plus the thickness of the button, plus a little for oversewing the ends of the hole.

Seam rippers are useful tools for helping you start to open up buttonholes

2 **CUTTING OUT** Sew a buttonhole stitch along either side of the mark and across the ends. Cut a hole at the end of the mark with a seam ripper or small, sharp scissors. Cut open the hole.

HAND-SEWN BUTTONHOLES

1 **CUTTING HOLE** Mark the position and length of the buttonhole as required with tailor's chalk or vanishing ink. Use a seam ripper or small, sharp pair of scissors to cut open the length of the buttonhole.

2 **STARTING EDGE** Thread a needle with buttonhole thread. Secure it at one end of the slit; if the hole is at a right angle to the edge, start at the end that will take the strain. Oversew across this end.

3 **STITCHING EDGES** Working in the buttonhole stitch (*see blanket stitch, page 13*), sew closely along one side of buttonhole. At the far end, oversew again. Work along second side and fasten off.

BUTTON LOOPS

First, sew the buttons in place on one edge of the opening. Pin the rouleau strip (*see page 25*) in place along the other edge of the opening, folding it to form loops. Adjust the loops to fit the buttons' size and spacing. Tack and oversew the rouleau in place.

ZIPPERS

Ideal for strength and invisibility, metal and plastic zippers are available in a wide variety of weights, lengths, and colors. They are suitable for all but the most lightweight furnishings.

Metal zippers are strongest, but plastic zippers are available in a wider color range and are more flexible, although you must take care not to damage them when ironing.

CENTERED ZIPPER

 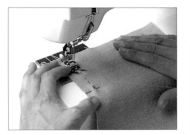  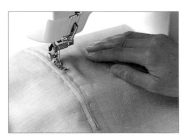

1 POSITIONING Select a zipper for the fabric, taking wear and tear into consideration. Make sure that the zipper is long enough for the task. Lay zipper on the seam line on the wrong side of the fabric, and mark the point where each end lies.

2 SEWING IN Pin, tack, and sew the fabric pieces at both ends of the zipper, starting at fabric edges and stopping at pin markers. Tack the opening for the zipper between the pins closed along the seam line, and press the seam allowances open.

3 PINNING ZIPPER Lay the fabric right side down with seam pressed open. Place the zipper right side down on the tacked part of the seam. Make sure that it is placed centrally, with the teeth lying on the join. Pin and tack the zipper in place.

4 SEWING ON ZIPPER Turn fabric right-side up. Using the zipper attachment on a sewing machine, sew through all layers of fabric around the zipper. Keep the stitching about ⁵⁄₁₆ in (8 mm) from the zipper teeth. Remove the tacking stitches.

OFFSET ZIPPER

1 TACKING IN PLACE Follow steps 1 and 2 for centered zipper. Place zipper on the tacked section and set to one side so that teeth are on one seam allowance. Pin and tack in place.

2 SEWING ON ZIPPER Turn fabric right side up. Using the zipper attachment on a sewing machine, stitch through all layers of fabric around the zipper. Follow the tacking stitches closely.

3 FINISHED ZIPPER Take out the tacking stitches. An offset zipper is less visible than a centered one, so this is a particularly useful way of hiding a zipper that does not match the fabric.

ZIPPER IN A PIPED SEAM

1 PIPED SIDE Lay one edge of the open zipper right side down on the inside of the allowance of the piped edge. Pin, tack, and sew ⅛ in (3 mm) from the zipper teeth, using the zipper attachment on a sewing machine.

2 PLAIN SIDE Close the zipper. Turn back the seam allowances of both edges. Lay the unpiped edge on the zipper to meet the piping. Pin, tack, and sew the zipper in place.

LAPPED ZIPPER AT THE END OF A SEAM

 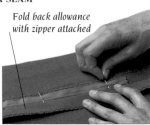 

Fold back allowance with zipper attached

1 PLACING Sew allowances wider than the zipper. Leave opening for zipper at seam end. Fold both allowances to one side. Lay fabric right side up, and fold back top piece. Pin, tack, and sew one side of zipper right side up on bottom allowance.

2 SECOND SIDE Lay the top fabric piece over the zipper, and line up the seam allowances. Turn the fabric pieces over. Pin and tack free edge of zipper to free seam allowance. Turn right side up again, open zipper, and sew along tacked edge of zipper.

3 FINISHED ZIPPER Seam allowances both lie to one side of seam, with the zipper between them, concealed beneath the top seam allowance. This method is generally used for slipcovers on chairs and sofas.

CURTAINS AND DRAPERIES

Because the window is often the focal point of a room, the style, color, and pattern of window dressing can help determine the overall interior scheme. As window coverings, draperies and curtains create privacy, conserve heat, and reduce external noise. There is a huge range of styles and fabrics to choose from, and modern improvements in hardware – rods, poles, rings, and tracks – have simplified curtain-making and installation. Whether you wish to make lined draperies or a simple curtain, a professional treatment is not difficult to achieve.

TAB CURTAIN
This unlined curtain is made from sheer panels of cerise fabric, machine-sewn with hems at the top and sides. The wide fabric tabs are stitched to the reverse side.

CHOOSING A STYLE

THERE ARE VARIOUS FACTORS to consider before making your draperies or curtains. There is an extensive range of fabrics to choose from, the latter determining the kind of hardware to be installed. Begin by examining your practical requirements. Take into account the shape and size of your windows, the need for privacy, and the overall decorative style and color scheme of the room. If you are at the point of decorating the room, you may wish to base everything around the curtain fabric. Bear in mind that curtains and draperies can set the style and mood of a room, and create the illusion of more, or less, space.

BAY WINDOW
(above) Bay windows add depth and interest to rooms but the amount of fabric required for full-length draperies can be expensive. To keep costs down, hang a panel of sheer fabric in the center of the bay to create a natural divide.

OPAQUE PANELS
(left) Simple striped tab curtains emphasize the ceiling and window height, while sheer, ungathered curtains on rods are permanently drawn across the large windows to maintain privacy.

SELF VALANCE
(opposite) To give a softer finish, a wide strip of fabric has been sewn to the top of each panel to produce a valance. When drawn back, the valance falls into the drapery folds, providing a neat finish and an unobstructed window view.

SCALLOPED VALANCE
(opposite) A vibrant gingham check is used to create a valance, while white pom-pom trimming, machine-sewn along the outer edge, stands out in contrast.

SIMPLE SWAG
(below) Attached to the cornice board above the window, this elegant swag conceals the plain curtain heading and track. The swag is lined with a paler fabric to emphasize its classical folds.

BANDS OF COLOR
(above) Two plain fabrics achieve a layered look without excessive frills. A narrow band of caramel-colored fabric, sewn at valance height, makes a deceptive but clever alternative heading. The deep band at the base provides a sense of balance for the full-length windows.

SHELL DETAIL
(left) Ungathered curtain headings are simple to hang from curtain hooks. For decoration, buttons, glass beads, or shells (like these shown here), can be attached to hooks and hung directly from the curtain pole or rod. Curtain hook decorations look best when used with plain voile or lightly woven fabrics for contrast.

CHOOSING A HANGING SYSTEM

BEFORE YOU BEGIN TO MAKE YOUR CURTAINS, you must decide on the type of hanging system you intend to use. It is important to make this decision first, because the hanging system and heading tape that you choose, along with the size of the opening to be covered, determine the measurements of the curtains. For a visible hanging system, choose a rod or pole made of wood or metal. Track systems, by contrast, are usually plastic and designed to be concealed by the curtain heading, a valance, or a cornice.

RODS AND POLES

Rods or poles with matching rings and finials are available in a wide range of woods – painted or natural – and brass and iron, and provide a decorative way to hang curtains. They can only be used to span straight openings. Choose an appropriate thickness of rod or pole to support the weight of fabric. Rods and poles are usually attached to the wall with two supporting side brackets, but when hanging heavy or wide curtains, you should consider attaching an additional central bracket.

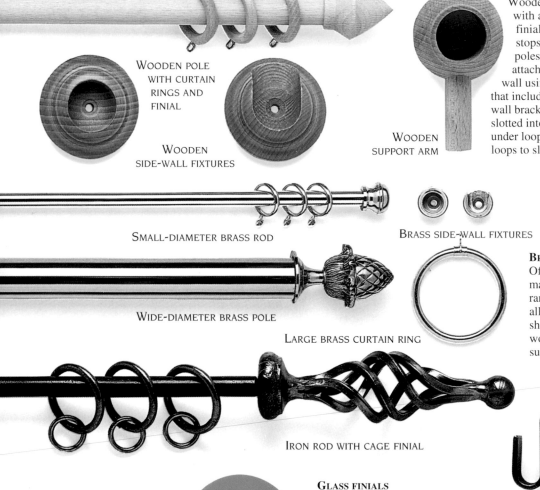

WOODEN POLE WITH CURTAIN RINGS AND FINIAL

WOODEN SIDE-WALL FIXTURES

WOODEN SUPPORT ARM

WOODEN POLES
Wooden poles are available with a range of decorative finials that act as end stops for rings. Many poles are designed to be attached to the face of a wall using a two-part system that includes support arms and wall brackets, but some can be slotted into side-wall fixtures. Tab-top gliders fit under looped curtain headings. They help the fabric loops to slide along the curtain pole without sticking.

TAB-TOP GLIDERS

SMALL-DIAMETER BRASS ROD

BRASS SIDE-WALL FIXTURES

BRASS SUPPORT ARMS

WIDE-DIAMETER BRASS POLE

LARGE BRASS CURTAIN RING

BRASS RODS AND POLES
Of all styles of curtain rod and pole, those made from brass are produced in the greatest range of diameters, making them suitable for all types of curtain fabric, from the lightest sheers to heavyweight insulated curtains. Like wooden poles, they can be mounted with supporting brackets or side-wall fixtures.

IRON ROD WITH CAGE FINIAL

WROUGHT IRON RODS
Iron, like brass, has become a popular metal for making attractive curtain rods. Iron rods are often available wrought to individual order and possess a decorative charm that makes them particularly suitable for elaborate finials. Iron curtain rods are narrow in diameter and strong, making it possible to use them without rings for curtains made with a simple slot heading.

GLASS FINIALS
Glass finials are available in colored spherical, scrolled, and shell shapes and, because they are hand-blown, each one has its own unique decorative surface detail. Glass finials are quite fragile so take special care when dusting.

SIDE VIEW OF IRON MOUNTING BRACKET

BRASS ROD WITH GLASS FINIAL

SIMPLE HANGING SYSTEMS AND TRACKS

When hanging lightweight, stationary curtains, choose a simple support such as a narrow-diameter rod. For other types of curtain and weights of fabric, several systems are available. Tracks can be mounted on a wall or ceiling using multipurpose brackets. Curtains hang from a track on slides with hooks, or combined slides and hooks.

SIMPLE HANGING SYSTEMS
For net and sheer curtains that remain in a fixed position, use a custom-made spring wire or sash rod. Both can be attached to the face of a wall or to a side wall using screw eyes or brackets. Spring-tension rods can be extended to fit a variety of openings.

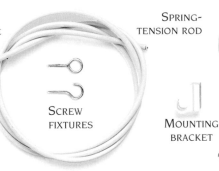

SCREW FIXTURES

SPRING-TENSION ROD

MOUNTING BRACKET

PLASTIC-COATED SPRING WIRE

SASH ROD

PULL-ROD AND CLIP

TRACK WITH CONCEALED SLIDES
This track conceals slides behind a flat fascia. Curtain hooks are inserted into the heading tape and hooked onto the slides. The end stop secures the last curtain hook.

WALL OR CEILING BRACKET

END STOP

TRACK AND SLIDES

TRACK WITH COMBINED SLIDES AND HOOKS
In this system, slides move along the track face and support separate hooks inserted into the tape, or they can be inserted directly into the tape.

END STOP AND WALL BRACKET

COMBINED HOOKS AND SLIDES

TRACK WITH COMBINED HOOKS AND SLIDES

VALANCE ROD
The simplest rod for supporting a valance in front of a curtain heading, with clip-on brackets and linking bars. This is adaptable for any length and shape of window.

COMBINED VALANCE HOOK AND SLIDE

METAL LINKING BAR

VALANCE ROD WITH COMBINED HOOKS AND SLIDES

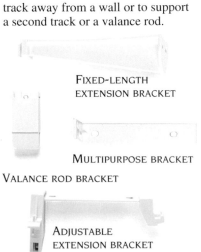

TRACK FIXTURES

Optional fixtures enable hanging systems to fit all openings. Extension brackets can be used to mount a track away from a wall or to support a second track or a valance rod.

FIXED-LENGTH EXTENSION BRACKET

MULTIPURPOSE BRACKET

VALANCE ROD BRACKET

ADJUSTABLE EXTENSION BRACKET

BUILT-IN VALANCE ROD
When making up a matching curtain and valance, it is possible to use a curtain track supplied with a built-in valance rod. This system is easy to assemble and can be mounted either on the wall or the ceiling.

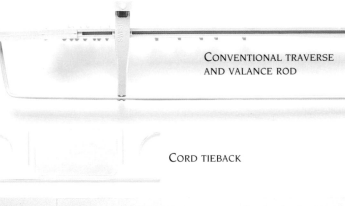

CONVENTIONAL TRAVERSE AND VALANCE ROD

CORD TIEBACK

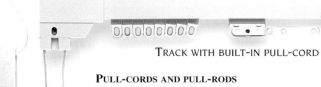

TRACK WITH BUILT-IN PULL-CORD

PULL-CORDS AND PULL-RODS
Track systems are available with pull-cords to ease the opening and closing of curtains, and a cord weight prevents pull-cords from entangling. A master slide with an overlap arm ensures that curtains overlap slightly in the center. Alternatively, pull-rods can be clipped to the master slide at the central edge of each curtain.

HANGING-SYSTEM ACCESSORIES

You may wish to add accessories and fixtures to your curtain hanging system that allow you to completely personalize your curtains. A variety of finials and support brackets is available for use with poles or rods. Similarly, there are several tieback accessories, which can be used for drawing curtains away from windows and securing them to walls.

FITTINGS FOR POLES
Choose from a range of decorative finials and support brackets to use in conjunction with your curtain pole or rod. Brass – or brass-effect – poles in particular can be purchased as lengths of tube, which you can accessorize with fixtures to complement your hanging system.

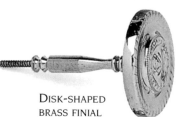

ACORN-SHAPED BRASS FINIAL

SPHERICAL BRASS FINIAL

DISK-SHAPED BRASS FINIAL

DECORATIVE BRASS END-SUPPORT BRACKET

MATCHING BRASS CENTRAL-SUPPORT BRACKET

TIE-BACK HOOKS AND CLASPS
If you wish to use tie-backs that are fitted with rings, you will need a pair of wall hooks to secure the tie-backs to the wall. These curtain accessories are available in both simple and elaborate designs. Alternatively, you can secure a curtain to a wall by means of various styles of metal clasp, or you can hold a curtain away from a window or other opening by draping it over a tie-back arm and knob.

SIMPLE TIE-BACK HOOK

FLEUR-DE-LIS TIE-BACK HOOKS

TIE-BACK ARM AND KNOB

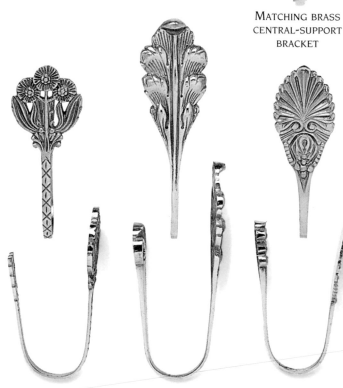

DECORATIVE BRASS CLASPS

CURTAIN HOOKS

Choose hooks best suited to your heading tape. Most ready-made tapes can be hung from universal plastic hooks. Elaborate pleats, however, require divided hooks, while handmade headings need pin-on or sew-on hooks, or even curtain clips, which offer a quick and easy no-sew solution.

STANDARD PLASTIC HOOKS

BRASS SEW-ON HOOKS

PIN-ON HOOKS

DIVIDED HOOKS

CLIPS

MOUNTING HANGING SYSTEMS

WHEN SECURING A HANGING SYSTEM TO A WALL, you should allow enough space for the apparatus to overhang on each side of the opening, so that the curtains can be drawn away from the window. The hanging system should be attached either to the wall or to the window frame. Rods and poles are meant to be seen; tracks are designed to be hidden by the curtain. Always be sure to align the pole, rod, or curtain track so that it is parallel to the top of the opening, or to the ceiling. Use a carpenter's level if your walls and windows are perfectly squared; if they are not, align the hanging system to the opening by eye.

MOUNTING RODS OR POLES

Metal or wooden rods and poles, complete with supports, are manufactured in a range of standard lengths and can be cut to size. First measure the width of the opening and frame, and add enough for the curtains to overhang on each side. Select a pole or rod at least as long as this measurement, and calculate the number of rings needed. Make a series of marks at least 2 in (5 cm) above the opening, and join these with a guideline the same length as the width of the opening, plus the overhang. Mount supports to the wall using a drill with a masonry bit, screw anchors and screws, and a screwdriver.

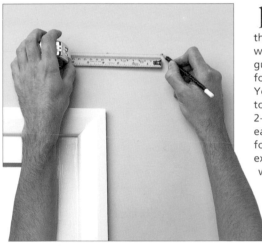

1 MARKING POSITION Mark the position for the wall bracket on the guideline, allowing for curtain overhang. You will also need to consider a further 2–4 in (5–10 cm) at each end of the pole for the finial, which extends beyond the wall bracket. Drill a hole in the mark and mount an anchor in it.

2 POSITIONING BRACKET Align the bracket with the anchor. Screw the wall bracket in place. Mount a wall bracket on the other side of the window. When hanging a long pole, prevent it from sagging under the weight of the curtains by attaching a central-support bracket above the window.

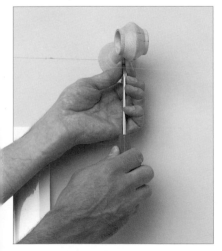

3 SECURING BRACKETS Slide the support brackets into the wall brackets. Secure with the small screws provided. Slide the pole through a support bracket. Place all but two rings on the pole. Push it into position through the second support bracket.

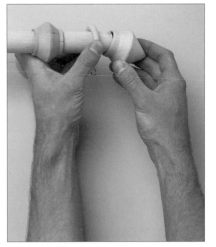

4 ADDING FINIALS Slide one of the remaining curtain rings over the end of the pole and push the finial into place on the end of the pole. Add the last curtain ring and the finial to the other end of the pole. Centralize the pole within the brackets.

5 SECURING POLE Finally, you should drive home the small screw provided by the manufacturer into the hole on the underside of each ring support bracket. Once the small screws have bitten into the wood, the pole will be held securely in position.

MOUNTING A TRACK TO A WALL

Choose the track most appropriate for the heading tape or handmade heading of the curtain *(see page 35)*. Measure the width of the window and add enough for an overhang on each side. If necessary, cut the track to the exact size. Tracks are held in place by small brackets. Use a tape measure, pencil, and straightedge to mark the positions of the brackets on the wall. Mount the brackets in place, using a power drill with a masonry bit, suitable anchors, screws, and a screwdriver.

1 MARKING TRACK POSITION Make a series of pencil marks along the top edge of the window, of equal distance from the ceiling. If mounting the track very close to the ceiling, you must ensure that there is sufficient room remaining for attaching and securing the track.

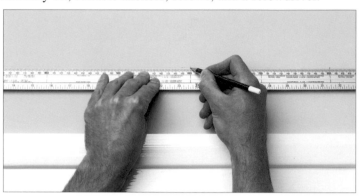

2 MARKING GUIDELINE Using a straightedge as a guide, join the measured marks with a pencil line directly on the wall. Refer to the track manufacturer's instructions to establish the minimum recommended distance between the mounting points for the brackets that will hold the track in place, and mark these on the wall.

3 POSITIONING ANCHORS Beginning at the side of the window, and allowing for the overhang, mark the drilling positions for the anchors with a pencil. Here, the overhang is 4 in (10 cm). The first point for a bracket should be 2 in (5 cm) in from the end of the track. Drill first position mark and push in an anchor.

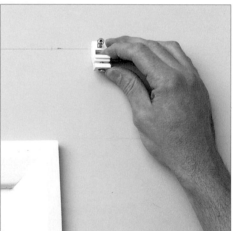

4 SECURING BRACKETS Place the track bracket and a suitable screw on the first fixing point. Lightly push the tip of the screw into the anchor, then drive it home with a screwdriver. Work along the mounting points, drilling, plugging, and screwing the brackets in place.

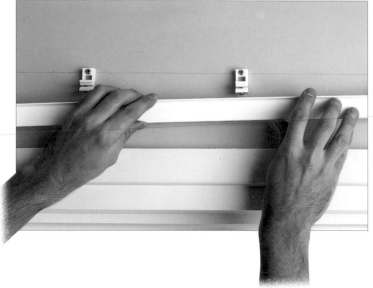

5 POSITIONING TRACK Make sure that each of the brackets is correctly aligned, then clip or slot the track into place. If the track is not centered above the window opening, remove the track and reposition it onto the brackets.

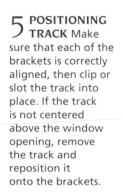

6 SECURING TRACK Once you have put the curtain track in the correct place, secure it to the wall fixtures by tightening the screws on each bracket.

FRAME-MOUNTED TRACK

As an alternative to fixing tracks to a wall, brackets can be mounted onto a wooden window frame, although the width of frame may make it difficult to draw curtains back fully. Mark bracket positions, make pilot holes, and screw brackets in place.

MOUNTING ON THE FRAME

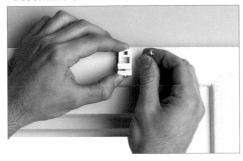

Consult the manufacturer's instructions for positioning the brackets. Mark the position of each bracket. Make a pilot hole in each mark with an awl or, for longer screws, an electric drill and wood drill bit. Push each screw into the bracket and screw it into place.

FRAME EXTENSIONS

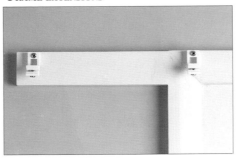

If you wish to draw the curtains away from the window to allow the maximum amount of daylight into the room, you can extend the width of the window frame by mounting a pair of short wooden battens onto the wall. Mount the brackets onto the extensions as before.

SLIDES AND END STOPS

Once the track has been correctly positioned and attached to the brackets, calculate how many slides you will need. You can then slide these onto the track. Fit the end stops or finials. When hanging the curtain, it is a simple task to remove an end stop and add or remove extra slides.

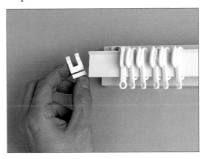

ATTACHING A WIRE TO A FRAME

Sheer and net curtains can be hung across a window or door opening with a lightweight hanging system, such as plastic-coated spring wire. This can be attached by a hook and eye at each end to the side or face of the frame. If you wish to use this system, first mark the positions for the eyes, then use an awl to make pilot holes for the fixtures. Cut the wire to the correct length with a pair of pliers.

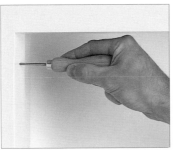

1 MAKING PILOT HOLES Push and twist the awl into the pencil marks on both sides of the window frame to make two small pilot holes to guide the threaded metal eyes.

2 SETTING SCREW EYES Screw eyes into the wood by hand, so that they lie flush with the frame. Measure the distance between the eyes and cut wire to this length, minus the hooks.

3 HOOKING WIRE Screw the hooks onto each end of the wire. Attach one hook to one of the eyes on the frame. Stretch the wire across the window and join the other hook and eye.

PUTTING UP A CORNICE BOARD

First determine the location for a cornice board by aligning it with the window or the ceiling. If the ceiling and window are not parallel, use a level as a guide. Drill into the wall with an electric drill and masonry drill bit. Attach the board to the wall above the window with brackets that are secured by screws and anchors.

1 MARKING DRILL HOLES Center the cornice board over the opening and, using a level as a guide for correct alignment, mark the drilling points through the bracket holes with a pencil. Remove the cornice, drill the holes, and push anchors into them.

2 ATTACHING BRACKETS Place the cornice board on the wall, align the brackets with the correct anchors, and screw them in place. You may need an assistant for a large cornice board.

PLANNING AND PREPARATION

HANGING FABRIC OVER A WINDOW or door creates a strong visual focus in any room. For the most part, the effect of a curtain will determine the character of a room. It is therefore well worth taking plenty of time to plan and prepare the look of a curtain in relation to its window or door opening, and to the whole of the room, before you begin working. The decorative appearance of a curtain is subject to a number of factors other than just the type of fabric that you choose, including the style of the curtain heading tape, the dimensions of the window or door opening, and the width and length of the curtains.

CHOOSING A HEADING TAPE

The type of heading tape determines the curtain's character by governing the way the fabric hangs in folds. Ready-made heading tapes are available in many gathered or pleated styles. They are easily applied to the fabric, and the pleats or gathers are made by drawing up sets of cords within the tape. These folds can be released to allow the curtains to be washed or dry-cleaned flat. Some tapes are constructed with rows of pockets into which the curtain hooks can be inserted.

SHEER AND NET TAPE

This tape forms thin pencil pleats on sheer or net fabrics. It is approximately 2½ in (6 cm) wide. Use standard curtain hooks, or slide a curtain rod through loops in the tape. For measuring, allow twice the track length.

SIMPLE GATHERED HEADING

Often used for small-scale curtains, this narrow tape – approximately 1 in (2.5 cm) wide – forms gathers. When using a track, position the tape to hide the fixture. Allow one and a half to two times the track length.

PENCIL PLEATING

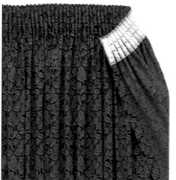

The most popular heading tape, pencil pleating is 3 in (7.5 cm) wide and produces multiple folds in the curtain fabric. Standard hooks can be placed in one of three rows of pockets. Allow two and a half times the track length.

CARTRIDGE PLEATING

Designed to produce rows of cylindrical pleats, cartridge tape, which is 3½ in (9 cm) wide, is suitable for curtains that have a long drop. Use divided hooks to hang this tape. Allow two times the track length when measuring.

TRIPLE PINCH PLEATING

A tape 3¼ in (8.5 cm) wide creates groups of triple pleats. Suitable for curtains with a long drop, it can be used with any fabric. Fit divided hooks into either of the two rows of pockets. Allow twice the track length.

BOX PLEATING

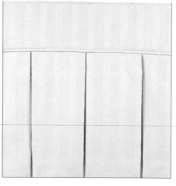

Box pleats can be sewn or formed by tape. The tape is 3 in (7.5 cm) wide, which allows you to hide the track. This tape has two rows of hook pockets, to be used with divided hooks. Allow for three times track length.

SMOCKED PLEATING

To produce a "smocked" effect for valances and curtains, use a heading tape 3 in (7.5 cm) wide. Standard hooks can be placed into one of two rows of hook pockets. Allow two and a half times the track length.

GOBLET PLEATING

Heading tape can be used to form deep, goblet-shaped pleats, which are ideally suited to full, floor-length draperies. You should use metal divided hooks with this heading tape. Allow two times the track length when measuring.

MEASURING

The amount of fabric needed is affected by the width of the opening, type of hanging system *(see pages 34–36)*, style of heading tape, length of the finished curtains, and size of any pattern repeats on the material. For floor-length curtains to clear the floor, deduct ½ in (12 mm) from the track-to-floor measurement (B). To bunch curtains on the floor, add 2–8 in (5–20 cm) to measurement B. For a window sill, hang the curtains either ½ in (12 mm) above the sill (C), or to an apron length of 2–4 in (5–10 cm) below.

The curtain heading should obscure, or stand slightly above, a track. If you are using a pole, curtains should hang just below it. From the curtain top or the hanging system, measure to the bottom edge of the required curtain drop. Add to this 3 in (7.5 cm) for top turnings and 6 in (15 cm) for the lower hem.

To find the fabric width, measure the span of the hanging system (A). If the curtains are to overlap, add the extra necessary. Multiply this by the fullness of the heading tape. Add 12 in (30 cm) for side turnings. Divide this by the fabric width to find the number of fabric panels needed for the curtain width. Round up to the next whole number. For the total amount of fabric required, multiply the number of panels needed by the length calculated above.

SILL-LENGTH CURTAINS

APRON-LENGTH CURTAINS

Floor-length curtains are very good insulators, but should not be hung too close to an electric heater

FLOOR-LENGTH CURTAINS

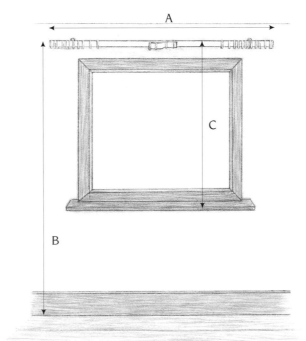

MEASURING REQUIREMENTS
The length of the hanging system and curtain are the bases for calculating the amount of curtain fabric needed. Use a wooden ruler or steel tape measure for accuracy. To calculate the width of fabric, measure the span of the hanging system between the end stops (A). To find the track-to-floor measurement (B), or the track-to-sill length (C), measure carefully, starting from the pole or track. You will need to add or deduct from B or C, depending on the required length of the curtains.

A HANGING SYSTEM LENGTH

B TRACK-TO-FLOOR MEASUREMENT

C TRACK-TO-SILL MEASUREMENT

MATCHING PATTERNS

When calculating the widths for a patterned material, allow for the pattern repeat so that you can accurately match the pattern across the curtain. You should always try to centralize the pattern on each curtain.

MEASURING PATTERN REPEAT

You will need to spread out the fabric onto a smooth, flat work surface and carefully measure the whole of one pattern repeat on the material. You can allow for the matching of the pattern across the seams and from one curtain to another by simply adding a single pattern repeat for each drop of curtain.

CUTTING OUT

Cutting out with accuracy is as important as taking careful measurements. Lay the fabric on a flat surface. Cut square and straight to the grain or, if necessary, the pattern. For cutting out fabric, you will need the basic sewing kit. When cutting loosely woven fabric, cut along a pulled thread.

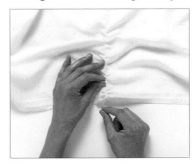

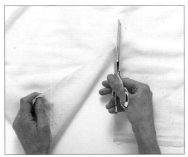

1 PULLING THREAD Make a small cut through the selvage. Pull out a single thread at this point and smooth the fabric.

2 CUTTING FABRIC Using the channel left by the pulled thread as a guideline, cut across the fabric with a pair of dressmaker's scissors.

SHEER AND NET CURTAINS

TRANSLUCENT FABRICS MAKE IDEAL CURTAIN MATERIAL when daytime privacy is desired. When drawn, sheer or net fabrics will obscure a window, but at the same time allow daylight to illuminate the room. Available in various weights and colors, sheers and nets can be made up as the only curtains in a window or as secondary daylight drapes accompanying a set of curtains in a lightproof fabric. Make a simple or specialized handmade heading *(see page 51)* or use a ready-made heading tape. Hang the curtains from a lightweight pole, sash rod, or plastic-coated spring wire, attached by hooks to eyes screwed into the frame *(see page 39)*.

MAKING THE CURTAIN

Choose a sheer or net heading tape, and calculate the quantity of fabric required *(see page 41)*. For translucent curtains, try to find a wide fabric needing few joins. Cut the fabric straight, using the pulled-thread method. Using a new, fine sewing needle, make joins with French seams. You will also need appropriate hooks and the basic sewing kit.

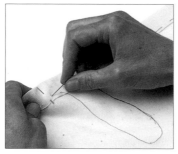

1 HEMMING EDGES Lay the fabric on a large, smooth, flat surface. To neaten the edges of the fabric, pin a ⅜ in (1 cm) double hem at each side edge. Tack, sew, and press the hems.

2 HEMMING BOTTOM EDGE Turn over and pin a ¾ in (2 cm) double hem at the bottom edge. Tack, sew, and press the hem. At the top, or heading, edge of the curtain, turn over the fabric the same width as the tape and pin the tape in position.

3 ATTACHING TAPE Turn under the raw ends of the heading tape by ¾ in (2 cm), and sew it to the wrong side of the curtain. Sew across the ends of the threads at the leading edge. Pull up loose gathers. Arrange fabric evenly across the curtain *(see page 50)*. Secure free ends of cords using a cord tie-back.

THE FINISHED CURTAIN

OTHER OPTIONS

The easy-to-work and lightweight nature of translucent fabrics allows for a wide range of curtain styles to be quickly made up and hung over a window or doorway. A simple effect can be quickly achieved with a narrow heading tape or sleeve. Sophisticated ideas include draping the curtain pole and cutting the drops too long so that the fabric cascades onto the floor.

CROSSOVER SHEER

Sew two curtains to one piece of heading tape. The leading edge of each should be the length of the diagonal of the window. The sides should be the sill length.

DEEP HEADING

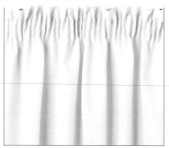

This is a formal style using wide heading tape on a sheer fabric. A deep frill such as this looks very effective and elegant on curtains with a long drop.

DRAPED HEADING

Drape a pole or rod above an opening with sheer fabric. The effect is purely decorative and is ideal for windows where privacy is not very important.

FLOPPY HEADING

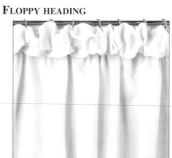

When using a wooden or metal pole or rod, attach heading tape below the top edge of the fabric so that the frill flops forward, revealing the hanging system.

LARGE WINDOWS
For living rooms with large windows, on the first floor or above, it is often unnecessary to have heavy draperies. The amount of fabric required will also make heavyweight draperies awkward to hang on tall windows. Instead, look for lightweight fabrics in pale colors to soften the window's outline without obscuring the view.

DECORATIVE CURTAIN
Decorative or ultra-dramatic draperies are designed primarily for effect. Here, a scarlet taffeta curtain with an elaborate tassel tie-back frames the window and achieves an opulent style with the rich red pillows piled up beside it.

UNLINED CURTAINS

WHEN MADE OF AN OPAQUE FABRIC, unlined curtains are the simplest and least expensive lightproof drapes for a window or other opening. Unlined fabric may be well suited to frequent washing, so curtains made from this material are particularly appropriate for the most extensively used rooms of a home, such as the kitchen and bathroom. An unlined curtain is also quick and easy to make, and it provides an ideal way to practice fundamental curtain-making techniques before attempting the more demanding lined varieties. To enable these curtains to hang properly, you may have to add chain or button weights in the hems or miters.

MAKING THE CURTAIN

Decide on the type of hanging system and curtain heading *(see page 40)* and the fabric fullness. Measure the window and calculate your fabric requirements *(see page 41)*. Clear a flat surface to work on and have ready the heading tape, matching hooks, and the basic sewing kit. Cut the fabric to size, allowing extra for joining panels. Remove the selvages.

1 JOINING PANELS Sew together panels of fabric, aligning any pattern *(see page 41)*. Fold the hem and sides of the fabric by ⅝ in (1.5 cm) to the wrong side and press in place. Fold the sides over again by 1 in (2.5 cm) and press. Fold up the hem by 3 in (7.5 cm) and miter the corners *(see page 19)*. Then slipstitch the side turnings.

2 TURNING TOP EDGE Along the top edge of the curtain, fold over, pin, and press a strip of fabric 1½ in (4 cm) wide to the wrong side. Cut the heading tape to the same width as the finished curtain, allowing ¾ in (2 cm) at each end for turning under.

3 ATTACHING TAPE Pin and tack heading tape in position, just below top fold of the curtain. Sew along both sides of the tape in same direction, and across leading edge to secure the drawstrings. Knot individual drawstrings to prevent them from being pulled through when you draw up gathers *(see page 50)*. Cut a length of medium-density chain weights to the curtain width.

4 SECURING WEIGHTS Unfold the hem so that the topmost fold is exposed. Lay the length of chain weights along the crease in the fabric. Then sew the weights in place at regular intervals.

5 FINISHING OFF To finish off the curtain, refold the hem and pin it in place. Then slipstitch along the hem to secure it. Fit the curtain hooks to the tape, and hang the curtain on the track, rod, or pole. Dress the finished curtain.

THE FINISHED CURTAIN

WEIGHTS

The draping quality of lightweight or opaque curtains will be improved by securing weights within the hem. Weights are available either as chains to lay along a hem or as button-shaped disks to secure in the miters.

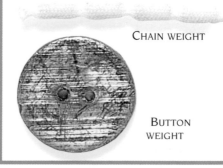

CHAIN WEIGHT

BUTTON WEIGHT

LINED CURTAINS

THERE ARE MANY ADVANTAGES to lining a curtain. First, the lining will give body to the main fabric so that the curtain hangs with pleasing fullness. Second, a curtain composed of layers will be much more lightproof than an unlined curtain. Last, if the appropriate interlining material is inserted between the two fabrics, the curtain will possess excellent insulating properties. You can line a curtain using the simple tube method *(see opposite),* which is best for small, light curtains, or by hand sewing the lining to the main fabric – a technique known as locked-in lining. This technique is best suited to wide, deep curtains.

LOCKED-IN LINING

You should use the locked-in lining technique to achieve the most professional finish, particularly when making wide and deep curtains from widths of fabric that need to be joined together. Lock the lining in place with rows of lockstitches *(see below)* running at regular intervals down the length of the back of the main fabric. You will need curtain and lining fabrics, heading tape, hooks, and the basic sewing kit. First

cut out the panels for the curtain, making joins with plain flat seams if necessary *(see page 14).* Next, cut out the panels for the lining 5 in (12.5 cm) shorter than the length of the curtain fabric. Allow 3½ in (9 cm) at the hem edge and 1½ in (4 cm) at the heading edge. Join the panels of lining fabric with plain flat seams, and trim 1½ in (4 cm) from each side edge of the completed lining sections.

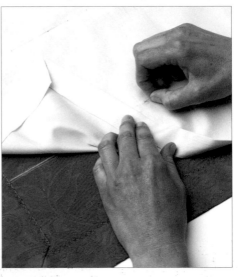

3 PINNING LINING Pin the lining material to the curtain fabric, wrong sides together, along each of the marked lines. Beginning 6 in (15 cm) from the top of the curtain fabric, tack the lining in position along the first of the vertical lines.

1 HEMMING FABRIC Turn fabric sides under by 1½ in (4 cm). Turn a 2 in (5 cm) hem along bottom edge and miter corners. Press hem and add weights. Herringbone stitch hem *(see page 18).* Turn sides and hem of lining under by ⅝ in (1.5 cm) and press.

2 MARKING GUIDELINES Using a triangle or straightedge as a guide, along with a vanishing-ink pen or tailor's chalk, draw full-length, vertical lines on the wrong side of the curtain fabric at intervals of about 12–20 in (30–50 cm).

4 LOCKSTITCHING LINING Fold back the lining and lockstitch along the first line of tacking, beginning 6 in (15 cm) from the top. To lockstitch, sew loose stitches wide apart to avoid puckering. Stitch the lining in place down the lines. Remove the tacking stitches.

5 FINISHING OFF Pin, tack, and slipstitch the lining fabric to the curtain at the sides and hem. Remove the tacking stitches. Finish off by applying the chosen heading tape *(see page 50).* Attach the appropriate hooks, then hang and dress the curtain.

THE FINISHED CURTAIN

TUBE LINING

This is a quick and simple means of lining a curtain, in which lining is attached to the main fabric, only by its side seams, to form a tube. Tube lining is best suited for small curtains and light fabrics. You will need curtain and lining fabrics, heading tape complete with hooks, and the basic sewing kit. Cut out the curtain and lining as described opposite.

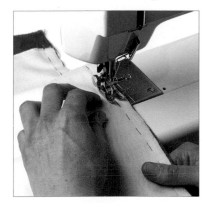

1 ATTACHING LINING Place the lining on top of the curtain, right sides together. The top edge of the lining should lie 1½ in (4 cm) from the top of the curtain. Pin, tack, and sew down one side with a plain flat seam, ⅝ in (1.5 cm) from the edge. Leave 6 in (15 cm) of the bottom of the lining unsewn to allow for turning up hems. Align the other side edge of the lining with the unsewn curtain edge. Pin, tack, and sew lining to curtain as before. Press both seams open.

2 HEMMING LINING Continue to work with the curtain laid wrong side out. Fold a double hem ⅝ in (1.5 cm) deep along the bottom edge of the lining. Pin, tack, and sew the hem in place.

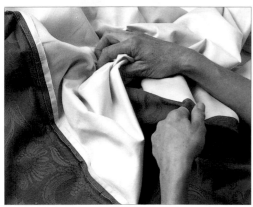

3 TURNING OUT Turn the curtain and lining right side out. Lay the tube flat, lining side up, and adjust it so that the side seams lie on the reverse of the curtain and the lining is centered. An equal amount of curtain fabric – about 1½ in (4 cm) – should be visible at each edge. Pin to hold in place if necessary and press. Turn up the curtain hem by ⅝ in (1.5 cm), and then by 3 in (7.5 cm), and press.

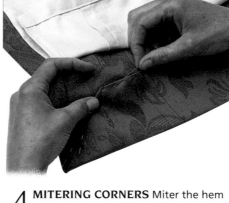

4 MITERING CORNERS Miter the hem corners *(see page 19)*, adding curtain weights if required *(see page 45)*. Then pin and tack the miters in position. Next, pin and tack the hem in place. Attach the heading tape *(see page 50)* and hang the curtain. Check the length of the lining and the curtain fabric and adjust if necessary.

OTHER LINING OPTIONS

SELF-LINED

Rather than using white or cream lining fabric, consider self-lining the curtain with the same material as the front. Here, for instance, the reverse of a brocaded fabric makes an ideal lining.

CONTRASTING PATTERN

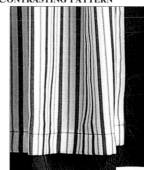

Fabrics with a pattern containing a range of colors harmonious with the curtain fabric or similar to it make an interesting lining. Suitably colored stripes and checks are possibilities.

5 FINISHING OFF Once the two fabrics have been correctly aligned, you can finish off the curtain by slipstitching the hem, the mitered corners, and the remainder of the lining in place. Remove any tacking stitches. Then press the curtain on both sides and rehang it.

THE FINISHED CURTAIN

INTERLINED CURTAIN

An interlining between a curtain fabric and lining provides efficient insulation and gives bulk and durability to a curtain. For an interlined curtain, you will need curtain and lining fabrics *(see page 6)*, interlining, heading tape with hooks, and the basic sewing kit. Measure and cut out the curtain, if necessary joining panels of fabric with plain flat seams.

1 CUTTING OUT Fold up the fabric hem by ⅝ in (1.5 cm), then by 3 in (7.5 cm) to the wrong side, and press. Fold in the other edges by 1½ in (4 cm) and press. Open out the turnings. Lay the interlining on the fabric and trim it to fit within hem folds. Cut lining to the same size as the interlining.

2 ATTACHING INTERLINING To join sections of interlining, simply overlap the edges of the pieces, and pin, tack, and sew through both. Attach the interlining to the curtain fabric with parallel vertical rows of lockstitching, as for locked-in linings *(see page 46).*

3 SEWING HEMS Fold hems over interlining and miter the corners. Use a herringbone stitch *(see page 18)* to hem the sides, and slipstitch the bottom hem to the interlining *(see page 12).* Stop short of the corners if you are using curtain weights.

4 ADDING WEIGHTS Sew curtain weights onto the inside of the corners of the bottom hem allowance, and finish slipstitching the hem. Hem the bottom of lining fabric by turning it up twice by ⅝ in (1.5 cm) and machine stitching it.

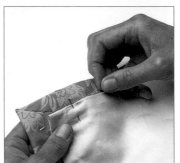

5 ATTACHING LINING Fold under the side edges of the lining by ⅝ in (1.5 cm) and press. Slipstitch the folded side edges to the curtain *(see page 46).* Fold the fabric over the lining at the top edge and attach the heading tape *(see page 50).*

THE FINISHED CURTAIN

LOOSE-LINED CURTAIN

Loose-lining is an easy way of adding a detachable layer to a curtain. To make up this curtain, you will need fabric and heading tape, lining fabric and lining heading tape, hooks for both tapes, and the basic sewing kit. Make up the curtain and cut lining to the size of the finished, ungathered curtain. Turn under the sides by ⅝ in (1.5 cm) twice and machine sew them.

1 POSITIONING TAPE Lining heading tape is folded double lengthwise. Slip the raw top edge of the lining into the fold in the heading tape. Check that the tape is the right way around, and that the raw edge is against the inside of the fold in the tape. Pin it in position.

Secure heading tape to lining fabric by sewing along top and bottom edges

2 ATTACHING TAPE When the lining is enclosed within the tape, tack along the top and bottom edges. Sew along the tacking lines, working in the same direction each time to prevent puckering. Remove the tacking stitches and gather the lining *(see page 50).*

3 HEMMING LINING Hook the lining to the curtain tape. Lay both layers flat, and trim the lining length so that a double hem of ⅝ in (1.5 cm) will make it 1¼–1½ in (3–4 cm) shorter than the curtain. Hem and attach the lining, and hang and dress the curtain *(see page 53).*

THE FINISHED CURTAIN

ADAPTABLE CURTAIN

Versatile curtains, ideal for seasonal use, can be made by layering fabrics. You will need curtain and sheer fabrics, fabric for binding edges and for ties, heading tapes, and the basic sewing kit. Measure for the curtains, and cut out fabric one and a half times the width of the finished curtain by the full length, plus 1¼ in (3 cm) for the heading. Allowances are not necessary for other edges, because they will be bound. Make joins with French seams *(see page 15)*. Cut out the sheer fabric to same fullness, adding 2½ in (6 cm) to the width and 5⅛ in (13 cm) to the length for turnings.

Attach pleated heading tape to hemmed top edge of sheer fabric

1 SEWING TAPE Fold, tack, and sew ⅝ in (1.5 cm) double hems on the sides and bottom of the sheer fabric. Fold a double hem 2 in (5 cm) deep at the heading edge, and press. Pin, tack, and sew a pleated sheer heading tape just below the top fold, and gather up the sheer curtain *(see page 50)*.

2 SEWING TIES Count how many ties you need, spacing them about 4 in (10 cm) apart with one at the very edge of each end. Mark the positions. Make ties *(see page 25)* long enough to hold the curtain at the right height when folded in half. Fold each tie double and slipstitch the fold to the tape.

3 SEWING BINDING Make a bias strip 1½–2½ in (4–6 cm) wide to go all around the heavier fabric, adding 4 in (10 cm) for joining ends. Fold ⅜ in (1 cm) of each long edge of the binding to the wrong side, and press. Bind the edges of the fabric *(see page 14)*. Join the ends of the binding on the bottom edge, where they will be least visible.

4 ATTACHING TAPE Measure and mark a line 1¼ in (3 cm) from the top of the main curtain fabric. Pin, tack, and sew a simple heading tape along this line, and gather it up. Estimate the positions for the ties, as for the sheer curtain, ensuring that they will alternate with the sheer ties. Fold the ties in half and slipstitch them to the tape's top edge.

5 HANGING CURTAIN Attach the ties of the sheer curtain and the main curtain to alternate curtain rings. Remove the main fabric and the rings to which it is tied during the summer months, when an insulating layer is not required. This leaves the sheer curtain in place to ensure privacy.

THE SHEER CURTAIN

THE TOP CURTAIN WITH SHEER LINING

HEADING TAPES

THE FINAL TASK, once you have assembled your curtains, is to attach the heading tape that you chose when deciding on the style of the curtains (*see page 40*). Every type of ready-made heading tape, from the simplest pencil pleat to the most sophisticated triple pinch pleat and goblet heading, is made of a strip of strong, stiff fabric. Ready-made heading tape has one or more rows of pockets, through which the curtain hooks are threaded, and two or more drawstrings that run along the length of the heading tape and are designed for gathering up the curtain fabric to the desired fullness.

APPLYING HEADING TAPE

You will need the curtain, the heading tape and hooks, and the basic sewing kit. Measuring from the bottom edge up, mark the desired length on the fabric at the top of the curtain. Turn the fabric down at the mark, and press. If necessary, trim the folded part to the depth recommended for the tape. Cut the heading tape to the width of the curtain, plus 1½ in (4 cm).

UNLINED CURTAIN

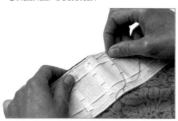

1 PLACING TAPE Lay the tape with its top edge just below the top fold. At the leading edge, knot the drawstring ends.

2 TACKING TAPE Turn under the fixed end of the tape by ¾ in (2 cm) and align the fold with the curtain edge. Tack the tape in place. At the side edge, turn the other end of the tape under by ¾ in (2 cm), leaving the drawstring ends free.

3 SEWING TAPE Machine sew along the top and bottom edges of the tape to secure it to the curtain. Sew in the same direction both times, to prevent the fabric from puckering. Sew across the ends of the tape, securing the knotted ends of the drawstrings at the leading edge and leaving them free at the side edge. Remove the tacking stitches.

LINED CURTAIN

1 FOLDING FABRIC Trim the lining fabric at the top, so that its edge aligns with the mark that indicates the top of the curtain drop. Fold the top of the curtain fabric over at the mark, covering the raw edge of the lining fabric. Pin the folded fabric in place over the lining, and press. Remove the pins.

2 SEWING TAPE Lay the heading tape along the top of the curtain, just below the top fold. Knot the drawstring ends at the leading edge, turn under the end of the tape by ¾ in (2 cm), and align the fold with the curtain edge. Pin and tack the tape. At the side edge, turn the end of the tape under but leave the drawstrings free. Sew the tape in place as for an unlined curtain.

GATHERING UP THE TAPE

1 PULLING STRINGS Grasp the free ends of the drawstrings at the side of the curtain. Hold the tape and curtain steady with your other hand, and pull the strings to one side. As you pull out the drawstrings, the tape will gather and form pleats. As you pull, ease the pleats along the whole length of the tape, until the curtain heading is gathered to the required width.

Use a ready-made cord tieback or a piece of cardboard

2 TYING OFF Tie the ends of the drawstrings in a slipknot to hold them. Wind the free lengths of drawstring around a cord tieback so that they will lie neatly out of sight. Do not cut off the drawstring ends: when the curtains are taken down to be cleaned, the drawstrings must be released and the heading tapes pulled out again so that the curtains will lie flat.

Use recommended hooks

3 THREADING HOOKS Distribute the curtain's fullness evenly along the width of the curtain by adjusting the pleats. Decide on the position and spacing of the hooks, and insert them into one of the rows of woven pockets in the tape.

HANDMADE HEADINGS

UNTIL RELATIVELY RECENTLY, the majority of headings were handmade, forming an integral component of a curtain. Nowadays, most types of pleated headings can be purchased as commercial heading tapes. There remain, however, a range of curtain headings that either can or must be made by hand. In some cases, for example the looped and scalloped treatments, this is because they are very specialized. In other cases, such as cased headings, it is because they are simple. Assembling your own handmade heading also allows you to customize curtains and maintain greater control over the look of your room.

CASED HEADING

A cased or slot heading provides the simplest method of hanging a curtain. It is suitable for treatments where the curtains will be held open with tie-backs, while the heading remains closed. You will need one and a half to two and a half times the width of the finished curtain (if necessary, join widths with French seams), the curtain rod or wire that you intend to use, and the basic sewing kit. Hem the bottom and side edges of the curtain first *(see page 42)*.

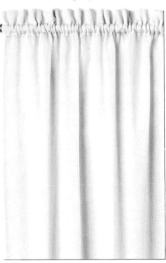

1 TURNING TOP Fold a double hem deep enough for the slot and the desired frill. Mark a seam line to the depth for the slot, which should fit the rod loosely, and tack along it.

2 TACKING HEADING Tack close to the bottom of the turning. This will now form the case, or slot, for the rod. Before sewing, check the fit of the casing, and adjust if necessary.

3 SEWING SLOT Machine sew along the tacked lines. Work in the same direction each time to prevent puckering. Remove the tacking stitches and press. Insert the rod, gather the curtain, and hang in place. A heading with a frill will hang better on a rod than on a wire.

THE FINISHED CURTAIN

OTHER CASED HEADINGS

Making a turning in the top edge of a curtain fabric to form a slot for a rod or wire is a simple and versatile heading technique. It can easily be adapted to make a variety of heading treatments, both plain and decorative. All of these headings are ideally suited for hanging sheer, net, or lightweight fabrics that are not intended to be drawn: cased headings do not draw very easily.

UNGATHERED CURTAIN

Some curtains, such as pictorial lace panels, look best if they are made up without any gathers at the heading. Cut the fabric slightly narrower than the width of the rod or wire to prevent wrinkles. Turn a double hem to fit the pole or wire, and stitch along its edge.

GATHERED CURTAIN

A simple casing will hang better on a wire than one with a frill. Cut the fabric to the fullness desired. Make a double turning for the slot, deep enough to fit loosely over the eyes at the ends of the wire. Tack and sew along the lower edge.

GATHERED DOUBLE FRILL

Press a turning in the top edge to wrong side for the slot. Fold two pleats wrong sides together for each frill. Align the inner fold of pleats with the raw edge of the slot. Sew two seams for the casing: bottom one through the slot fold; top one through raw edge and pleats.

SCALLOPED HEADING

A fabric heading cut into a scalloped pattern is popular for ungathered café curtains covering the lower half of a window. Be sure to cut the fabric straight, particularly when using a striped pattern. Estimate the width desired for the scallops and the strips between them. The strips should be no less than 2 in (5 cm) wide, and the scallops about 4¾ in (12 cm) wide.

Divide the finished curtain width by combined measurement of scallop and strip, remembering to make one more strip than scallops to provide a strip at each end. You will need curtain and lining fabrics to the width of the window and depth desired plus allowances for hems, cardboard for the template, café curtain rings, and the basic sewing kit.

1 MAKING TEMPLATE Use a compass to draw a circle to the width of the scallop on a piece of cardboard. Draw a pencil line across the cardboard at the required depth, and cut out the template.

2 MARKING UP Pin curtain and lining right sides together. Lay fabrics with lining facing up. Mark seam line ⅝ in (1.5 cm) from raw heading edge. Mark width of one strip in from side of curtain. Place template against the mark, straight edge against heading seam line, and draw around it. Work along curtain top, spacing scallops one strip-width apart. Pin and tack along scalloped line.

Use a vanishing-ink pen to mark pattern on fabric

3 SEWING SCALLOPS Sew along the pinned and tacked line of scallops and continue around the other sides of the curtain. Leave a gap in one of the seams, large enough for the whole curtain to be turned right side out through it.

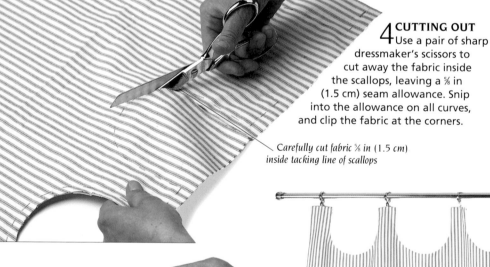

4 CUTTING OUT Use a pair of sharp dressmaker's scissors to cut away the fabric inside the scallops, leaving a ⅝ in (1.5 cm) seam allowance. Snip into the allowance on all curves, and clip the fabric at the corners.

Carefully cut fabric ⅝ in (1.5 cm) inside tacking line of scallops

5 TURNING OUT Turn the whole curtain right side out through the opening left in one of the seams. Gently push out all the corners to a neat point – a blunt knitting needle is ideal for this task. Slipstitch the opening closed and press the curtain.

6 SEWING RINGS Sew café curtain rings in place at the center of each of the strip between the scallops. If you are using café clips, follow the manufacturer's instructions. Slide the pole or rod through the rings, mount the end stops, and hang the curtain.

THE FINISHED CURTAIN

LOOPED HEADING

Flat or gathered curtains can be given a heading of simple fabric loops (tabs). Cut the curtain fabric to the size required, joining pieces with flat fell seams *(see page 15)*, if necessary. Hem the sides and bottom *(see page 18)*. The loops should be stitched to the wrong side of the top of the curtain, and the ends covered with a facing strip. Decide on the number and

size of loops required. Cut each fabric strip for the loops to double the distance from the top of the curtain and pole and double the width required, plus ⅜ in (1.5 cm) all around for seam allowances. Allow enough fabric for a facing strip 2½ in (6 cm) wide, and as long as the curtain width, plus 1¼ in (3 cm) for turnings. You will also need the basic sewing kit.

1 SEWING LOOPS Fold each strip in half lengthwise, right sides together. Pin, tack, and sew each strip ⅜ in (1.5 cm) from the edge to form a tube. Press the seam open.

2 TURNING OUT Turn each strip right side out. For narrow strips, stitch a piece of thread to one end, pass it through the tube, and pull. Press flat, with the seam in the middle of one side.

3 ATTACHING FACING Fold the loops in half, seams to the inside. Lay them along the right side of the curtain, their ends aligned with raw top edge. Pin and tack in place. Pin the facing to the curtain, wrong side up and with the raw edges aligned, sandwiching the loops. Leave ⅜ in (1.5 cm) extra facing at each end.

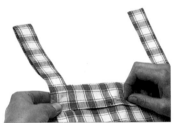

4 SEWING Tack and sew a seam ⅜ in (1.5 cm) from the top, securing the fabric, the loops, and the facing. Fold under ⅜ in (1.5 cm) on the other edges of the facing strip. Press and tack.

5 FINISHING FACING Press the facing strip and curtain wrong sides together, with the loop end hidden. Slipstitch the folded edges of the facing to the curtain. Press the curtain.

THE FINISHED CURTAIN

ADDING BOWS
To decorate the loops with fabric bows, make up rouleau strips *(see page 25)* to the required length, and tie them around the base of each loop to form bows. Alternatively, you could use ribbon or cord.

HANGING AND DRESSING CURTAINS

To achieve the best results, finished curtains must be hung correctly, and then dressed. Hang heavy curtains for at least 24 hours before hemming to allow the fabric to stretch fully.

Dressing curtains involves tying the folds in place: bind the folds securely, but not so tightly that the fabric will crease. After the ties have been removed, the curtains will hang in neat folds.

INTEGRAL CURTAIN HOOKS

To ensure that the hooks will be evenly spaced, count the pockets to be hooked and mark them before hanging the curtain.

HOOKS AND EYELET RUNNERS

Curtain hooks are threaded through pockets in the header tape and hooked through eyelets in the bottom of each runner.

DRESSING CURTAINS

1 ARRANGING FOLDS Fold curtain into an accordion. Grasp each fold at heading. Pull down in one smooth motion.

2 BINDING Bind folds with fabric strips tied at the top, center, and bottom. Leave for 48 hours, then remove ties.

DOOR COVER
A curtain across a door minimizes the cold and drafts of winter months, and maintains privacy. This curtain drapes onto the floor and is swept back to give a full outline. The painted tie-back knob helps to maintain the fullness of its gathers, while still allowing people to pass through the door with ease.

TIE-BACKS

TIE-BACKS ARE USEFUL AND DECORATIVE curtain accessories. A tie-back holds a curtain away from a window, allowing as much daylight as possible to enter a room during the day, and it also breaks up the straight vertical line of a curtain. Hooks or cleats are fixed to the wall to anchor the tie-back, and should be positioned far enough out from the window to pull the curtain clear, and high enough to allow a generous sweep of fabric to hang below them. Ready-made tie-backs of cord and rope, complete with tassels, can be bought, or you can make your own out of fabric in a variety of shapes.

MEASURING

Hang and dress the curtain, then draw it to one side. Hold a tape measure around the curtain at the chosen level for the tie-back. Hold the ends of the tape against the wall where you want the hook. Decide on the size and position for the tie-back. Note the measurement around the curtain, and mark the hook position on the wall.

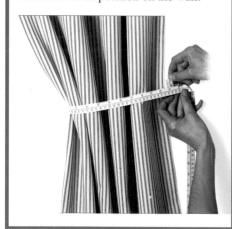

SIMPLE V-SHAPED TIE-BACK

To make the V-shaped tie-back, you will need the fabric for the tie-back, and lining if desired, interfacing, suitable rings and hooks for fixing the tie-back round the curtain and to the wall, as well as the basic sewing kit.

1 **MAKING PATTERN** Measure for the tie-back and mark a rectangle on the paper that measures half the required length by 11 in (28 cm) wide. Mark a point 5½ in (14 cm) up from the bottom left-hand corner of this rectangle, and mark a straight line from this point to the top right-hand corner. Measure 2 in (5 cm) down from the top right-hand corner, and mark a straight line from this point to the bottom left-hand corner. Cut out the wedge shape for the paper pattern.

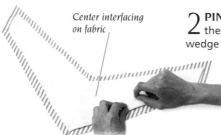

Center interfacing on fabric

2 **PINNING PIECES** Fold the fabric double, and lay the paper pattern on it with the wider end of the wedge on the fold. Cut out the fabric, adding ⅝ in (1.5 cm) all around for seam allowances. Cut out a piece of lining fabric in the same way. Cut a piece of interfacing to the exact size of the paper pattern. Unfold the fabric piece and lay it right side down on a flat surface. Unfold and place the interfacing on the fabric, and pin and tack in place.

3 **SEWING FABRIC** Place the tie-back fabric and the lining right sides together. Pin, tack, and sew them together, keeping close to the edge of the interfacing. Leave a gap in the seam large enough to turn the tie-back right side out.

4 **FINISHING** Trim corner seam allowances to reduce bulk. Pull the tie-back right side out and press it. Turn in the raw edges of the gap and slipstitch the edges together. Topstitch ¼ in (6 mm) in from around the edge to hold interfacing in place.

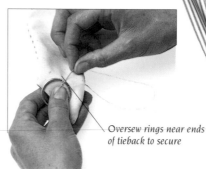

Oversew rings near ends of tieback to secure

5 **FIXING RINGS** Attach rings at either end of the tie-back, oversewing to secure. The rings can be positioned far enough in so that they are almost hidden, or at the ends to make them visible. Fix the hook to the wall, and hang the tie-back in place.

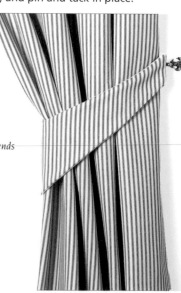

THE FINISHED TIE-BACK

PADDED TIE-BACK

The padded tie-back, a simple tube with filling, can add a three-dimensional feel to your finished curtain. Determine the length of the tie-back required, as described opposite, and decide on the width of the tie-back. Cut out the fabric to the length of the tie-back and double the width, adding ⅝ in (1.5 cm) all around for seam allowances. To make this tie-back, you will need fabric for the tie-back, padding, rings and retaining hooks, and the basic sewing kit.

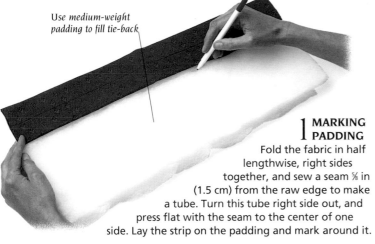
Use medium-weight padding to fill tie-back

Tie a thread to one end of padding to help pull it through fabric tube

1 MARKING PADDING
Fold the fabric in half lengthwise, right sides together, and sew a seam ⅝ in (1.5 cm) from the raw edge to make a tube. Turn this tube right side out, and press flat with the seam to the center of one side. Lay the strip on the padding and mark around it.

2 FILLING TUBE Cut out the padding to the same size as the strip. Tie a strong thread around one end of the padding and pass the thread through the tube. Carefully pull on the thread to ease the padding into the tube.

Rings are attached to ends of tie-back

3 SECURING ENDS When the padding is in position and well into the tube, remove the thread from it. Turn the two raw ends of the tie-back fabric to the inside, and then slipstitch their folded edges together.

4 FIXING RINGS Place the securing rings at each end of the tie-back and mark their positions according to whether you want them to be visible or not. Oversew them securely in place. Fix the hook to the wall and hang the tie-back in place.

THE FINISHED TIE-BACK

ROPES, TASSELS, AND CLASPS

Ready-made ropes and cords with tassels are available in a wide variety of thicknesses, colors, textures, and sizes to match or attractively contrast with every type of curtain fabric. Often, these rope tie-backs incorporate one or more elaborate tassels. Fixed hooks and holdbacks can be found in a range of finishes and styles, and they can provide another decorative means for holding a curtain open.

HOLDBACKS
Hooks and knobs are available in both wood and metal, often made to match decorative curtain poles. These fixtures are usually sold with screws and anchors for mounting them to a wall. Hook the curtain fabric behind the holdback and move it up and down the wall to determine the best position.

ROPES AND TASSELS
These elegant tie-backs can be bought ready-made in standard lengths, but you could buy tassels separately and combine colored cords to make a tie-back to match your curtains. Attach the hook to the wall and loop the rope around the curtain, leaving the tassel to hang down against folds.

CRESCENT TIE-BACK WITH CORDED EDGE

The edge of a tie-back can be decorated with a range of trimmings to highlight its shape. To make this tie-back, you will need fabric, decorative cord, iron-on interfacing, lining if required, rings, hooks, and the basic sewing kit. Measure for the tie-back. On a piece of pattern paper, mark a strip 4¼ in (11 cm) wide by half the length required.

1 MAKING PATTERN Draw half a crescent, tapering to a width of about 2 in (5 cm) at the end, on the paper strip. Cut it out, fold the fabric double, and place the wider end of the crescent pattern on the fold. Cut out the fabric with a ⅝ in (1.5 cm) seam allowance all around. Cut another piece in the same fabric or in a lining fabric in the same way, and cut a piece of interfacing to the exact size of the pattern. Iron the interfacing to the wrong side of one tie-back piece, leaving a ⅝ in (1.5 cm) border.

Attach edging just inside seam line

2 TACKING EDGING Unfold the fabric and measure around the seam line to find the length of cord required. Cut the cord to this length, adding 1 in (2.5 cm) extra for overlapping the ends. Pin and tack the cord just inside the seam line on the right side of the piece of fabric that will be the outside of the tie-back.

Pin and tack pieces together along seam line

3 ALIGNING PIECES Lay the back piece of fabric on top of the front piece, right sides facing, and align the edges. Pin and tack the fabric pieces together along the seam line, sandwiching the corded edging between them.

4 SEWING PIECES Machine sew along the tacking line on the tie-back, stitching through the corded edging to secure the pieces together. Remember to leave a gap large enough to allow the tie-back to be turned right side out through it.

5 CLIPPING ALLOWANCES Using a pair of sharp dressmaker's scissors, make snips into the seam allowance around the tie-back to ease the fabric and reduce bulk *(see page 14)*. Turn the tie-back right side out through the opening and press flat.

6 FINISHING OFF Fold in the raw edges of the opening and slipstitch it closed. Sew the curtain rings securely in their required positions at the ends of the tie-back, then mount the hook to the wall and wrap the tie-back around the finished curtain. Adjust and dress the curtain as necessary.

Make sure slipstitching is on inside when hanging tie-back

THE FINISHED TIE-BACK

BOW-TRIMMED TIE-BACK

To add a bow to a tie-back, you will need fabric for both, iron-on interfacing, rings, hooks, and the basic sewing kit. Cut two strips the length of the tie-back by 3⅛ in (8 cm) wide, plus ⅝ in (1.5 cm) for allowances. Cut out interfacing to the same size minus the seam allowance. Iron it to the wrong side of one of the fabric strips, leaving a ⅝ in (1.5 cm) border.

1 SEWING TIE-BACK Lay the tie-back strips right sides together and pin, tack, and sew together ⅝ in (1.5 cm) from the cut edge, close to the edge of the interfacing. Leave an opening in one side for turning the band right side out. Trim the seam allowances to ¼ in (6 mm) and clip at the corners.

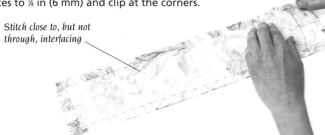

Stitch close to, but not through, interfacing

Pull tie-back band right sides out through opening in seam

2 FINISHING TIE-BACK Turn the tie-back band right side out through the opening in the seam, and press flat. Finish making the tie-back by neatly slipstitching closed the opening in the seam.

3 MAKING BOW BAND Lay two cut strips of fabric – 1 yd x 4¼ in (93 x 11 cm) – right sides together. Pin, tack, and sew ⅝ in (1.5 cm) from edges. Leave a gap. Trim seams to ¼ in (6 mm), and clip corners. Turn right sides out and press. Slipstitch the opening closed.

4 CROSSING ENDS Fold the strip in half, bringing the ends together, and mark the center of it with a pin. Fold the ends of the strip over each other across the center mark, to form a bow shape. Adjust the placing to change the size of the loops and tails.

5 STITCHING BOW When the bow is the shape desired and the loops and tails are even, pin layers in place at the center. For a bigger bow, just use larger pieces of fabric. Try out your bow with inexpensive material before cutting it out in the fabric.

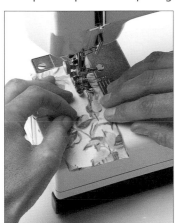

6 SEWING CENTER STRIP Cut out a 4¼ in (11 cm) square of fabric. Fold it in half, right sides together. Pin, tack, and sew ⅝ in (1.5 cm) from the long edge of the rectangle to make a tube. Turn right side out, and press flat with the seam in the center of one side.

7 SECURING BOW Wrap strip around center of folded band, with seamed side inside. Overlap and fold under ends at back. Bring together folded ends to grip center of bow. Slipstitch ends together.

8 ATTACHING BOW Lay the completed tie-back band face up on a flat surface and mark the center. Sew the bow in place at the mark, making sure that it lies straight on the tie-back. Sew the rings in place at the ends of the tie-back and wrap it around the finished curtain. Hook the tie-back to the wall and dress the curtain as necessary.

THE FINISHED TIE-BACK

CORNICES AND VALANCES

A CORNICE OR A VALANCE PROVIDES an additional decorative finish to the heading of a curtain and also helps to prevent drafts from coming through a window. A cornice is made of rigid or semi-rigid panels covered with fabric, which usually matches the curtain fabric. It is hung or tacked over the window on a board that is held on right-angled brackets, with side pieces attached under the board at each end. The cornice board does not need to be very strong, because it carries little weight. A valance is a deep frill of fabric that either hangs over the curtain heading on a rod or is attached to the curtain fabric itself.

SIMPLE CORNICE

The cornice should be slightly wider than the curtains, so that they do not look cramped by it, and its front should be far enough away to ensure that the curtains do not drag against it when they are opened or closed. The depth of the cornice will depend on the length and style of the curtain: a good rule is to make the cornice one-eighth of the depth of the finished curtain. To make up this cornice, you will need the curtain and lining fabric, medium-weight interlining, buckram, Velcro, a permanent marker pen, a decorator's brush, heavy-duty shears, staple gun, and the basic sewing kit.

1 CUTTING BUCKRAM Measure and cut the buckram to the length (including the sides, or returns, of the cornice) and depth required. Use heavy-duty shears – buckram is very tough and will blunt good dressmaker's scissors.

2 SCORING SIDES Mark lines on the buckram at the point where the sides meet the front corners of the cornice. Score along these two lines with the back of a scissor blade. Cut out the interlining and the lining ⅝ in (1.5 cm) larger than the buckram panel all around. Assess the placement of any design motifs and pattern repeats on the cornice's covering fabric, and ensure that the straight grain will run straight on the finished cornice. Cut out the curtain fabric 1¼ in (3 cm) larger than the buckram panel all around.

3 DAMPENING EDGES Lay the buckram centrally onto the interlining, and lightly dampen its edges with water: a small decorator's paintbrush is ideal for this purpose. The dampened buckram will be lightly adhesive.

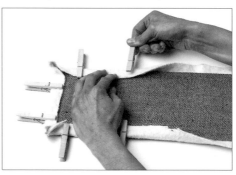

4 CLAMPING INTERLINING Fold the edges of the interlining over and then onto the dampened edge of the buckram panel. Press the interlining edges down firmly with your fingertips, and fix it in place with clothespins.

5 TRIMMING INTERLINING Press the edges with an iron over a damp cloth, removing the pins as you work around the buckram panel. The heat from the iron will cause the interlining to adhere to the buckram. Trim off the excess interlining at the corners so that the cornice's covering fabric will fit easily and smoothly over the interlining.

6 ATTACHING FABRIC Lay the panel centrally on the wrong side of the fabric. Dampen the edges of the buckram to the inside of the interlined edge. Fold the fabric over the panel, overlapping the interlining. Miter it at the corners. Smooth fabric taut and pin in place. Iron the edges over a damp cloth.

7 ATTACHING LINING Turn lining edges ¾ in (2 cm) to wrong side. Miter corners and press. Pin lining to the back of the panel and slipstitch in place.

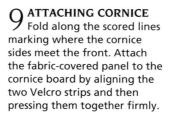

9 ATTACHING CORNICE Fold along the scored lines marking where the cornice sides meet the front. Attach the fabric-covered panel to the cornice board by aligning the two Velcro strips and then pressing them together firmly.

8 MOUNTING VELCRO Attach the frame over the window *(see page 39)*, ensuring that the cornice will cover the curtain heading. Cut Velcro to the length of the frame. Staple the hooked strip along the frame. Slipstitch the fuzzy strip to the top edge of the back of the cornice.

THE FINISHED CORNICE

CASTELLATED CORNICE

Cut buckram to the size of the panel, including sides. Make a pattern to the size of the front of the cornice. Fold in half and mark the center, then fold into quarters or eighths. You will need curtain and lining fabric, medium-weight interlining, buckram, Velcro, a marker pen, tape, decorator's brush, heavy-duty shears, and the basic sewing kit.

1 DRAWING PATTERN Draw a right-angled shape from the side to the bottom edge of the paper pattern. If you draw the shape from the side that has the marked central fold, there will be an indentation at the center of the panel; if, however, you draw from the other side of the paper pattern, there will be a castellation at the center, as below.

2 CUTTING PAPER Cut out the pattern and open up the paper. If the pattern shape was half the width of the folded paper, the castellations and indentations will be of equal size.

3 TRACING PATTERN Secure the pattern on the buckram with tape. Draw around the pattern with a marker pen. At each end of the pattern, mark on the buckram where the sides of the cornice meet the front.

4 CUTTING BUCKRAM With the back of a scissor blade, score along the lines that mark where the sides of the cornice meet the front. Cut out the pattern along the bottom edge of the front of the buckram panel, using heavy-duty shears – do not use good-quality dressmaker's scissors on buckram.

5 CUTTING INTERLINING Cut the interlining, lining, and fabric ⅝ in (1.5 cm) larger than the buckram all around, carefully assessing the placement of pattern repeats and the alignment of the straight grain on the cornice fabric before cutting. Lay the buckram centrally on the interlining, and snip the internal corners.

6 TRIMMING EXCESS Dampen the buckram edges with a brush, and clothespin the interlining in place. Press the interlining over a damp cloth. Trim the excess at the corners. Lay the panel centrally on the wrong side of the covering fabric and carefully snip the internal corners.

7 ATTACHING FABRIC Fold the fabric over the cornice edge and pin it to the interlining. Smooth the fabric taut and sew it to the interlining with small tacking stitches. Trim excess fabric at corners. Hang the cornice as for a simple cornice.

THE FINISHED CORNICE

SHAPED WOODEN CORNICE

Decide on the size of the cornice *(see page 60)*, then cut panels of board to shape for the front and sides. Cut out lining and interlining to the same shape, but ⅝ in (1.5 cm) larger all around than the panels. To make a shaped cornice, you will need thin board, curtain and lining fabrics, interlining, curtain rings, cord, fabric glue, tape, and the basic sewing kit.

1 ATTACHING INTERLINING Lay the front board panel centrally on the interlining, and clip the edges of the interlining all around the curves and corners. Spread fabric glue along the edge of the board, and fold the edges of the fabric onto the glue, pressing down firmly with your fingertips. Attach the interlining to the two side panels in the same way.

2 CUTTING FABRIC Taking into account the alignment of any patterns and the straight grain of the fabric, lay the panel in position, interlined side face down, on the wrong side of the fabric. Cut out the fabric 1¼ in (3 cm) larger than the panel all around. Repeat this procedure for the side pieces.

3 ATTACHING FABRIC Clip fabric edges at the curves and fold them over the interlined edges. Pin in place, stretching the fabric taut and laying it square on the panel. Secure fabric edges to the panel with glue, and press. Cover side pieces in the same way.

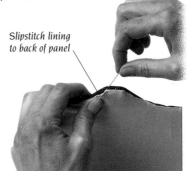

4 PREPARING LINING Lay out the lining fabric for the front and the side panels. Clip the edges around the curves and fold all edges under to the wrong side by ¾ in (2 cm). Miter the corners, and press.

Slipstitch lining to back of panel

5 ATTACHING LINING Lay the lining fabric right side up on the back of the prepared front panel. Slipstitch it in place along the edge, leaving a section at one end unstitched. Repeat for the two sides, leaving the front edges open.

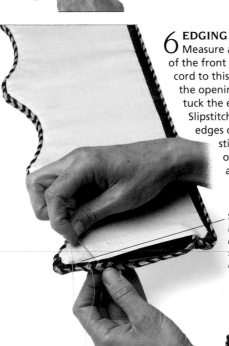

Slipstitch through lining, fabric, and cord to secure together at open end

6 EDGING FRONT PANEL Measure around the edge of the front panel and cut the cord to this length. Starting at the opening in the lining seam, tuck the ends under the lining. Slipstitch the cord to the edges of the front panel, stitching through the open section to close it as you attach the cord.

7 EDGING SIDES Measure around the top, back, and bottom edges of each side piece, and cut cord to size. Slipstitch the cord to the three edges of the sides, tucking in the ends and closing the opening as for the front panel. Slipstitch the lining to the fabric along the front edges.

8 MOUNTING RINGS Mount screws into the top of the cornice board. Sew curtain rings in place on the back of the front and side panels, below the cord, to align with these fixtures. Hang the panels on the board by the rings.

THE FINISHED CORNICE

SIMPLE VALANCE WITH BOUND EDGE

For this technique, you will need fabric, lining fabric, bias strip, heading tape, curtain rod, hooks, and the basic sewing kit. Decide on the heading tape and estimate the fabric width (the valance should have more fullness than the curtain). For joins, center the largest panel of fabric, joining panels with plain flat seams. Decide on the valance length and cut out the valance fabric, allowing 1 in (2.5 cm) for side turnings and 1½ in (4 cm) for the heading turning. Cut out the lining fabric ¾ in (2 cm) smaller all around than the fabric. Place the fabric and lining right sides together, aligning bottom edges. Pin, tack, and sew both side seams. Press seams open and turn right side out. Press flat, centering the lining so that the seams lie on the lined side, ¾ in (2 cm) in from the folded edges. Fold the top 1½ in (4 cm) of fabric down over the lining, and press.

1 ATTACHING HEADING Lay the heading tape on the valance to align it with the top edge. Pin, tack, and sew the tape in place as for a curtain heading *(see page 50)*.

2 BINDING EDGE Make up bias strip to the length of the bottom edge of the valance. Attach the bias strip *(see page 14)*. Gather and secure the heading tape, attach the hooks, and hang the finished valance on the separate curtain rod.

THE FINISHED VALANCE

INTEGRAL VALANCE

You will need a tube-lined curtain without heading tape, fabric, fringe, binding, heading tape, and the basic sewing kit. Cut the fabric to the curtain width, plus 4¼ in (11 cm) for turnings and joins. For the length, allow one-sixth to one-fifth of the curtain drop, adding ⅝ in (1.5 cm) for turnings: cut lining 3⅛ in (8 cm) less in width and to the same depth. Cut a fringe strip to 2¼ in (5.5 cm) less than length of the valance hem edge. Attach fringe to right side of fabric, ⅝ in (1.5 cm) from hem edge, facing away from the edge. Lay lining and fabric right sides together, aligning top edges, and sew a ⅝ in (1.5 cm) seam at the sides. Press seams open and turn right sides out. Fold fringed edge allowance to wrong side and press.

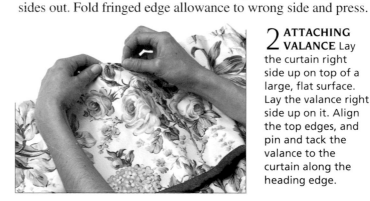

1 ATTACHING LINING Turn the bottom edge of the lining under by ⅝ in (1.5 cm). Press the turning and slipstitch it in place along the back of the fringed edge.

Slipstitch bias strip to lined side of curtain

2 ATTACHING VALANCE Lay the curtain right side up on top of a large, flat surface. Lay the valance right side up on it. Align the top edges, and pin and tack the valance to the curtain along the heading edge.

3 FIXING BINDING Cut bias strip to the length of the curtain heading edge and valance. Lay the strip along the curtain top edge and valance and align raw edges. Pin, tack, and sew the binding. Trim seam allowance to ⅛ in (3 mm).

4 STITCHING BINDING Fold the bias strip over the raw edges of the valance and curtain, and pin. Slipstitch in place along the seam line on the lined side of the curtain.

5 ATTACHING TAPE Pin, tack, and sew the heading tape to the curtain just below the bound edge, sewing through all the layers of fabric. Gather the heading tape, fit the hooks, and hang and dress the finished curtain *(see page 53)*.

THE FINISHED VALANCE

SWAGS AND CASCADES

AMONG THE MOST SOPHISTICATED and luxurious window dressings, swags and cascades (also called tails or jabots) complement and enhance functional curtains. To benefit from their full decorative effect, swags and cascades should preferably be hung over a long window in a room that has a high ceiling. Swags and cascades are constructed individually and then attached to the cornice board above a window using a staple gun to form an independent curtain furnishing. It is appropriate to make them in the same fabric as the curtain – the edges of the cascades can be highlighted with a frill, contrasting piping, or ribbon.

MAKING UP A SWAG

For the swag and binding, you will need the same fabric as used for the curtain, lining fabric, masking tape, a cornice board with sides in position *(see page 39)*, and the basic sewing kit. Measure the front panel of the cornice: this will be the width of the finished swag. To calculate the drop, measure the height of the window. The drop at the deepest point of the finished swag should be between one sixth and one eighth of this measurement.

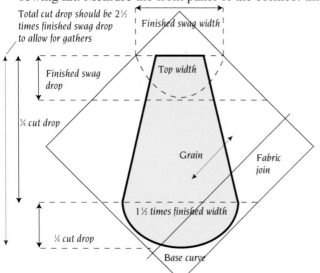

Total cut drop should be 2½ times finished swag drop to allow for gathers

Finished swag width

Finished swag drop

¾ cut drop

Top width

Grain

Fabric join

1½ times finished width

¼ cut drop

Base curve

1 DRAWING PATTERN
Using the diagram as a guide, draw a pattern on paper to the proportions shown for use as a template, adding ⅝ in (1.5 cm) for seams. You will need to cut out the pattern and pin it in place on the bias of the lining fabric.

2 CUTTING FABRIC Cut out the lining fabric around the pattern. Remove the pattern. Pin the lining fabric to the main fabric, again on the bias. Cut out main fabric, making joins, if necessary, on the straight grain with plain flat seams *(see page 14)*.

3 TURNING HEM Remove pins. Turn ⅝ in (1.5 cm) hem to wrong side along all edges of main fabric. Tack and sew, using herringbone stitch *(see page 18)*. Clip the seam allowance along the base curve to reduce its bulk *(see page 14)*. Turn a ⅝ in (1.5 cm) hem to the wrong side along lining fabric edges, and press.

4 TACKING FABRICS With the wrong sides together, tack the lining fabric to the main fabric along the three straight edges.

5 STITCHING BASE CURVE On the finished swag, the base curve will be visible. Make sure lining does not show on the right side of the swag by slipstitching panels together along base curve.

6 HANGING FABRIC Using masking tape, attach a strip of spare fabric longer than the ultimate width of the swag to the edge of a table. Mark the center and the ultimate width of the finished swag on the fabric strip as a guide. Pin the central point of the top edge of the swag to the marked center of the fabric strip. Pin the outer edges of the swag to marked width points on the fabric strip.

7 FOLDING FABRIC Working toward the center, make even folds up one long side of the fabric, allowing the fold nearest to the center to lie over the top edge of the center swag. Repeat on the other long side, mirroring the fold at the center to create a symmetrical swag. Pin all the folds securely in place. It may also be helpful to mark the fold edges at the top with a vanishing-ink pen. Remove the pins securing the swag to the tabletop fabric.

8 SEWING FOLDS Tack and sew along the tops of the folds to hold them firmly in place. To bind the top edge of the swag, cut a strip of the main fabric 2 in (5 cm) wide, and to the same length as the cornice, plus 1¼ in (3 cm). Lay one edge of binding (*see page 14*) against top edge of the swag, right sides together. Sew the binding ⅝ in (1.5 cm) from the edge.

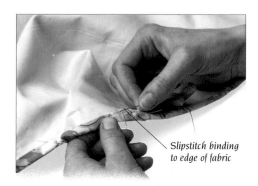

9 STITCHING BINDING To complete the swag, fold the binding over the edge of the main fabric. Tuck in the raw edges of the binding, and slipstitch along the edge to secure.

Slipstitch binding to edge of fabric

MAKING UP CASCADES

Cascades are fitted to the cornice board and fall at each side of the swag. They can be self-lined or lined with contrasting fabric. As well as cascade and binding fabrics, you will need to use a staple gun and the basic sewing kit. Make cascades in mirroring pairs. Decide on finished length of cascades (A).

The length of the shorter edge (B) should be about 6 in (15 cm). Estimate width of top edge (C), allowing for the sides of the cornice to be covered. Select the number of pleats and their width. Double the number of pleats, and multiply this by the pleat width to give finished width of the top edge.

1 MAKING PATTERN Draw and cut out a full-size paper pattern to the required dimensions for a cascade, adding ⅝ in (1.5 cm) all around for seam allowance. Use a try square to draw the corners.

B C A (pattern diagram)

2 CUTTING OUT FABRIC Pin the pattern to the straight grain of the lining fabric. Cut out the fabric. Remove the pattern from the lining fabric, and pin it in place on the straight grain of the main fabric, aligning designs, if necessary. Cut out the fabric. Make the piping (*see page 20*) to the length of the leading edge.

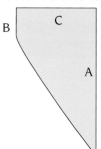

3 TRIMMING PIPING Pin and tack piping to right side of main fabric, then trim ends. Lay right sides of main and lining fabrics together. Pin, tack, and sew along three edges. Leave top open for turning out. Use zipper foot to sew along piped edge. Turn right side out, and press. Tack top edge.

Use pins to mark fold positions

4 MARKING FOLDS Lay the fabric on a flat surface, with the right side facing up. Starting from the short edge, measure and then mark the positions for the folds with pins along the top edge.

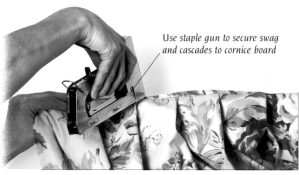

Use staple gun to secure swag and cascades to cornice board

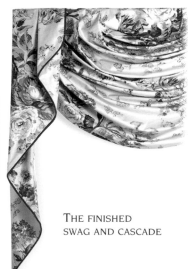

5 PINNING FOLDS Pin the folds in place, leaving the last fold open in order to position it around the side of the cornice board. Tack and sew along the top edge to secure the folds. Cut out a strip of the same fabric 2 in (5 cm) wide by the width of the top edge for the binding. Attach the binding as in steps 8 and 9, above.

6 FITTING SWAG AND CASCADES Secure the swag and cascades to the cornice with staples or tacks. Make sure that the swag is correctly centered, and staple or tack it in position along the top edge of the cornice front. Attach the cascades to the top edge of the sides and front of the cornice.

THE FINISHED
SWAG AND CASCADE

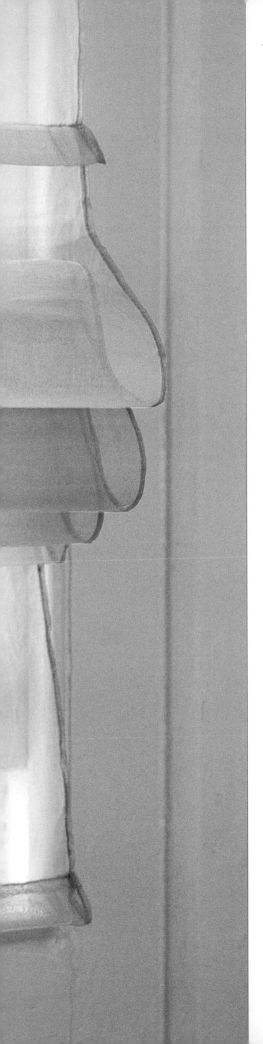

SHADES

CONCEIVED MORE THAN FOUR CENTURIES AGO, THE FIRST SHADES

WERE LITTLE MORE THAN PIECES OF FABRIC DRAPED OVER

WINDOWS, DESIGNED TO PROTECT FURNISHINGS FROM THE

DESTRUCTIVE EFFECT OF SUNLIGHT. TODAY, BY CONTRAST, SHADES

ARE FIRMLY ESTABLISHED AS A POPULAR ALTERNATIVE FOR

DECORATING WINDOWS. AS WELL AS BEING INHERENTLY

PRACTICAL, SHADES ARE EASY TO MAKE IN A VARIETY OF STYLES,

SIZES, AND MATERIALS, RANGING FROM PLAIN ROLLER SHADES TO

THE ELEGANT, GATHERED AUSTRIAN OR BALLOON SHADES. IN THIS

CHAPTER, YOU WILL FIND ALL THE INFORMATION YOU NEED TO

MAKE AND FIT ROLLER, ROMAN, AND GATHERED SHADES.

ROMAN SHADE IN COTTON VOILE
Where privacy is not a top priority, a sheer voile shade
can add color and allow natural daylight to filter into
the room. Fine seams and transparent hems maintain a
delicate look to soften the window's outline.

CHOOSING A STYLE

WINDOW SHADES can be categorized into two basic groups: plain and gathered. The first category is comprised of roller, simple tied, hooked, and Roman shades, all of which give a flat surface of color when lowered. Plain shades have a simple, tailored appearance, and roll up to allow maximum daylight to enter a room. Gathered shades include Austrian and balloon shades, and provide fuller, more opulent window dressings than plain shades. When choosing a style of shade, bear in mind that even when fully raised, a gathered shade will always obscure part of the window and block out some light.

SPLIT CANE SHADES
(above) Cane shades are relatively inexpensive and easy to cut and fit. They are particularly suitable for small or awkwardly shaped windows. Although they can be painted to match any color scheme, if left unfinished they harmonize with natural wood interiors, complementing the safari-style theme of this room. Where cane shades are the only means of window dressing, it is possible to line them with a fine cotton or voile to offer more insulation and privacy.

SKYLIGHT SOLUTION
(above) Light entering the room from overhead skylights make an area look airy and fresh, but can cause fabrics to deteriorate or fade over time. The effects of sunbleaching can be reduced with the right choice of window treatment. Here, a maneuverable natural cotton shade allows this room to remain cool.

NATURAL LINEN
(right) If the room receives plenty of natural light, and the shade is made from a loose-textured weave, leave a section of the shade on view to maintain a visual link with other fabrics and fixtures.

TRIPLE SHADES
(opposite) Adding a border to a shade will emphasize its shape and give a tailored finish to the window area. The fixtures for these Roman shades have been installed behind the recess and fit flush with the lowered ceiling for a neat finish. Pull cords would spoil the clean lines of the shades so they are secured to the window frame when not in use.

MODERN MATERIALS
(top) Denim is a hard-wearing, popular fabric, making it a good choice for contemporary interiors. Teamed with a leather pull, the roller shade will require strong hand- or machine-stitching.

SOFT FOLDS
(above) Simple tie shades are suited to lightweight fabrics that fall easily into soft folds. Leave the fabric unlined or it will become bulky and the gathering uneven.

RECESSED SHADES
(opposite) When making a shade to fit within a recess, you will need to leave a ¼ in (6mm) gap between the sides of the shade and adjacent wall to allow it to move freely. Side-winding shade mechanisms may require more space.

COTTON PRINT
(above) Once treated with a stiffening fluid, cotton print fabrics can easily be made into roller shades. The treatment dries clear leaving a durable and wipe-clean finish. In kitchen and bathroom areas prone to dampness and condensation, make sure that the stiffener contains a fungicide to prevent mold from discoloring the fabric.

PUNCHED-HOLE SHADES
(left) A fresh mix of bright canary-yellow and white paintwork gives this window a sunny look. The shade's fabric is punched with holes that create an interesting play of light when drawn. The hem has been cut away and a plastic rod serves as a pull and as a weight to keep the hem rigid.

MAKING SHADES

ONE OF THE FIRST CRITERIA for deciding on which style of shade to choose is the effect it will have when lowered and raised. When lowered, roller, Roman, tie-up, and hooked shades present flat surfaces of fabric. They also expose a greater window area when raised than gathered shades. Balloon and Austrian shades, on the other hand, are more shapely and pronounced at full length, dominating the window and its surrounding area. When raised, they remain gathered and highly decorative. Regardless of which shade you are making, it is important to take accurate, relevant measurements of the window area before starting.

TOOLS AND EQUIPMENT

To construct roller, Roman, simple, or gathered shades, you will need the basic sewing kit, plus equipment from a household tool kit. Attach fabric to poles or boards using a staple gun and staples, or small tacks and a tack hammer. Cut doweling, battens, and rollers with a crosscut saw. Use a tack hammer to secure the cap and round pin into place at the cut end of a roller. Hanging systems are mounted to a window frame with screws or to a wall using a tape measure, carpenter's level, awl, electric drill and drill bits, screwdriver, metal detector, and screw anchors.

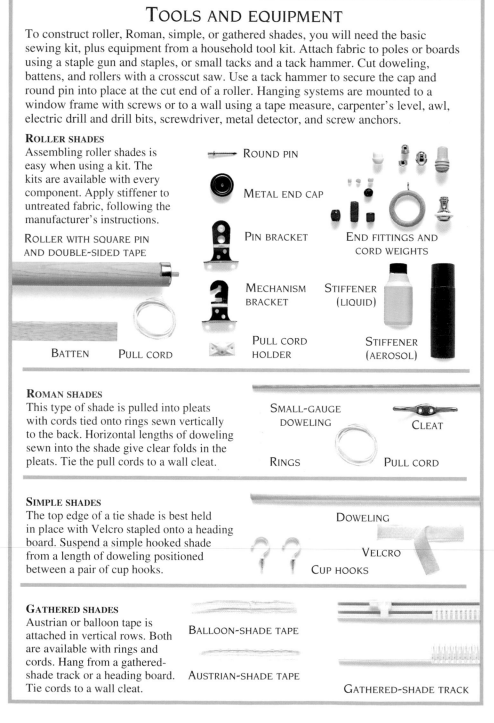

ROLLER SHADES
Assembling roller shades is easy when using a kit. The kits are available with every component. Apply stiffener to untreated fabric, following the manufacturer's instructions.

ROLLER WITH SQUARE PIN AND DOUBLE-SIDED TAPE

ROUND PIN

METAL END CAP

PIN BRACKET

END FITTINGS AND CORD WEIGHTS

MECHANISM BRACKET

STIFFENER (LIQUID)

PULL CORD HOLDER

STIFFENER (AEROSOL)

BATTEN   PULL CORD

ROMAN SHADES
This type of shade is pulled into pleats with cords tied onto rings sewn vertically to the back. Horizontal lengths of doweling sewn into the shade give clear folds in the pleats. Tie the pull cords to a wall cleat.

SMALL-GAUGE DOWELING

CLEAT

RINGS

PULL CORD

SIMPLE SHADES
The top edge of a tie shade is best held in place with Velcro stapled onto a heading board. Suspend a simple hooked shade from a length of doweling positioned between a pair of cup hooks.

DOWELING

VELCRO

CUP HOOKS

GATHERED SHADES
Austrian or balloon tape is attached in vertical rows. Both are available with rings and cords. Hang from a gathered-shade track or a heading board. Tie cords to a wall cleat.

BALLOON-SHADE TAPE

AUSTRIAN-SHADE TAPE

GATHERED-SHADE TRACK

MEASURING WINDOW AREA

If the shade is to fit inside the recess, measure from the mounting position to the windowsill for the drop required. The finished width should be 1¼ in (3 cm) less than the width of the recess. For a shade hanging outside the recess, measure from the top of the hanging system to 2 in (5 cm) below the windowsill for the drop. The finished width should be 2 in (5 cm) wider than the window at the sides to keep light from spilling in around the shade.

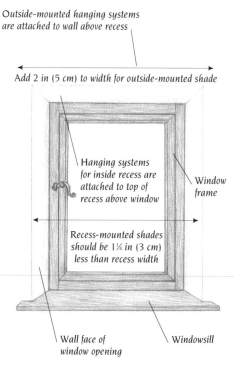

Outside-mounted hanging systems are attached to wall above recess

Add 2 in (5 cm) to width for outside-mounted shade

Hanging systems for inside recess are attached to top of recess above window

Window frame

Recess-mounted shades should be 1¼ in (3 cm) less than recess width

Wall face of window opening

Windowsill

ROLLER SHADES

THE SPRING OR SIDE-WINDER MECHANISM that causes a roller to raise and lower the fabric is what distinguishes this type of shade from others. At its full length, the shade should cover the window while allowing some daylight into the room – providing the fabric is not too thick. When the roller is attached above the window and the shade is rolled up, the entire window will be on view. You can embellish a roller shade with a decorative edging along the bottom.

SIMPLE ROLLER SHADE

Choose from a range of roller-shade fabrics, or apply stiffener to thin fabric. Brackets can be mounted to a window frame or to a wall. Purchase a roller that is too long – you can cut it down to size. When mounting the brackets, align them horizontally with the window. Cut the roller to the distance between the mounted brackets, less ⅛ in (3 mm), to allow for the end cap. Fit the end cap and hammer the pin home, following the manufacturer's instructions. Measure for the shade *(see opposite)*, checking that the roller hangs correctly in the brackets. Add 12 in (30 cm) to the length to allow for the roller to be covered with fabric when the shade is down, and for the hemmed channel for the batten at the lower edge.

1 ATTACHING BRACKET If mounting the hanging system within a window recess, allow a space of ¾ in (2 cm) from the brackets to the top of the recess. Mount the bracket for the square pin to the left of the window, and the bracket for the round pin to the right. In a wooden frame, mark the positions for the screws, then awl the holes before driving home the screws. On a wall, use a metal detector to confirm that there are no electrical wires. Mark, awl, drill holes, and insert an anchor into each hole.

2 MARKING FABRIC Measure the shade and mark the dimensions *(see opposite)*. Cut out the fabric, making sure that the corners are at perfect right angles so that the shade will hang and roll correctly. Join widths by overlapping edges by ⅜ in (1 cm) and sewing close to the raw edges (take such measurements into account when calculating the fabric).

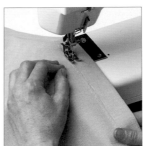

3 SEWING CHANNEL Zigzag stitch the lower edge *(see page 14)*. Place batten on wrong side of fabric. Fold lower edge over it. Mark the turning. Remove the batten. Press, tack, and sew near the stitching to form a channel. Leave sides open.

4 TAPING ROLLER Lay the fabric flat, right side up. Mark the place for the roller. Center it along the top edge of the fabric. Align the roller with the mark. Tape the top of the fabric along its length, or attach using double-sided tape, if supplied.

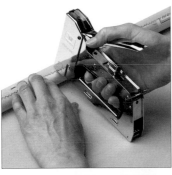

5 ATTACHING FABRIC Work a half-roll of fabric onto the roller, ensuring that the fabric is aligned. Using small upholstery tacks or staples, attach it to the roller, following the manufacturer's instructions.

6 ATTACHING CORD Cut batten ¼ in (6 mm) shorter than shade width. Center it in the channel. Secure cord in cord holder, and attach this to center of batten on wrong side of the fabric.

7 ATTACHING WEIGHT Thread the cord weight and end fitting onto the cord, and knot to secure. Wind the fabric onto the roller. Fit the roller into the brackets. Test the operation of the shade, altering the amount wound around the roller in order to obtain a perfect drop; if necessary, adjust the tension, following the manufacturer's instructions.

THE FINISHED SHADE

FRINGE-EDGED ROLLER SHADE

To give a roller shade a decorative lower edge, you will need the edging and the basic sewing kit. Measure for and make a roller shade *(see page 73)*. Consider the edging size in relation to the window, allowing for the edging to drop below the sill if the roller is to be mounted onto the molding or wall, or to the sill if it is to be recess-mounted.

1 NEATENING FRINGE Cut out the fringe to the same width as the shade, adding 2 in (5 cm) for turnings. Trim the raw edges at each end, turn them to the wrong side, and oversew to secure.

2 ATTACHING FRINGE Remove the batten and lay the lower edge of the shade on a flat surface. Using matching thread, slipstitch the fringe to the lower edge of the batten channel, with the wrong side facing the right side of the shade. Finish the shade by following steps 4–7 on page 73.

THE FINISHED SHADE

SCALLOP-EDGED ROLLER SHADE

There are several shapes, such as scallops, that can be used to decorate the lower edge of a roller shade. For this technique, you will need fabric for the shade and the facing strip, iron-on interlining to give body to the lower edge, a saucer for use as a template, and the basic sewing kit. Measure for the shade *(see page 72)*. Add the desired depth of the scallops to the dimension for the shade drop. The scallop depth here is 1¼ in (3 cm). Cut out and stiffen the shade fabric *(see page 63)*.

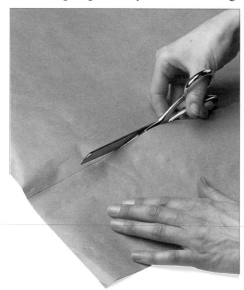

1 CUTTING PATTERN Cut out a strip of pattern paper to the width of the shade by the depth of the batten plus 3 in (7.5 cm), adding 1¼ in (3 cm) for the depth of the scallops.

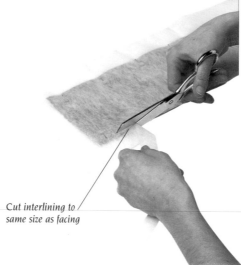

Cut interlining to same size as facing

2 TRIMMING INTERLINING Cut out a strip of fabric for the facing to the same size as the paper pattern. Cut a strip of interlining to match the facing. Press the interlining to the wrong side of the facing.

3 MARKING BATTEN LINE Machine sew a row of zigzag stitches *(see page 14)* along the top edge of the facing. Mark lines on both sides of the facing ⅜ in (1 cm) from the top edge. Mark a second line away from each marked line equal to the batten width. The batten used here is 1¼ in (3 cm) wide.

4 **DRAWING CURVE** Fold the paper pattern into equal lengths. Place the saucer on the folded pattern and draw a smooth curve for the scallop outline.

5 **CUTTING PATTERN** Hold the folded pattern firmly in one hand and cut out the scallops, carefully following the marked line.

Cut out scallops in pattern by following marked lines

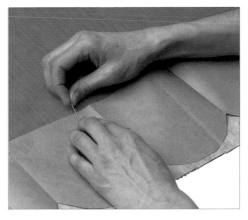

6 **PINNING PATTERN** Pin the facing and shade fabric right sides together, aligning the raw edges. Unfold the paper pattern and pin it to the facing, aligning the straight edge of the pattern with the neatened edge of the facing.

7 **MARKING FACING** Use a vanishing-ink pen to trace the outline of the scallops onto the facing. Remove the pattern. Sew a row of tacking stitches ¼ in (6 mm) inside the scallop line.

8 **SEWING FABRIC** Machine sew along the tacked line. Cut out the scallops, following the marked line. Notch the curved seam allowances (*see page 14*). Turn the shade fabric and the facing right sides out, and press.

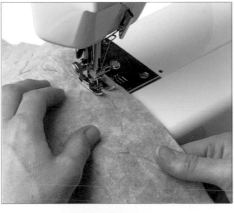

9 **STITCHING BATTEN LINE** Sew facing and shade fabric together along the lower batten line (*see step 3*). Lay out the shade and place the batten between the fabric pieces and against the stitched line. Fold the facing over the batten to check that there is space left for the batten.

10 **FINISHING CHANNEL** Remove the batten. Complete the batten channel by machine sewing the fabric close to the zigzag stitching. Finish the roller shade by following steps 4–7 on page 73.

Sew near zigzag stitch to finish batten sleeve

THE FINISHED SHADE

VIBRANT COLOR PANELS
Cool, off-white walls are given an injection of color with blocks of orange, lime, and cobalt-blue roller shades. A square detail across the weighted base of each shade acts as a clever linking device and also echoes the prints on the walls. Set within the window recesses, the shades create a strong visual contrast against the white frames.

SIMPLE SHADES

SIMPLE SHADES are well suited for covering windows in rooms where privacy is needed, such as bathrooms. These basic shades are easy to assemble, and they lend themselves to various decorative style options. The tie shades consists of unlined fabric held up by strips of fabric or ribbon, and is attached to a heading board with Velcro. The double-sided, hooked shade is more versatile than the tie shade. It is suspended from a piece of doweling supported between hooks attached above the window frame, and can be lowered, drawn halfway, reversed, and removed easily from the window.

TIE SHADE

To make this simple shade, you will need fabric for the shade, ribbon, Velcro strips, and the basic sewing kit. Alternatively, you can make ties from the fabric scraps. Measure the width and drop required, allowing for a 2 in (5 cm) overlap at all edges if the shade is to hang outside the recess. Add 2½ in (6 cm) to the width and drop measurements for turnings. Mount the heading board in position.

1 SEWING HEM Cut out the fabric. Sew a double ⅝ in (1.5 cm) hem to the wrong side on the sides and lower edge. Make four fabric ties to the width required, 2 in (5 cm) longer than the shade (see page 25).

2 MARKING FABRIC Lay out the fabric on a flat surface. Measure and mark a quarter of the shade width from both corners on the top edge.

4 ATTACHING VELCRO Cut the Velcro strip that has the tiny, smooth loops to the width of the shade. Turn 1¼ in (3 cm) of the shade fabric to the wrong side along the top edge and press. Pin, tack, and sew the Velcro strip to this turned edge of the fabric.

5 STAPLING VELCRO STRIP Staple the other Velcro strip to the heading board. Hold the shade up to the board, align the Velcro strips, and push the shade into place. To tie up the shade, gather the fabric loosely and knot the ties at the required height.

ATTACHING A HEADING BOARD

Upon deciding the position for the shade, look at the window setting and choose where to mount the heading board. If the shade is to be fitted inside the recess, mount the board to the top face of the recess with screws, as shown here. If the shade is to be fitted to the outside of a window, mount a board using angle brackets, as for the curtain cornice (see page 39). The heading board shown here is also used for hanging Roman or gathered shades – the shade cords are threaded through the eyes screwed into the underside of the board.

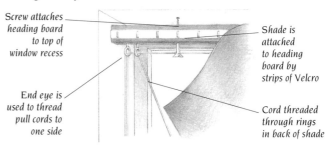

Screw attaches heading board to top of window recess

End eye is used to thread pull cords to one side

Shade is attached to heading board by strips of Velcro

Cord threaded through rings in back of shade

3 POSITIONING TIES Pin, tack, and sew the four ties to the top edge of the fabric on both sides, aligning them with the quarter marks.

THE FINISHED SHADE

REVERSIBLE SHADE

This shade works well when lined with a complementary fabric, since the back of the shade is visible when the shade is folded up. Here, the back of the shade is bordered with the main fabric. To make this shade, you will need the main fabric, lining fabric, braid edging, and the basic sewing kit. For securing the hanging system to the window frame, use two lengths of ½ in (12 mm) doweling for the top and bottom edges of the shade, a crosscut saw, two cup hooks, and an awl. For securing the hanging system to the wall, use a drill, drill bits, and screw anchors. Measure as for the Roman shade *(see page 80)*, allowing space within a recess for the doweling to protrude ¾ in (2 cm) at each end of the shade width, top and bottom. If hanging the shade outside the recess, allow a 2 in (5 cm) overlap at each side to exclude the light.

1 CUTTING OUT FABRIC Cut out the main fabric to the required measurements, adding a border allowance, here 3 in (7.5 cm) all around. Cut out the lining fabric to the exact size of the finished shade.

Turn each edge ⅝ in (1.5 cm) to wrong side

2 TURNING EDGES Lay out the main fabric wrong side up. Fold a ⅝ in (1.5 cm) hem to the wrong side on all edges, and press.

3 FOLDING AGAIN Turn the folded edges of the fabric by 2 in (5 cm) to the wrong side. Fold and press a miter in each corner *(see page 19)*.

4 MITERING CORNER Unfold the 2 in (5 cm) hems. Lay the lining fabric and main fabric wrong sides together. Align the raw edges of the lining within the creases of the hems of the main fabric. Refold the 2 in (5 cm) hems and the mitered corners, and pin in place.

Refold edges and corners once lining has been positioned

Stitch folded edge to lining to form border

5 STITCHING EDGES Tack and slipstitch close to the inner folded edge to form the border. Leave the inside edges of the mitered corners at the top and bottom unsewn to form a sleeve for inserting the pieces of doweling.

6 ATTACHING BRAID For the braid edging, measure and cut a length of braid to the same length as the inner edge of the border. Slipstitch the braid in place along this edge.

7 INSERTING DOWELING Measure width at the top and bottom edges of the shade. Cut two lengths of doweling to these dimensions, plus 1½ in (4 cm). Insert doweling into top and bottom sleeves.

Insert shade-width doweling into top and bottom sleeves

8 MOUNTING CUP HOOK Add ⅜ in (1 cm) to the shade width dimension, and mark this on the wall or window frame for the hook positions. With an awl, make pilot holes in a wooden frame, then screw the cup hooks into position. On a wall, mark, awl, drill, and use screw anchors to secure the hooks. Hang the doweling between the hooks.

THE FINISHED SHADE AT FULL LENGTH

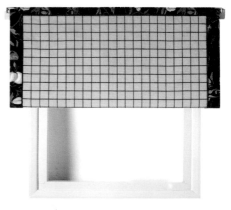

THE FINISHED SHADE WHEN FOLDED UP

ROMAN SHADES

ROMAN SHADES ARE THE MOST ELEGANT of the flat-faced shades and complement almost any decorative scheme. When raised, Roman shades gather into folds of deep horizontal pleats; these are formed by pieces of doweling that are sewn into sleeves in the lining fabric. Because the doweling gives firmness to this type of shade, there is no need to treat the fabric with stiffener. The hanging system for a Roman shade includes pull cords that run vertically up the back of the fabric and are threaded through a series of metal eyes screwed into a heading board. The same hanging system can also be used for gathered shades.

MAKING A ROMAN SHADE

Decide on the shade position and measure the window width. If the shade is to hang outside the recess, add an extra 2 in (5 cm) for a light-excluding overlap. Mount the heading board *(see page 78)*. Measure the drop from the heading board to the windowsill, or 2 in (5 cm) below if the shade is to hang outside the recess. To make this shade, you will need shade fabric, lining fabric, pull cords, crosscut saw, doweling, screw eyes, rings, Velcro strips, cleat, and the basic sewing kit.

CONSTRUCTION OF THE SHADE
The pull-up system applies to Austrian, balloon, and Roman shades. Cords are attached near the lower edge and threaded up through rings sewn to sleeves containing pieces of doweling. At the top, the cords are worked through eyes screwed into the underside of the heading board. These eyes are aligned with the vertical rows of rings at the back.

An extra eye is screwed to the side on which the cords will hang. The distance between the topmost piece of doweling and the top of the shade should be greater than the distances between the other pieces of doweling. This part is made larger so that the rest of the shade will pull up neatly behind it.

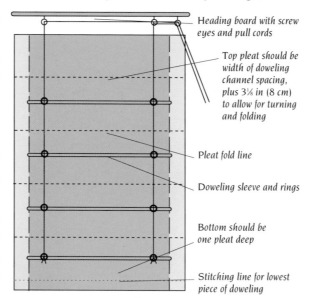

Heading board with screw eyes and pull cords

Top pleat should be width of doweling channel spacing, plus 3⅛ in (8 cm) to allow for turning and folding

Pleat fold line

Doweling sleeve and rings

Bottom should be one pleat deep

Stitching line for lowest piece of doweling

1 CUTTING FABRIC Cut out the fabric on the straight grain to the required size, adding 2½ in (6 cm) to the length and width. Cut the lining to the same size as the main fabric, less 3⅛ in (8 cm) widthwise, and add the sleeve widths – the circumference of each piece of doweling, plus ¼ in (6 mm) – to the length. You will need a piece of doweling for the bottom of the shade and for each sleeve. The top of the shade does not require a piece of doweling.

2 STITCHING SIDE HEM Lay out the lining fabric and turn the side edges by ⅝ in (1.5 cm) to the wrong side. Press, pin, tack, and sew both of the hems.

3 MARKING SLEEVE POSITIONS On the right side of the lining, mark a line 1¼ in (3 cm) from the bottom. From there, measure and mark the sleeve positions. The distance between the pieces of doweling will be twice the pleat depth.

4 FOLDING SLEEVE Following the sleeve marks, pinch the sleeves together, wrong sides facing. Pin, tack, and sew along these marks. Turn and press the sides and bottom edge of the main fabric 1¼ in (3 cm) to the wrong side.

5 MARKING SLEEVE Fold the bottom corners of main fabric into miters *(see page 23)*. From the lower folded edge, make a mark for each sleeve position. At lower edges of the fabrics, mark the midpoints.

6 PINNING FABRICS Lay the fabrics right sides together, aligning the midpoints. Sew a plain flat seam 1¼ in (3 cm) from lower edge. Trim seams to ⅝ in (1.5 cm). Fold lining and main fabric wrong sides together. Press along lower edge of seam line.

7 ALIGNING SLEEVE MARKS Align the sleeve seam line on the lining with the sleeve marks on the main fabric. Pin the lining to the main fabric along the edges.

8 ATTACHING LINING Tack together the lining and main fabric, just above or below each sleeve line and close to stitching. For the bottom doweling, tack a line 1/16 in (2 mm) plus the diameter of the doweling from the lower edge of the shade.

9 SEWING LINING Sew the lining and the main fabric together along the tacked lines. Cut doweling pieces, except the bottom one, ⅜ in (1 cm) shorter than the sleeve length. Cut the bottom doweling to the width of the shade, less ¼ in (6 mm).

10 STITCHING SIDES Insert each piece of doweling into a sleeve, including the longer piece at the bottom. Slipstitch the ends closed. Slipstitch the sides of the lining to the sides of the main fabric.

11 ATTACHING RINGS Sew the rings to the doweling sleeves, 4 in (10 cm) from the edges and 12–16 in (30–40 cm) apart. Make sure that they are aligned vertically. At the top edge of the shade, turn the fabric 1¼ in (3 cm) to the wrong side, press, and tack. Cut strips of Velcro to the same width as the shade.

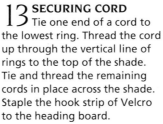

12 STITCHING VELCRO Sew the loop strip of Velcro to the top hem. Cut each cord length to twice the shade length plus the necessary amount for the cord to run along the top of the shade to the pull-up side.

13 SECURING CORD Tie one end of a cord to the lowest ring. Thread the cord up through the vertical line of rings to the top of the shade. Tie and thread the remaining cords in place across the shade. Staple the hook strip of Velcro to the heading board.

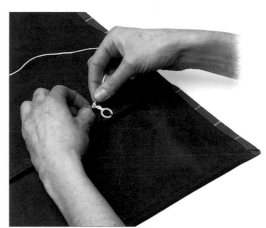

14 SECURING EYES Mark on the heading board the placement for the screw eyes. All of the eyes, except one, should line up with the rows of rings. Screw the eyes to the underside of the board corresponding with these dimensions. Fit one eye at the edge of the board on the side you wish the cords to hang. Attach the shade to the board.

15 MOUNTING SHADE Thread the cords through the eyes on the heading board, working toward the side where the cords will hang. Let the shade hang down and tie the cords together at the top, 1 in (2.5 cm) from the last eye. Trim the cords at the bottom and knot together again to neaten. Draw the shade, and mark and attach the cleat to the wall or window frame.

THE FINISHED SHADE WHEN DRAWN

GATHERED SHADES

THERE ARE TWO TYPES OF GATHERED SHADES, the Austrian and the balloon, and the headings of both are gathered in the same way as a curtain heading. Although the shades are similar in appearance, a balloon shade is gathered only at its lower edge, while an Austrian shade is gathered along its entire length. Gathered shades are drawn up by a system of parallel rows of cords threaded through rings or loops that are attached to the back of the shade, in the same way as a Roman shade *(see page 80)*. You can make gathered shades with or without a lining. Of the two shades, the balloon type is more suitable for heavy fabrics. To enhance the ruffled effect of the shade, add a frill or fringe at the lower edge and sides.

BALLOON SHADE

Measure the window and estimate the size of the finished shade *(see page 72)*. Decide on the shade fullness, and the width and number of finished swags – lightweight fabric provides the fullest swags. You will need shade fabric, lining fabric, heading tape *(see page 40)*, fringe, shade tape strips with loops or rings, pull cords, a cleat, a hanging system, heading board, and the basic sewing kit. Cut the main fabric to the required drop, adding 1½ in (4 cm) to the length for turnings and 6–24 in (15–60 cm) for gathering at the bottom edge. For the width, cut fabric to one to two and a half times desired width, depending on the fabric used and on the heading, plus 1¼ in (3 cm) for side turnings. If it is necessary to make joins to the fabric, allow 1¼ in (3 cm) for French seams *(see page 15)*. Join panels by making seams along the vertical lines where the edges of the swags will fall, and place half widths at the sides. Cut the lining to the same size as the main fabric, and stagger joins in the lining and main fabric to ease the gathering of the shade.

1 ATTACHING LINING Place the lining fabric and the main fabric right sides together. Pin, tack, and sew a seam ⅝ in (1.5 cm) from the side and lower edges of the material. Clip the corners *(see page 14)*. Turn the fabrics right side out and press.

2 ATTACHING HEADING Lay the shade out on a flat surface, with the lining side up. Turn the heading edge allowance by 1½ in (4 cm) to the wrong side, then press. Pin, tack, and sew the heading tape in place *(see page 50)*.

3 POSITIONING TAPE Mark the positions for the tape strips on the lining, beginning 1¼ in (3 cm) in from the sides. Decide on the spacing for the strips. If the fabric is one and a half times the finished shade width, the strips should be positioned apart one and a half times the finished swag width. Cut the strips to the length of the shade less the heading, allowing ⅝ in (1.5 cm) at ends for turning.

4 POSITIONING LOOPS Pin and tack the first tape strip in position with a line of stitching down each side. Turn under raw ends. Attach the remaining tape strips, making sure that the loops align horizontally. Measure from the lower edge of the shade and mark the loop positions.

5 ATTACHING TAPE Sew each of the tape strips in position, again making sure that the loops align across the shade.

6 FITTING EDGING For the fringe edging, measure the width of the shade, adding 1¼ in (3 cm) at each end for turnings. Cut the fringe to this length.

7 SECURING ENDS Turn each end of the fringe ⅝ in (1.5 cm) twice to the wrong side. Slipstitch the ends to secure them in place, taking care since the fringing can unravel easily. Slipstitch the length of fringe along the bottom edge of the front of the shade.

Slipstitch turned ends of fringe to secure in place

8 ATTACHING CORD Cut a length of cord for each tape strip to twice the finished shade length, plus the necessary amount for the cord to run along the top of the shade to the pull side. The cords are used to pull up and gather the shade.

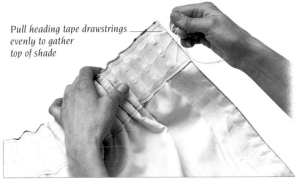

9 THREADING LOOPS For each strip, tie one end of the cord to the loop nearest to the base of the shade. Leave a long end free when tying off – this loose end will be secured to a loop two or three loops from the bottom to make the bottom swag. Thread the cord up to the heading edge through the loops in the tape strip.

Pull heading tape drawstrings evenly to gather top of shade

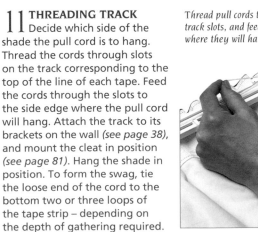

10 GATHERING HEADING
Pull up the heading tape and wind the drawstrings around a cord tie-back *(see page 50)*. Insert the curtain hooks and hang the shade on a track, or attach it to a heading board as for Roman shades *(see page 81)*.

11 THREADING TRACK Decide which side of the shade the pull cord is to hang. Thread the cords through slots on the track corresponding to the top of the line of each tape. Feed the cords through the slots to the side edge where the pull cord will hang. Attach the track to its brackets on the wall *(see page 38)*, and mount the cleat in position *(see page 81)*. Hang the shade in position. To form the swag, tie the loose end of the cord to the bottom two or three loops of the tape strip – depending on the depth of gathering required.

Thread pull cords through corresponding track slots, and feed cords to side where they will hang

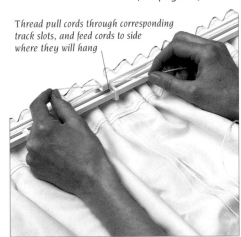

THE FINISHED SHADE

PIPED AND FRILLED AUSTRIAN SHADE

You will need fabric for the shade, frill, and piping, lining fabric, piping cord, shade tape, pull cords, cleat, and the basic sewing kit. Mount a hanging system *(see page 38)*, and measure as for a balloon shade *(see page 82)*. For the gathers, multiply the finished length by up to three for sheer and fine fabrics or one and a half for heavier materials. Add 1½ in (4 cm) for the heading tape. Cut the lining to the same size as the shade fabric. For the piping, measure the length of the shade fabric, multiply by two, and add the width. Cut a bias strip and make the piping *(see page 20)*. Multiply the piping length by two to give the frill length. Cut fabric for the frill to this length by twice the width of frill required, plus 1¼ in (3 cm). Join fabric with plain flat seams *(see page 14)*. Press the seams open. Turn each end of the frill ⅝ in (1.5 cm) to the wrong side. Press, then fold in half lengthwise. Sew across each end ¹⁄₁₆ in (2 mm) from the edges.

1 **ATTACHING PIPING** Lay the shade fabric right side up on a flat surface. Pin and tack the piping to the shade fabric along the two side edges and the lower edge.

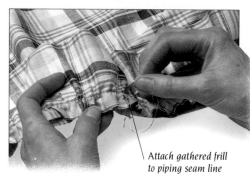

2 **TACKING FRILL** Gather the frill at the raw edges *(see page 22)*. Pin and tack the frill to the shade right sides together along the piping seam line. Start and finish the frill 1½ in (4 cm) from the top edge of the shade.

Attach gathered frill to piping seam line

3 **PINNING LINING** Lay the lining and shade fabrics right sides together. Pin, tack, and machine sew them together along the piping and frill seam, using a zipper foot. Leave heading end open. Turn right side out and press.

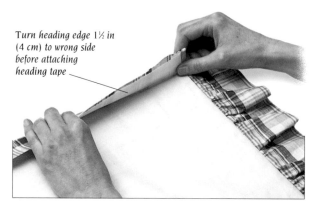

Turn heading edge 1½ in (4 cm) to wrong side before attaching heading tape

4 **TURNING HEADING EDGE** Turn the allowance at the heading edge 1½ in (4 cm) to the wrong side, and press.

Turn under end of tape ¾ in (2 cm) and align fold with edge of shade, but leave drawstrings free

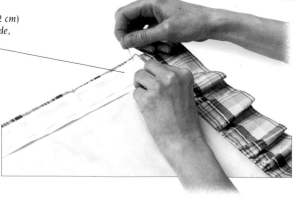

5 **ATTACHING HEADING TAPE** Apply the chosen heading tape to the wrong side of the top edge of the shade *(see page 50)*.

6 **POSITIONING TAPE** Lay the shade out flat with the lining side up. Mark positions for the tape strips, starting 1¼ in (3 cm) from the side edges. When the shade has been made to two and a half times the width of the window, the tape strips will need to be positioned two and a half times the required finished scallop-width apart from each other. Cut the number of tape strips required to the length of the shade, less the heading, allowing ⅝ in (1.5 cm) at each end for turning under raw edges.

7 PINNING TAPE
Pin, tack, and sew tape strips in position with a line of stitching down each side, turning under raw edges. Make sure that the loops (or rings) are aligned horizontally by measuring and marking loop positions from the shade's lower edge.

8 SECURING TAPE ENDS
Sew across the bottom edge of each tape strip to secure the ends of the gathering cords. When all the tape strips have been sewn in place, draw the gathering cords until the shade measures the required length.

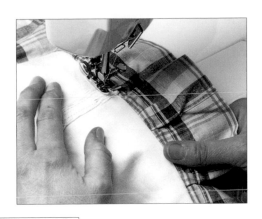

9 SECURING CORDS
Tie ends of gathering cords to themselves and roll spare cord neatly. (Do not cut the ends, since it will be necessary to ease out the gathers for cleaning.) Cut a length of pull cord for each tape strip to twice the finished shade length, plus the necessary shade width.

10 ATTACHING CORDS
Tie the end of each pull cord securely to each bottom loop of the tape strips. Thread each of the pull cords vertically through each row of loops.

Thread pull cord through tape strip and secure at bottom loop

11 TYING DRAWSTRINGS
Gather the heading tape. Do not cut the drawstrings – you can neaten them by winding them onto a cord tie-back. Insert the curtain hooks and hang the shade on the track.

Thread pull cords through corresponding track slots

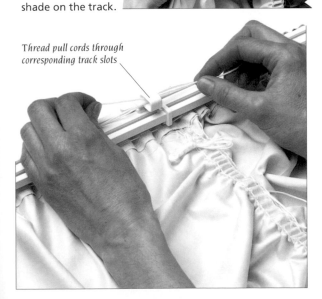

12 ATTACHING TRACK
Decide on which side of the track the pull cords will hang. Following the manufacturer's instructions, position slots on the track to align with the top of each tape strip. Thread the cords through the slots, then to the sides toward the edge where the cords will be. Attach the track to its brackets *(see page 38)*. Mount the cord cleat *(see page 81)*.

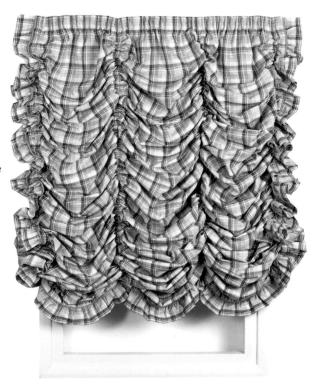

THE FINISHED SHADE

BED FURNISHINGS

THE CENTERPIECE OF THE MOST PERSONAL ROOM IN THE HOME,

A BED AND ITS FURNISHINGS SHOULD BE CHOSEN WITH AN

ATTENTION TO DETAIL THAT REFLECTS THE PREFERENCES OF ITS

OWNER. WHETHER YOU WISH TO FURNISH A SIMPLE DAYBED OR

AN ORNATE FOUR-POSTER, THERE ARE MANY PLAIN OR PATTERNED

FABRICS TO CHOOSE FROM. THIS CHAPTER DESCRIBES HOW TO

MAKE PILLOWCASES, DUVET COVERS, SHEETS, VALANCES, AND

BEDSPREADS THAT ARE BOTH PRACTICAL AND ATTRACTIVE.

PILLOWS AND BOLSTERS
The simplest of pillows is transformed
when tucked inside a handmade pillowcase.
Scalloped, frilled, or flanged edges are easy to
make and will give your bed a luxurious look.

CHOOSING A STYLE

BECAUSE A BED forms the focal point in a bedroom, bed furnishings should fulfill two functions: they should make a bed comfortable and warm to sleep in, as well as complement its size and the overall decorative scheme of the room. You can use plain or discreetly patterned fabrics to create a crisp, tailored look. To achieve a more sumptuous effect, use ornately patterned fabrics with contrasting piping, borders, or ruffles. Coordinating valances will add decorative touches while concealing unsightly bases. To create a unified look to bed furnishings, always make sure that the bedlinen complements the style of the coverings.

LINEN AND LACE
(above) Pure linen lasts a lifetime and is often passed down from one generation to the next. Sheets that have worn thin in places can gain a new lease on life when cut up to make pillowcases or covers for bolster cushions. An assortment of lacework adds to the appeal of a collection of pillows, so pile them up against the headboard to accentuate the variety you are displaying.

MACHINE QUILTING
(right) Using a basic straight stitch, herringbone quilting is easy to do by machine. For added interest, the center panel of the quilted bedspread and pillowcases have been stitched in a machine-sewn criss-cross design.

CRISP BEDLINEN
(above) Pure white cotton has a fresh, crisp style. Achieve this by making flange-edged pillowcases for square pillow pads and by sewing together cotton sheets to make duvet covers. Once finished, the pillow edges can be left plain or can be trimmed with cotton lace. For a sophisticated edge, hand- or machine-sew double-row stitching around the flange. Alternatively, embroider white-on-white initials on the bedlinen.

STRIPES AND FLORALS
(opposite) This bedlinen, mixing stripes and florals, is color-matched so, whichever is dominant, the look remains cohesive. Here, the two fabrics are brought together in a cottage-style bedroom. The room's appearance could be altered with stripes for pillowcases and florals for sheets.

MULTI-LAYERED LOOK
(right) A combination of sheets, bedspreads, and throws offers the perfect solution for arriving at the right degree of warmth at bedtime. Define the layers by starting with plain white or off-white cotton sheets, then choose a richer color for the pillowcases and duvet. The sheeting color complements the quilt, folded back to display the saddle stitch and button detail. A soft wool throw completes the bed's relaxed, comfortable style.

FLORAL DETAIL
(left) Having successfully made a plain pillowcase and button-up duvet cover, it is relatively easy to add an embroidered floral motif. Make a template of the design and copy it onto the fabric. Then, machine-embroider the design onto the pillow and duvet cover using threads in matching colors. For more instant results, paint on a floral design with fabric paints, which can be bought from most specialized arts and crafts shops.

RICH COLOR THEMES
(left) Lace-trimmed linen sheets teamed with plaid wool blankets work well with an antique cast iron bedframe to give this room rich contrast in style. Several pillows in rich ruby red are piled on top of white ones to continue the red theme, and a generous red tablecloth and lampshade on the bedside table complete the room.

WARMTH WITH COLOR
(below) Vibrant colors instantly give a sense of warmth and well-being to a room. Here, scarlet and purple bedspreads are balanced by warm pine paneling. The bed on the far side of the room uses bold purple blocks of color while the bed in the foreground is trimmed with purple. Although both beds are presented differently, the wide bands of color work together to give a harmonious look.

PILLOWCASES

MAKING YOUR OWN COLORFUL PILLOWCASE is a simple and inexpensive method of decorating a bed. Only a small amount of fabric is needed for assembling a pillowcase, and you can choose the fabric from a great variety of durable and easy-to-wash sources, ranging from elegant linens to printed dress materials. A pillowcase can be fastened with a concealed inner fold of fabric or by means of simple or fanciful buttons or ties. In addition to decorative fastenings, you can give a pillowcase a personal touch by adding an edging, such as a flange or a frill, to complement your bed furnishings.

PLAIN PILLOWCASE

This simple pillowcase is made from a continuous length of fabric and is therefore quick and easy to make up. One end of the fabric is folded over to the inside, forming a hidden flap that holds the pillow in position. To make this pillowcase, you will need suitable fabric that is more than twice the length of the pillow itself, plus the basic sewing kit.

1 MEASURING Measure the pillow length and width. Cut out fabric to twice the length, adding 9½ in (24 cm) for turnings and the fold-over flap. Add 1¼ in (3 cm) to the pillow width for seam allowances. Turn, pin, and tack a ⅝ in (1.5 cm) double hem along the width at one end of the fabric, and press.

2 MAKING HEM Turn the fabric around so that you are working at the opposite end, then fold over a hem to the wrong side by ⅜ in (1 cm), followed by a 2 in (5 cm) turning, to form a wide-hemmed edge. Pin, tack, and sew.

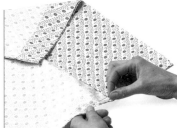
Pillowcase fabric should be durable and easy to care for

3 MAKING POCKET Turn the fabric around again so that you are working at the ⅝ in (1.5 cm) double hem. Make the internal pocket that will hold the pillow by folding over a 6 in (15 cm) flap of fabric to the inside. Pin and press. Fold the fabric in half along the width, so that the wrong sides are together.

Wide internal pocket of fabric will act as fastening

4 SEWING SEAMS Align the sides then the wide-hemmed edge with the edge of the flap. Pin, tack, and sew a ¼ in (6 mm) seam on each long side of fabric – this is the first stage of a French seam *(see page 15)*. Trim the seams and remove all of the tacking stitches.

5 ENCLOSING EDGES Turn the pillowcase wrong side out, and press before pinning and tacking the long sides of the fabric together, ⅜ in (1 cm) from the first seam. This second seam will enclose the raw edges.

6 COMPLETING SEAMS Complete the French seams by machine sewing along the two long sides of the pillowcase, again working ⅜ in (1 cm) from the first seam. Remove the tacking stitches. Turn the completed pillowcase right side out and press.

THE FINISHED PILLOWCASE

PILLOWCASE WITH FLANGE EDGING

Unlike the plain pillowcase opposite, this is constructed from separate sections of fabric and incorporates a fastening consisting of buttons and a strip of looped rouleau. Select the fabric for the pillowcase, and have ready the basic sewing kit.

Measure the pillow, then cut out one piece of fabric to the same size, plus ⅝ in (1.5 cm) all around. For the facing strip, which conceals the pillow, cut a length of fabric to the same width as the pillow, plus ⅝ in (1.5 cm), by 2½ in (6 cm) wide.

1 MEASURING FABRIC Mark and cut out the fabric for flanged-edge panel to the same size as pillow, plus 5 in (12.5 cm) all around. Make a rouleau strip 2 ft (60 cm) long *(see page 25)*.

2 HEMMING STRIP Turn, press, and pin a ⅜ in (1 cm) double hem on a long edge of facing strip. Take smaller panel and mark ¾ in (2 cm) intervals along right side of a short edge.

3 POSITIONING ROULEAU Pin and tack rouleau strip to this edge, making loops between marks. Lay facing strip over rouleau, with right sides together. Match the raw edges.

4 PINNING FACING STRIP Secure the facing strip in place over the rouleau strip by pinning, tacking, and sewing it ⅝ in (1.5 cm) from the edge of the panel of fabric.

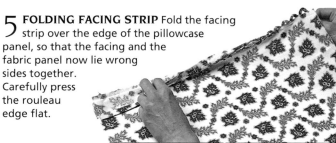

5 FOLDING FACING STRIP Fold the facing strip over the edge of the pillowcase panel, so that the facing and the fabric panel now lie wrong sides together. Carefully press the rouleau edge flat.

6 FOLDING EDGES Take the larger of the two panels, fold over the edges by ⅝ in (1.5 cm) to the wrong side, and press flat. Fold the edges over again to the wrong side by 2 in (5 cm) and press.

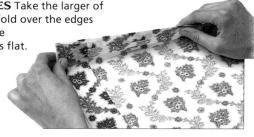

Tuck straight edge of back casing under flange fold

7 MITERING CORNERS Neaten the folds of the fabric at the corners by machine mitering *(see page 19)*.

8 TRIMMING CORNERS Trim the excess fabric at the mitered corners *(see page 19)*. Press the seams open. Turn the corners right side out, and press.

9 JOINING SECTIONS Lay the pillowcase back with the rouleau onto the mitered pillowcase front, wrong sides together. Line up the rouleau edge with the inside edge of the flange on one of the short sides. Tuck the other three edges of the back under the fold of the flange. Pin in place and tack.

10 STITCHING EDGES On three sides, topstitch around the edges close to the turning edge of flange. Do not sew over the rouleau edge. After the first row, topstitch a second row ¼ in (6 mm) in from the first.

11 ATTACHING BUTTONS Sew the buttons to the flange edge, corresponding to the rouleau. Make sure the buttons are aligned with the loops. Press the finished pillowcase.

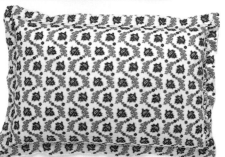

BUTTON AND ROULEAU FASTENING

THE FINISHED PILLOWCASE

FRILLED PILLOWCASE WITH TIE FASTENINGS

To make this pillowcase, you will need suitable fabric and the basic sewing kit. First, cut out two panels to the same size as the pillow, plus ⅝ in (1.5 cm) all around. Cut out a strip of fabric for the internal flap; the length should measure the same as the pillow's width, plus ⅝ in (1.5 cm), by 6 in (15 cm) wide. Cut out a piece of fabric for the frill to twice the entire perimeter of the pillow. The width of the frill fabric should be twice the width of the finished frill, plus 1¼ in (3 cm) for seam allowances. Make the frill as a continuous strip (see page 22). Mark divisions at the frill seam-line with tailor's tacks in order to align the frill with diagonally opposite corners; this will ensure an even distribution of gathers.

1 MEASURING TIES Cut out ties from the pillowcase fabric. The number required depends on the size of the pillowcase. Here, there are three pairs of ties, made from six fabric pieces, each 2 x 10 in (5 x 25 cm). Make ties to the size required (see page 25).

2 ALIGNING FRILL Take one of the panels and, on the right side, align the tailor's tacks made on the frill to one corner of the panel, and pin the frill to the panel at this point. Align the tailor's tacks to the corner diagonally opposite, and pin.

3 GATHERING FRILL Pull ᴏʀ gathering stitches from pinned corner so that one long and one short side of frill is same length as corresponding sides of panel. Arrange gathers so they are evenly distributed (see page 22). Pin and tack. Align, pin at corners, gather, and secure other half of frill to remaining two sides.

4 TURNING HEM On the back panel of the pillowcase, turn under and pin a double hem of ³⁄₁₆ in (5 mm), followed by ⅜ in (1 cm), to the wrong side of one short edge. Press, tack, and sew along this hemmed edge – this will be the open edge. Remove tacking stitches.

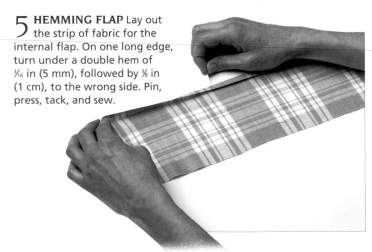

5 HEMMING FLAP Lay out the strip of fabric for the internal flap. On one long edge, turn under a double hem of ³⁄₁₆ in (5 mm), followed by ⅜ in (1 cm), to the wrong side. Pin, press, tack, and sew.

6 ATTACHING TIES Pin and tack three of the fabric ties to the frilled edge of the pillowcase opening. Position one of the ties centrally, and the other two ties equidistantly to either side.

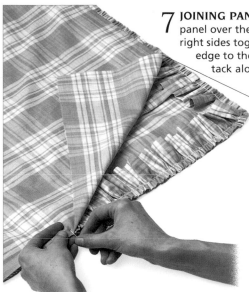

7 JOINING PANELS Lay the pillowcase back panel over the front panel on top of the frill, right sides together, matching the hemmed edge to the seam line of the frill. Pin and tack along the three unhemmed sides.

Match seam lines on three sides of pillowcase

8 ATTACHING FLAP Place the flap fabric, right side down, at the open end of the pillowcase, on top of the frill, ties, and hemmed edge of the back panel. Pin and tack in place, taking care not to sew through the hemmed edge of the opening. Machine sew all around the pillowcase, ⅝ in (1.5 cm) from the edges. Remove the tacking stitches, and turn the pillowcase right side out.

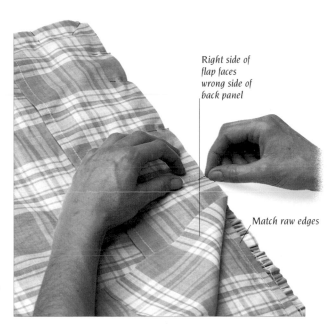

Right side of flap faces wrong side of back panel

Match raw edges

9 COMPLETING TIES Complete the fastenings by pinning, tacking, and sewing the other three ties to the open edge of the pillowcase, adjacent to the ties secured within the frill. Press the finished pillowcase.

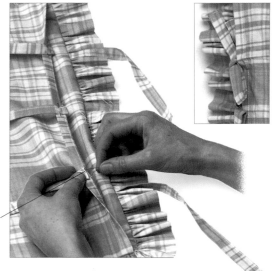

Pin ties to underside of open edge

THE FINISHED PILLOWCASE

ENGLISH EMBROIDERY

As an alternative to making a frill, you can use a piece of ready-made edging, such as English embroidery, for this type of pillowcase. English embroidery does not need to be gathered as much as a frill; use a strip one and a half times the length of the pillow's circumference. To make this pillowcase, you will need fabric, English embroidery, and the basic sewing kit.

1 JOINING ENGLISH EMBROIDERY Tack the strips of English embroidery together, right sides facing.

2 SEWING FRENCH SEAMS Sew a French seam ³⁄₁₆ in (5 mm) from the edge. Remove the tacking stitches, trim the seams, and press.

THE FINISHED PILLOWCASE

SCANDINAVIAN INFLUENCE
A red-and-white checked cotton patchwork quilt on a traditional sleigh bed makes an eye-catching feature in a simply furnished room. White bedlinen decorated with red cross-stitch embroidery also adds to the simple charm. To give a handmade quilt a more relaxed style, sew together a mixture of rectangular and square pieces of fabric rather than identically-sized pieces.

DUVET COVERS

DUVETS ARE WARM IN THE WINTER and lightweight in the summer, and in many households a duvet has taken the place of blankets and a top sheet as a comfortable and decorative bed covering. When combined with a fitted bottom sheet, a covered duvet allows for easy and quick bedmaking, needing only to be lightly shaken or turned over each morning. To cover a duvet, you can use either an extra-wide sheeting fabric or other easy-care material. It is well worth bearing in mind that many fabrics will have to be seamed to make up the required width.

BUTTONED DUVET COVER

Made from one length of fabric, this simple duvet cover is suitable for all types of duvet. Measure length and width of your duvet, which should overlap the bed by about 10 in (25 cm). Cut out a piece of fabric to twice the duvet length, adding 6 in (15 cm), by the width of the duvet, adding 4 in (10 cm). These allowances are for seams and fastenings, and provide space for the duvet, which is important if it is filled with feathers and down. In addition to the cover fabric, you will need buttons and the basic sewing kit.

Turn a hem twice along each short side of unfolded fabric

1 PINNING HEM Lay the covering fabric right side down on a flat surface and turn under the two short sides of the fabric by ⅜ in (1 cm) and then ⅝ in (1.5 cm) to the wrong side. Press, pin, tack, and sew these hems. Remove the tacking stitches.

2 SEWING SEAMS Fold fabric in half along width, wrong sides together. Align hemmed edges. Pin, tack, and sew first part of French seam (see page 15) down each side ³⁄₁₆ in (5 mm) from edges. Trim allowances to ⅛ in (3 mm) along sides. Turn wrong side out and press seams. Finish French seam at each side, ⅜ in (1 cm) from the folded edge.

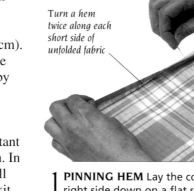

3 MARKING OPENING Using a tape measure, triangle, and vanishing-ink pen, measure and draw a line on the wrong side of the fabric along both sides of the cover 2 in (5 cm) from, and parallel to, the folded edge of the hemmed opening.

4 SEWING OPENING From each edge of the cover, pin, tack, and sew 8 in (20 cm) along the marked guideline. This will leave an opening in the cover large enough to insert the duvet. Remove the tacking stitches.

5 FOLDING OPENING Fold both unsewn edges of the duvet cover at the opening end to the wrong side along the marked guidelines. Press the folded edges. Turn the duvet cover right side out and press again. Mark the positions for the buttonholes along one edge of the folded opening. Make the buttonholes to the appropriate size (see page 26).

6 ATTACHING BUTTONS Use the buttonholes as a guide to mark the button positions on the opposite edge, then sew the buttons in place. Fill the cover with the duvet, shake it into place, and fasten the buttons.

THE FINISHED DUVET

BUTTON FASTENING

PIPED DUVET COVER WITH TIE FASTENINGS

This duvet cover with piping is made up of two panels of material, with a side opening secured by matching fabric ties. Begin by cutting out two pieces of fabric to the dimensions of your duvet, adding 4 in (10 cm) all around for seam allowance. Make piped edging to the circumference of the cover at seam line, adding 4 in (10 cm) for joining (see page 20). To make the duvet cover, you will need fabric for the cover, facing, ties, and piping, and the basic sewing kit.

1 ATTACHING PIPING Pin and tack the piping to the right side of the front cover panel along the seam line. Clip the corners of the piping and join the ends (see page 21).

2 SEWING PANELS Place the fabric panels right sides together. Pin, tack, and sew them together along the seam line, leaving an opening of approximately 1 yd (1 m) in the center of one side seam. Clip the excess fabric at the corners (see page 14).

3 MAKING FACING Cut out a strip twice the length of the opening, adding 1¼ in (3 cm) to the length for allowances, and 7½ in (19 cm) to the width. Sew a ⅝ in (1.5 cm) double hem to the wrong side along a long edge of the strip. Join the fabric length with a seam ⅝ in (1.5 cm) from short edges. Make ties from eight strips (see page 25), each measuring 2 x 14 in (5 x 36 cm).

4 ATTACHING TIES Mark four equidistant points on each side of the opening to show the positions for the ties. Pin and tack the ties in place, making sure that they are aligned in pairs.

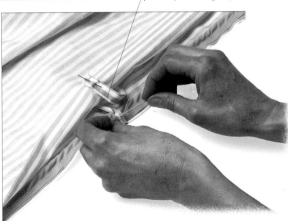

Ties should be aligned in pairs before sewing in place

5 POSITIONING FACING Turn the facing strip right side out and tuck it into the cover opening. Pin and tack the facing strip to the inside of the cover opening along one side. Make sure you have aligned the raw edges of the facing with the raw edges of the opening.

6 SECURING FACING Machine or hand sew the facing strip in place, ensuring that the raw edges are aligned. When you have finished sewing, remove the tacking stitches. Turn the duvet cover right side out.

7 TUCKING IN FACING Tuck the facing strip inside the cover opening. Press the finished duvet cover and fill it with the duvet. The corners of the cover should be well filled with the duvet. Tie the fabric ties neatly into secure but decorative bows.

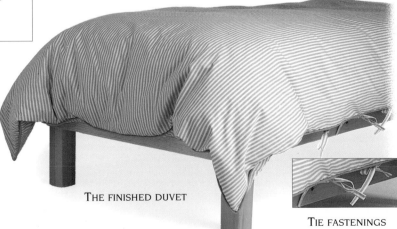

THE FINISHED DUVET

TIE FASTENINGS

SHEETS

MAKING YOUR OWN SHEETS is an economical and satisfying project. You can use any fabric that is light, durable, and easy to care for. Fabrics that are too narrow for your mattress can be joined lengthwise. Reduce the impact of the seams by making up a central full-width panel seamed with cut-down side panels. Extra-wide fabric made especially for sheeting is also available in a range of widths, such as 7½ or 9 ft (228 or 274 cm). Traditional flat sheets are the most versatile type of sheet because they can be used as either top or bottom sheets. Bottom sheets with fitted corners are, however, much easier to handle when making a bed.

FLAT SHEET WITH DECORATIVE STITCHING

If you are going to use a flat sheet as a top sheet, consider decorating the top seam line of the fabric with a satin stitch sewn in a matching or contrasting colored thread. Choose fabric from a range of suitable cottons, linen, or poly-cottons, and calculate the amount of fabric needed. To make this sheet, you will need fabric for the sheet and the basic sewing kit.

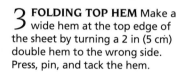

1 CALCULATING FABRIC Measure the length and width of the mattress. Add 16 in (40 cm) to the width (A), plus twice the mattress depth (B), and 20 in (50 cm) to the length (C), plus twice the mattress depth (B). Add a ¾ in (2 cm) allowance for side hems, if these are required.

2 SEWING HEMS Turn and press ⅜ in (1 cm) double hems to the wrong side along each long edge. Pin, tack, and sew. Turn the fabric around and fold a ⅝ in (1.5 cm) double hem to the wrong side along the bottom edge. Press, pin, tack, and sew.

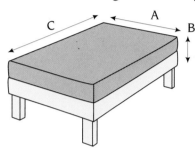

Wide hem will make an attractive band at top edge of sheet

3 FOLDING TOP HEM Make a wide hem at the top edge of the sheet by turning a 2 in (5 cm) double hem to the wrong side. Press, pin, and tack the hem.

4 STITCHING TOP HEM Machine stitch the wide hem edge, using satin stitch, which is a close, tight zigzag *(see page 14)*. Remove the tacking stitches and press the finished sheet.

THE FINISHED SHEET

FLAT SHEET WITH PIPED TOP SEAM LINE

To make this flat sheet, you will need sheet fabric, piping cord, a bodkin, and the basic sewing kit. Select piping cord to the width of the fabric, plus 2 in (5 cm). Make a flat sheet *(see above)*.

Topstitch along, and ⅜ in (1 cm) in from, the edge of the wide hem at the top edge of the sheet. Topstitch again, ½ in (12 mm) from the first row of stitches, to form a narrow channel.

1 THREADING CORD Thread the piping cord onto a bodkin, then ease the cord through the channel in the top seam line.

2 TRIMMING CORD Once the piping cord is positioned along the length of the channel, cut off the excess cord close to the edge of the sheet.

3 SECURING ENDS Secure the ends of the cord by oversewing either by hand or with a sewing machine. Press the finished sheet.

THE FINISHED SHEET

FITTED BOTTOM SHEET

A fitted bottom sheet requires slightly less material overall than a flat sheet, because the elasticized corners keep the sheet firmly in place. Fitted sheets also greatly facilitate the task of making up a bed. To make this type of sheet, you will need fabric for the sheet, 1 yd (1 m) of elastic that is ¼ in (6 mm) wide, as well as the basic sewing kit.

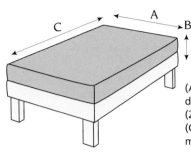

1 CALCULATING FABRIC

Measure the length and width of the mattress. Add 8 in (20 cm) to the width (A), plus twice mattress depth (B), and 8 in (20 cm) to the length (C), plus twice the mattress depth (B). Cut out the sheeting fabric to these dimensions.

2 REMOVING CORNERS

Lay fabric wrong side up. From corner along each edge, mark mattress depth plus 4 in (10 cm). Form a square at the corner by drawing lines from each marked edge. Draw lines ⅝ in (1.5 cm) to inside of first lines. Cut along the second set of lines. Repeat on remaining three corners.

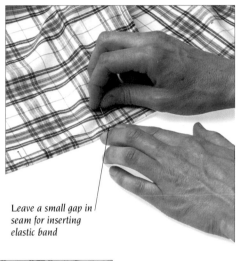

3 SEWING CORNERS

Position wrong sides of cut edges of corner together, and pin, tack, and sew a seam ³⁄₁₆ in (5 mm) from edge, as first part of a French seam (see page 15). Trim allowance to ⅛ in (3 mm). Turn right sides together, press, and finish French seam. Repeat on three remaining corners.

Leave a small gap in seam for inserting elastic band

4 PINNING HEM

Turn a ³⁄₁₆ in (5 mm) and then a ⅜ in (1 cm) hem to the wrong side along all edges of the sheet. Pin, tack, and sew the hem. Along each edge, leave a ⅜ in (1 cm) gap in the seam, 6 in (15 cm) from all four corners. You will insert the elastic band through these gaps to form the fitted corners. Remove the tacking stitches.

5 INSERTING ELASTIC

Cut four 10 in (25 cm) lengths of elastic and thread each through corner hems from gap to gap. To do this, pin one end and pull the other end to gather corners. Oversew to secure elastic at openings. Sew up openings. Repeat at other corners. Press finished sheet.

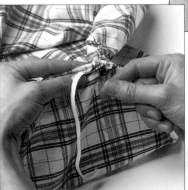

THE FINISHED SHEET

FITTED TOP SHEET

Cut fabric to mattress width, adding twice mattress depth plus 16 in (40 cm), and to length of mattress, adding mattress depth plus 8 in (20 cm). Cut out and sew two corners at the foot end as above. Sew a ⅜ in (1 cm) double hem along the long edges and one short end of the sheet, leaving gaps for elastic at two corners as described above. Insert and secure the elastic.

HEMMING TOP EDGE

Next, turn the fabric to work at the raw edge. Neaten this edge by turning a 2 in (5 cm) double hem to the wrong side. Finish the top sheet by pinning, tacking, pressing, and sewing the hem in place.

VALANCES

A VALANCE IS A BED FURNISHING accessory that provides a decorative cover for the sides and foot of a bed, particularly those with a solid base. You can choose to make a valance with either an informal-looking gathered skirt or a plain-sided panel, complete with corner pleats. The style that you opt for will depend on the character of your bedroom. For both types of valance, the technique involves sewing a three-sided skirt onto a piped top panel that fits over the bed base and under the mattress.

GATHERED VALANCE

Choose a decorative fabric for the gathered skirt; for economy, use a plain material for the top panel, which will be hidden from view, and edge it with a border of the same fabric as the skirt. You will also need prewashed piping cord, piping fabric, and the basic sewing kit. Prevent uneven shrinkage by prewashing both the skirt and the panel fabrics. Measure the length and width of the bed, and cut out a piece of plain fabric for the top panel to this size, less 8 in (20 cm) all around. To choose the length of the skirt drop, measure from the bed base down to where you want the skirt to finish.

B / Facing over end of bed-head
Bed base
C
Piping
A
Top panel with border strips
Gathered skirt

1 MEASURING Cut out a length of fabric for the skirt to three times length of top panel (A), plus one and a half times its width (B), by the skirt drop (C). If necessary, join fabric using French seams (*see page 15*). Cut out five strips of fabric, all 5 in (12.5 cm) wide: two to length of A, plus 1¼ in (3 cm); two to length of B, minus 9¼ in (23 cm); and one to length of B, plus 1¼ in (3 cm), for facing.

2 SEWING ENDS Pin, tack, and sew a short border strip to each end of the top panel, right sides together, ⅝ in (1.5 cm) from edges. Press seams open.

3 ATTACHING SIDE STRIPS In the same way, attach a long border strip to each side of the top panel to form an edging. Press the seams open.

4 MARKING CORNERS Use a saucer or a glass to draw a curve at each corner. Cut along the curves. Make up piping (*see page 20*) to twice the length of A, plus B, adding 9½ in (24 cm) for the two corners at the bed-head end. Cut the piping cord ¾ in (2 cm) short of the bias strip at each end. Turn ¾ in (2 cm) at the ends to the wrong side.

5 STITCHING PIPING Fold the bias strip over the piping cord at each end, and slipstitch the edges together so that the ends of the cord are enclosed.

6 ATTACHING PIPING Pin and tack piping to the right side of the top panel. Turn the extra around the head-end corners. Turn ⅝ in (1.5 cm) double hems at the ends and bottom edge of the skirt. Press, pin, tack, and sew hems.

7 SECTIONING SKIRT On the top edge of the skirt fabric, measuring from one hemmed end, mark a point at one and a half times the length of A, plus 7 in (18 cm). This section will fit one side of the top panel. From this point, measure one and a half times the length of B and mark, to correspond with the opposite corner. The remaining length of fabric fits the other long side of the panel.

8 SEWING GATHERING STITCHES Sew gathering stitches between the marks along the top of the skirt fabric, ⅝ in (1.5 cm) from the edge (*see page 22*). Overlap the stitches at the corners to make it easier to pull up the gathers.

9 PINNING SKIRT Align one end of the skirt with one end of the piping on the top panel, with the right sides of the fabric together. Pin ⅝ in (1.5 cm) from the edge.

10 ALIGNING MARKS Match the first mark to the first corner, and pin at this point. Pull up the gathers. Distribute evenly along the fabric. Repeat along the remaining sections of the skirt, finishing at the other end of the piping. Tack and sew the skirt in place, using the zipper attachment on the machine.

11 HEMMING FACING On one long edge of the strip of fabric for the facing, turn, pin, tack, and sew a double hem of ³⁄₁₆ in (5 mm), followed by ⅜ in (1 cm).

12 ATTACHING FACING Pin, tack, and sew, right sides together, the raw edge of the facing to the head end of the top panel, over the border strip and along the skirt seams.

13 FITTING VALANCE Turn right side out. The facing strip lies over the head end of the top panel and neatens the valance's appearance. Press the valance, and fit it in place.

THE FINISHED VALANCE

CORNER-PLEATED VALANCE

This plain-sided bed valance is constructed with corner inserts that together form box pleats. Make up the top panel by following the directions to the end of step 6, opposite, but do not cut out the fabric for the skirt. For this valance, you will need three separate pieces of fabric for the skirt. Two pieces should measure the length of the bed, plus 8 in (20 cm); the length of the third piece should be equal to B (see diagram opposite), plus 8 in (20 cm). Measure the length required for the skirt drop (C), and add 1¼ in (4.5 cm). This measurement is the width of the three skirt panels.

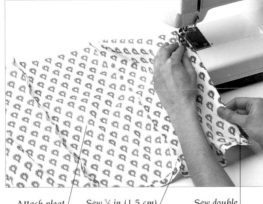

2 ATTACHING INSERTS Starting at the bed-head end, pin, tack, and sew a top corner panel to a pleat insert, ⅝ in (1.5 cm) from the edge, right sides together. Join this insert to one of the side skirt panels in the same way. At the foot corner, join this side skirt panel to another pleat insert. In this way, continue around the valance, finishing with the other bed-head corner panel. Trim all seam allowances.

1 MEASURING Cut out four panels for the pleat inserts to the same width as the skirt fabric, by 8 in (20 cm). For the corner panels at the bed-head end, cut two panels to the same width as the skirt, by 10½ in (26.5 cm) wide.

Attach pleat inserts to skirt panels

Sew ⅝ in (1.5 cm) double hems on lower edges of all skirt panels

Sew double hems to wrong sides on edges of corner panels

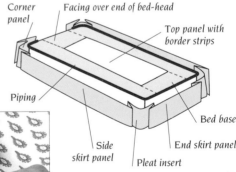

Corner panel

Facing over end of bed-head

Top panel with border strips

Piping

Bed base

Side skirt panel

End skirt panel

Pleat insert

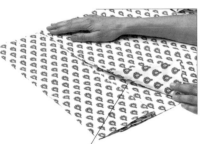

Fold ends of side panels to center of inserts to form box pleats, and press, pin, and tack ⅝ in (1.5 cm) from top edge to secure pleats while attaching them to top panel

3 FOLDING PLEATS At each corner, fold side panels to centre of insert to form a box pleat. Press, pin, and tack 1.5 cm (⅝ in) from top edge to secure them in place while attaching to top panel.

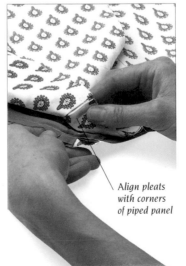

4 ATTACHING SKIRT Pin, tack, and sew the skirt with pleated corners, right sides together, to piped edge of the top panel. Turn a double hem of ³⁄₁₆ in (5 mm), followed by ⅜ in (1 cm), on one long edge of the facing panel. Pin, tack, and sew the facing panel to the head end of the top panel, right sides together, along top edge and skirt seams. Turn right side out and press. Trim all seams before fitting valance in place.

Align pleats with corners of piped panel

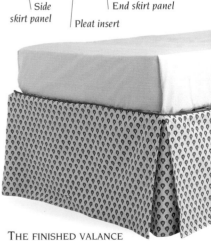

THE FINISHED VALANCE

BEDSPREADS

THE PURPOSE OF A BEDSPREAD is primarily to decorate a bed when it is not in use. A throw cover is easy to prepare and presents a casual, comfortable dressing. This style of cover can be made in a heavyweight fabric, so that it can double as an extra blanket. Alternatively, fitted covers, which are made to fit the shape of a mattress exactly, neaten the appearance of a bed, allowing you the option of using it as a seat. For a tailored finish, you can make a cover with a straight skirt and box-pleated corners. Choose a cover with a gathered skirt and contrasting piping for a more relaxed effect.

REVERSIBLE THROW COVER

To make a reversible cover, use matching or contrasting fabrics for the top and lining panels. If you wish the bedspread to have insulating properties, either quilt material *(see page 15)* or select a medium- to heavyweight fabric. Allow the fabric to drape to the length you wish. Select a fabric for the binding, and have the basic sewing kit ready.

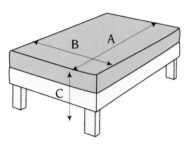

1 MEASURING With the bed linen in place, measure the length of the bed (A) and the width (B). Decide on the length of drop you require (C). Add to A the measurement of C; if you wish the cover to extend over a pillow, add a further 6 in (15 cm) to A. Add to B twice the length of C. Cut the top and lining panels to these dimensions, if necessary allowing for joins *(see page 17)* and pattern matching.

2 MARKING CORNERS Using a circular template, round off the four corners on the wrong side of both the fabric panels. Cut along the curved lines. Fold both pieces of fabric in half and line up the edges in order to check that all the corners are the same shape.

3 JOINING PANELS Lay the wrong sides of the top and lining fabrics together. Pin and tack the two fabrics to each other all around, ⅜ in (1 cm) from the edges.

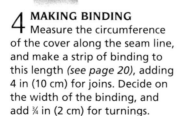

Fold ⅜ in (1 cm) to wrong side on both edges, and press flat

4 MAKING BINDING Measure the circumference of the cover along the seam line, and make a strip of binding to this length *(see page 20)*, adding 4 in (10 cm) for joins. Decide on the width of the binding, and add ¾ in (2 cm) for turnings.

5 ATTACHING BINDING With the right sides together, pin, tack, and sew one edge of the binding to the top panel of fabric, ⅝ in (1.5 cm) from the edge, along the fold line of the binding. Trim the seam allowance to ⅜ in (1 cm), or just under half the finished width.

6 COMPLETING BINDING Turn the cover over. Fold the binding over the edge. Pin, tack, and slipstitch the folded edge of the binding to the lining ⅝ in (1.5 cm) from the edge.

7 TOPSTITCHING BINDING You may prefer to finish the binding by machine topstitching. These stitches will, however, be more visible. Press the finished cover and place it over the bed.

THE FINISHED BEDSPREAD

FITTED BEDSPREAD WITH GATHERED SKIRT

When choosing fabric for a fitted cover for a daybed, choose a durable material that will withstand wear and tear. You will also need prewashed piping cord, fabric for the piping – the one shown here is in a complementary color to the main fabric – and the basic sewing kit. Measure the dimensions of the bed with the bed linen in place to make sure that the finished cover fits neatly. To find the dimensions of the top panel of fabric, measure the length (A) and width (B) of the bed, and then add 1¾ in (4.5 cm) to the length for seams and hem, and 1¼ in (3 cm) to the width for seams.

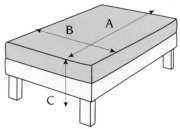

1 MEASURING SKIRT For the width of the skirt fabric, measure the skirt drop (C), and add 1¾ in (4.5 cm) for seams and hem. The length should be three times the length of the bed (A), plus one and a half times the width (B), plus 2½ in (6 cm) for hems. If you need to join fabric, add ⅝ in (1.5 cm) for seams.

Turn double hem along edge of top panel piece

2 HEMMING PANEL Lay the top panel right side down on a flat surface, and turn and press a ⅝ in (1.5 cm) double hem along its top edge.

Turn ¾ in (2 cm) to wrong side at end, and slipstitch folded edges

3 SEWING PIPING Cut a bias strip to twice A, plus B. Add 1½ in (4 cm) for turnings. Make up piping (see page 20), leaving 1½ in (4 cm) unsewn at each end.

4 ATTACHING PIPING Pin and tack the piping to the right side of the top panel, along one short and two long edges, matching raw edges of fabric.

5 HEMMING SKIRT EDGE Join skirt fabric using French seams (see page 15). Turn, pin, tack, and sew a ⅝ in (1.5 cm) double hem to the wrong side.

6 HEMMING SKIRT ENDS At both ends of the skirt, turn ⅝ in (1.5 cm) double hems to the wrong side. Pin, tack, and sew the hems.

7 MARKING SKIRT Divide up the top edge of the skirt into three parts to ensure the gathers will be evenly distributed. Measure from one end and mark a point one and a half times the length of A. From this point, mark another point at one and a half times the length of B. The remaining part will be one and a half times the mattress length.

8 SEWING GATHERING STITCHES Sew a line of gathering stitches (see page 22) ⅝ in (1.5 cm) from the top of the unhemmed edge of the skirt. Sew separate lines of stitching along each of the three marked lengths. Overlap the lines of gathering stitches at the corner marks, so that the fullness will not be lost when gathering up.

9 GATHERING SKIRT Align the ends of the skirt with the ends of the piped top panel, and pin in place at these points. Align the corner marks on the skirt with the corners of the panel, and pin in place at these points. Starting at one of the long edges, pull up the gathers, distribute evenly, and pin and tack the skirt in place along the piped edge. Repeat this procedure on the remaining two sides.

10 ATTACHING SKIRT Machine sew the skirt to the piped panel along the tacking using the zipper foot. Trim the seam allowances. Press the cover, and fit it to the bed.

THE FINISHED BEDSPREAD

FITTED BEDSPREAD WITH BOX PLEATS

To make this bedspread, you will need fabric for the spread and piping, piping cord, and the basic sewing kit. Cut out the fabric for the top panel to the width (A) and length (B) of the mattress, adding 1¼ in (3 cm) to the width for seams and 1¾ in (4.5 cm) to the length for seams and hems. At the foot end of the top panel, use a vanishing-ink pen to round off corners (see page 102). For the sides, cut out three strips of fabric to the mattress depth (C). Add 1¼ in (3 cm) to the width for seams. Cut two strips to B, adding 1¾ in (4.5 cm) for hems and seams, and one strip to A, adding 1¼ in (3 cm) for seams.

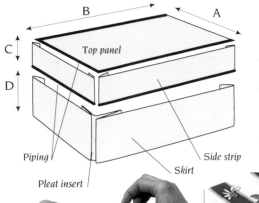

1 CUTTING OUT SKIRT Measure drop (D) from lower edge of mattress to floor, adding 1¾ in (4.5 cm) for hems and seams. This is the required width of skirt pieces. Cut out two pieces to this width by same length as B plus 1¼ in (3 cm) for top edge hem, adding 4 in (10 cm) to each for pleats. Cut one piece of fabric to D by same length as A, adding 8 in (20 cm). For corner pleat inserts, cut two pieces to D by 8 in (20 cm). Cut out two bias strips for piping to twice B plus A, adding 1¾ in (4.5 cm) for turnings. Make two strips of piping (see page 20).

2 ATTACHING PIPING Pin and tack one length of piping to the right side of the top panel, matching the edges of the piping allowance and the top panel. Clip the piping seam allowance at the corners (see page 14).

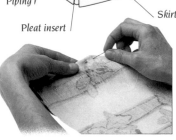

3 SEWING STRIPS Sew a long side strip to a short side strip along their widths, right sides together. Leave a ⅝ in (1.5 cm) seam. Similarly, attach other long strip to other side of short strip.

4 PINNING SECOND PIPING Pin and tack the second length of piping to the edges of the mattress side strips. In step 9 below, the skirt piece will be attached to these edges.

5 ATTACHING PANEL Place unpiped edges of side strips and piped edges of top panel right sides together. Pin, tack, and sew them to each other, leaving a ⅝ in (1.5 cm) allowance.

6 TURNING HEM Turn a ⅝ in (1.5 cm) double hem to the wrong side of the bottom edges of the three skirt pieces, and the insert pieces.

7 SEWING INSERTS Sew insert pieces to ends of short skirt piece, leaving a ⅝ in (1.5 cm) seam. Attach each long skirt piece to insert pieces on either side of short skirt piece, leaving a ⅝ in (1.5 cm) seam. Trim seams.

8 FOLDING PLEATS At each corner, fold side panel to center of insert to form a box pleat. Press, pin, and tack ⅝ in (1.5 cm) from top edge to secure the pleats in place while attaching the skirt.

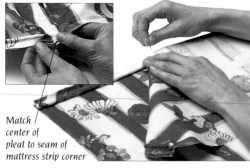

Match center of pleat to seam of mattress strip corner

9 ATTACHING SKIRT Pin, tack, and sew the top edge of the skirt to the piped edge of the mattress side strip, right sides together. Match the centers of the pleats to the seams of the mattress strip corners. Press all seams and hems and, where necessary, trim seams.

10 SLIPSTITCHING END At the bed-head end of the cover, trim away any excess fabric to form a straight line along the edge. Turn a ⅝ in (1.5 cm) double hem to the wrong side of the bed-head end, and pin, tack, and slipstitch it in place. Press the cover and fit it to the mattress and bed.

THE FINISHED BEDSPREAD

PATCHWORK PATTERN
The warm pinks and reds in the fabrics used to make this hand-stitched quilt provide the focus of attention in this pure white room. The color detail is concentrated within the center panel, where floral, sprigged, and plain cotton fabrics are used to fill in square and diamond shapes. Beyond the center panel the quilt is plain, but hundreds of tiny hand-stitches form indentations that catch the light to give a tufted or dimpled texture.

COMFORT ZONE
In addition to pillows in crisp white cases, a selection
of pillows in different styles have been piled on top of
the bed for comfort, creating a relaxed style. The
combination of fabric textures softens what might
otherwise appear to be an austere tonal palette of gray,
white, and black, and breaks up the geometric lines.

PATCHWORK AND QUILTING

PATCHWORK COVERS enable you to combine patterns, colors, and shapes to create your own personalized furnishings. When you are contemplating the design for your patchwork, let your imagination take over, and do not be afraid to use the shapes and colors that inspire you. Bear in mind that a patchwork cover made up of simple shapes such as squares can be machine stitched, but that more complex patchworks have to be sewn together by hand. Quilting the fabric provides effective insulation for the cover. This is a simple technique that involves layering wadding between two fabrics (*see page 15*).

SQUARE PATCHWORK SPREAD

This bedspread is easy to make up by machine but, as with all patchwork, needs careful preparation. Accuracy in measuring and cutting out is essential. To make this spread, you will need fabric for the patches, lining fabric, and the basic sewing kit. Decide on the sizes of the bedspread and the patchwork squares. Consider the scale of the squares in relation to the size of the bed. Calculate the number of squares needed to fill the cover area, adjusting the quantity to the nearest square. After you have cut out the squares, lay them on a flat surface and work out the placement of the squares.

1 CUTTING OUT SQUARES
Add ⅝ in (1.5 cm) all around to the required finished size of each square. On the fabric, carefully measure and draw out the number of squares required for the patchwork. Cut out the squares.

2 JOINING SQUARES
Assemble the patchwork by working across the width of the cover, one row at a time. Pin, tack, and sew the squares right sides together, and 1.5 cm (⅝ in) from their edges. To prevent seams from pulling apart, secure the stitching by reversing the sewing at start and end of seams. Press open seams.

Sew rows of patchwork together ⅝ in (1.5 cm) from edges

3 SEWING ROWS
Once the rows are completed, pin, tack, and sew them right sides together, ⅝ in (1.5 cm) from the edges. Press the seams open. Measure the finished spread and cut a panel of fabric for the lining to the same dimension.

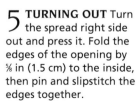

4 ATTACHING LINING Lay the lining and cover right sides together. Pin and tack ⅝ in (1.5 cm) from edges. Leave a 20 in (50 cm) gap in a seam for turning the spread right side out.

5 TURNING OUT Turn the spread right side out and press it. Fold the edges of the opening by ⅝ in (1.5 cm) to the inside, then pin and slipstitch the edges together.

Try using a lining fabric that is decorative and will complement colors in your patchwork

THE FINISHED BEDSPREAD

HEXAGONAL PATCHWORK BEDSPREAD

Decide on the finished design. The patches can be sewn together randomly, arranged in patterns of color, or carefully placed to form configurations. Measure the size of the finished bedspread, and choose the appropriate size of the patchwork pieces. Estimate the number required to fill the area of the spread. Because the patchwork will not form a straight edge around the cover, make a straight line by cutting out partial hexagons, or choose a backing fabric for the border. As well as the fabrics and the basic sewing kit, you will need a piece of stiff cardboard, and a standard compass.

1 DRAWING PATTERN Make a pattern to the size required. Draw a circle on the cardboard. Mark the circumference with six equally spaced points. Join the points with straight lines to form a hexagon. Cut out pattern. Use it to draw the number of hexagons required on paper.

Draw circle on cardboard with compass

Mark six equidistant points, and draw straight lines between them

2 CUTTING OUT PATCHES Cut out the paper hexagons. Pin them to the wrong side of the chosen fabrics. Cut out the hexagonal patches, leaving a ⅝ in (1.5 cm) allowance all around.

3 SEWING SEAMS Leaving the paper in position, fold the seam allowances over the edges of the paper, and tack and press. Make sure that the hexagons are identical in size and shape.

4 STITCHING PATCHES Lay out the patches in the pattern you have chosen. Working on the wrong side, slipstitch the edges together. It is worth taking the time to do this very carefully.

5 REMOVING PAPER After patches have been stitched together, press and remove tacks and paper pieces. Measure length and width at widest points of panel. Cut out lining to these dimensions, plus diameter of one hexagon, plus 1¼ in (3 cm) all around.

6 MARKING LINING Lay patchwork and lining wrong sides together. Mark outermost edges of patches on the lining. Fold lining to wrong side under the patchwork along the marked points. Fold the corners into miters *(see page 19)*, and press.

7 STITCHING LINING Keeping the lining and patchwork wrong sides together, pin, tack, and slipstitch the lining and the patchwork together along all the edges.

THE FINISHED BEDSPREAD

REVERSIBLE QUILTED BEDSPREAD

The size of this spread depends on the bed dimensions and on whether or not the spread reaches to the floor. To calculate the fabric dimensions, measure the length and width of the bed with the bedclothes in place. Add the required amount for the drop to the length measurement, and twice this amount to the width. Add 2 in (5 cm) to the length and width to allow for the fabric that gets taken up in quilting. Cut the top and lining panels to this size. Make any joins in the fabric with plain flat seams *(see page 14)*. You will also need fabric for the binding, wadding, a quilting pencil, and the basic sewing kit.

1 CUTTING WADDING Cut out a section of wadding to the same size as the fabric panels. When it is necessary to join pieces of wadding, use large herringbone stitches *(see page 18)*.

Make small overlap on wadding and secure widths with large herringbone stitches

2 TACKING WADDING Sandwich the wadding in between the wrong sides of both layers of fabric panels. Carefully match all the edges, and pin and tack the fabric panels and wadding together.

3 MAKING SECURING TACKS Lay the quilt flat. Using long tacking stitches, tack along the center from the top to bottom, and across the width, from the center of one side to the other. Use tacking thread of the same color as the sewing thread that you intend to use. Repeat the process, this time tacking halfway between the previous tacking lines and the edges of the quilt. These tacks will prevent the fabrics and wadding from slipping while you make the quilting tacks.

4 TACKING QUILTING LINES Decide on the style and size of the quilting pattern. Measure and mark lines for the quilting on the top panel of the fabric, using a quilting pencil. Tack along these marked lines through all the layers.

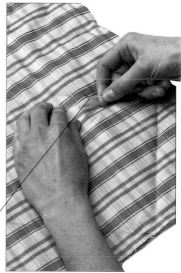

Tack along quilting lines through all layers of fabric and wadding

5 SEWING QUILT Sew along the tacking lines. Remove the tacking. Measure the perimeter of the quilt. Cut bias fabric for the binding to this length, adding 4 in (10 cm) for the join. The width of the binding fabric should be the ultimate binding width, plus 1¼ in (3 cm).

6 TACKING BINDING Fold the long edges of the binding by ⅝ in (1.5 cm) to the wrong side, and press. With the right sides together, pin and tack the edge of the binding to the edge of the top side of the quilt. At corners, snip the binding to fit. Miter, and join the ends of the binding *(see page 19)*. Trim the seam edges to ⅜ in (1 cm). Fold the binding over the edge of the cover. Pin and slipstitch the folded edge.

THE FINISHED BEDSPREAD

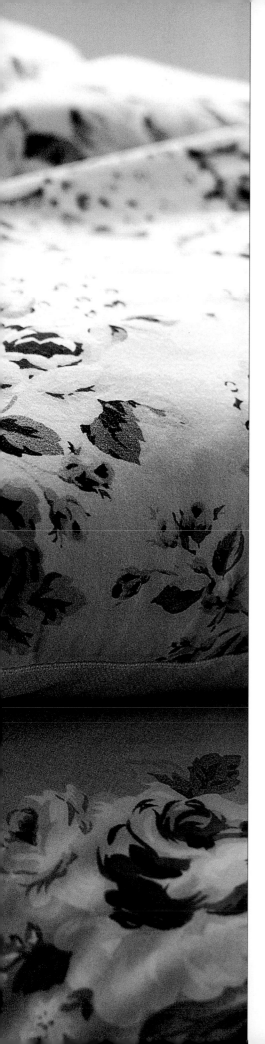

PILLOWS AND CUSHIONS

Because of their mobility and versatility, cushions and throw pillows are among the most useful accent pieces, providing comfort for seating areas like sofas, chairs, and floors, and bringing decorative focal points of color, texture, and pattern to a room. There are two basic types of cushion. Tailor-made styles such as box seat cushions are used where a fitted shape is required. Throw pillows, on the other hand, are not made to fit, and can be moved around. In the following instructions, we will use the terms cushion and pillow interchangeably.

CUSHION AND PILLOW COLLECTION
Decorative throw pillows can be made from small remnants of fabric. If you have a piece large enough to cover only one side, select a plain coordinating fabric for the reverse.

CHOOSING A STYLE

ADDING A FEW DECORATIVE PILLOWS to your room can instantly change its character. When grouped together on a sofa or bed, pillows can provide bright accents of color and texture, perhaps echoing the style of a picture above them, or complementing the neutral color scheme of a room. Because so little fabric is needed when making up pillows, any type of material can be used without being prohibitively expensive. Sumptuous fabrics such as raw silk create a sophisticated modern interior, while fake fur and hand-embroidered motifs on linen supplement an overall informal design theme or stand out as contrasts.

WINDOW SEAT
(above) Rose-colored *toile* has been chosen for this tailor-made box cushion seat, pillows, and draperies. The seat pad is made with fire-retardant foam padding and self-welting.

PASTELS
(left) Linen cushions in a range of pastel shades are scattered along this settee for comfort. Flanged edges, embroidery, and buttons add detailed interest, while a zipper hidden in the seam of each cover ensures their easy removal for cleaning.

FLORALS AND STRIPES
(opposite) Armchair cushions and pillows covered in floral motifs and striped cotton prints work well together. These covers can be unzipped, dry cleaned, or washed when necessary.

DRESS FABRICS
(opposite) Pillows made in unusual and unexpected materials, like beaded, sequinned, or studded dress fabric remnants look striking when set against a conventional barrel chair. Keep the shape and style of the pillows simple so that you can focus on the light-reflecting qualities of the fabric.

BUTTON FASTENINGS
(above) Ideal for understated style, self-covered buttons add a chic tailored look to plain cushions. On a practical level, button openings are also useful fastenings for heavy or stretchy fabrics where zippers may cause the material to pucker. Here, linen covers in delicious shades of chocolate, caramel, cream, and toffee have been chosen. The linen-covered buttons and mink-colored tabs contribute a simple but important element to the overall design.

ANIMAL PRINT PILLOWS
(above) These fake-fur pillows with their bold pattern become the focal point when placed on a pure white sofa. By edging the animal print pillows with self-welting, a more professional finish is achieved. When choosing a suitable pillow fabric, bear in mind the amount of wear it is subjected to; this synthetic fur must be dry cleaned only.

WINDOW SEAT WITH BOLSTER
(left) The directions showing you how to make a simple bolster and box cushion can be combined to make a comfortable window seat. Self-welting and covered buttons provide the detail for the bolster cushion, while a layer of quilted polyester wadding gives a deep, soft look to the cushion.

CUSHION FILLINGS

TODAY, FINDING READY-MADE INNER PADS for cushions is a simple task. If, however, you would rather make your own, you must consider which filling is most suitable for the pad. This choice depends on the desired decorative effect and on the type of cushion you are planning to make. In the past, feathers and down, animal hair, and plant fibers such as cotton and kapok were the only stuffing used for cushions and upholstery. Nowadays there is a wide range of material available. Polyester and cotton batting, as well as foam blocks and chips, can all be used to fill cushions.

CHOOSING FILLINGS

Fillings are available as loose material and are usually sold by weight. For comfort and durability, choose natural-fiber fillings, such as cotton. Feathers and down give real luxury, but they are messy to work with. Synthetic fillings are not as soft as natural ones and tend to lose their shape over time. They are easy to work with, however, and are hypoallergenic.

POLYSTYRENE BEADS
These tiny balls of polystyrene provide lightweight but firm fillings for cushion pads. They are best used for stuffing cushions that are unusually shaped, or for large floor cushions, such as bean bags.

FIBER FILL
This form of filling, made of acrylic or polyester, is fully washable once inside a fabric casing. Loose filling must be packed tightly to prevent clumps from forming, but it is a popular choice for making cushion pads, especially those of an unusual shape.

FEATHERS AND DOWN
Down is small, fluffy feathers of birds and is the softest, lightest, and most resilient filling. Feather-and-down mixtures are less expensive than pure down. They are also not as soft, but provide more body for a firmer cushion. When working with down or feathers, use a down-proof casing fabric such as ticking, and sew it with French seams.

KAPOK
This vegetable fiber filling has long been used for quilting, upholstery padding, and seat cushions. Kapok is not washable, and it tends to become lumpy over time.

FOAM
Foam is available in sheets, blocks, and chips, and in a variety of qualities. Foam blocks are easy to cut to a defined shape and are ideal for seat-cushion padding. Foam should always be enclosed in an inner lining, because it tends to crumble with age. Make sure the foam label states that it is flame retardant.

TEASING

If you use polyester or acrylic padding, it may be necessary to tease out the fibers before filling a cushion pad, in order to separate the fibers and break up any lumps and clumps. Hold each portion of padding in one hand, and gently tease the clumps of fibers apart between the fingers and heel of your other hand.

MAKING A SQUARE INNER PAD

Cushion pads can be made in all shapes and sizes, which means that you do not need to be restricted to the shapes of ready-made pads. Make the inner pad ⅝ in (1.5 cm) larger all around than the cushion cover for a plump effect. You can choose among various casing fabrics, such as ticking for feathers, or heavy muslin, lining material, or even old sheeting (see page 6). To make a cushion pad, you will need a suitable filling, the casing fabric, and the basic sewing kit.

1 MARKING PATTERN Mark out a paper pattern to the required size plus a ⅝ in (1.5 cm) seam allowance all around, using a tape measure, pencil, and triangle. Pin the pattern to the casing fabric, making sure that its edges lie along the straight grain of the fabric.

CUTTING WITHOUT A PATTERN
If you wish, you can measure up and mark the measurements for the inner pad directly onto the casing fabric, using a tape measure, triangle, and vanishing-ink pen or tailor's chalk. Again, allow ⅝ in (1.5 cm) for seams, and draw the cutting lines on the straight grain of the fabric. A triangle is useful for marking both paper patterns and fabrics.

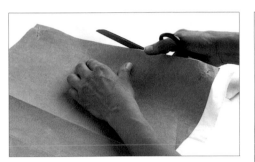

2 CUTTING OUT Use a pair of sharp dressmaker's scissors to cut out the fabric, following the paper pattern pinned to the material or the outline drawn onto the fabric. Cut out two identical pieces of fabric for the front and back panels of the casing.

3 SEWING TOGETHER Place the panels of fabric for the casing right sides together. Pin, tack, and sew the panels together ⅝ in (1.5 cm) from the edge along three sides only. On the fourth side, sew seams 2 in (5 cm) from each corner.

4 CLIPPING CORNERS Clip the corners of the seam allowance to ¼ in (6 mm) from the seam. On a round pad, you will have to clip the allowances as appropriate (see page 14).

5 STUFFING PAD Turn the casing right side out and lay it on a flat surface. Stuff the chosen filling through the opening in the fourth side seam. Make sure that the filling is pushed well into each corner and distributed evenly across the whole pad.

THE FINISHED PAD

6 FINISHING OFF When the casing has been filled to the required thickness and weight, slipstitch the opening closed. If more filling or a change of filling is required at a later date, unpick this slipstitched seam, and when the pad has been restuffed slipstitch it closed again.

OTHER PAD SHAPES

The instructions for making the square cushion pad can be applied to cushions of various designs – such as bolsters or round cushions – to fit in with your decorative scheme.

BOLSTER PAD   ROUND PAD

SQUARE CUSHIONS

PERHAPS THE MOST USEFUL and versatile soft furnishing, square cushions offer instant comfort as well as an elegant highlight to chairs and sofas. When covered in patterned, brightly colored fabric, a group of square cushions of different sizes can be an attractive decorative contrast to plain furniture upholstery. A variety of edging treatments, such as piping, flange, and frills, can add texture and detail, particularly to simple-patterned fabric. Fastening choices vary, from visible and attractive fine buttons and fabric ties to concealed zippers, snaps, and slipstitches.

SLIPSTITCHED FASTENING

A simple square cushion can be used almost anywhere. Square cushion pads are available ready-made in numerous sizes. Alternatively, they can be easily made at home using a range of stuffings *(see page 118)*. Unless the cover needs to be cleaned frequently, the simplest fastening is a slipstitch. To make a simple square scatter cushion with a slipstitched fastening, you will need the cushion fabric, an inner pad, and the basic sewing kit.

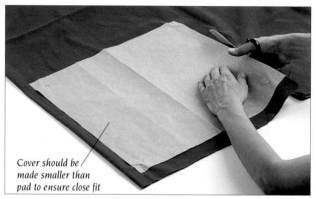

Cover should be made smaller than pad to ensure close fit

1 CUTTING OUT PANELS Using a tape measure and drafting triangle, make a paper pattern to the same size as the pad. Lay pattern piece on a double layer of cushion fabric. If the fabric that you are using has a pattern with large designs, or a nap, check that they are aligned correctly. Pin the paper pattern in place, and cut out the fabric pieces.

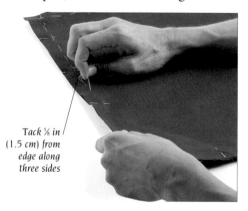

Tack ⅝ in (1.5 cm) from edge along three sides

2 TACKING PANELS Lay the fabric pieces right sides together. Ensure that the grains of both pieces align. Pin the panels together along all four sides. Tack ⅝ in (1.5 cm) from the edge along three sides of the square. On the fourth side, stitch only 2 in (5 cm) from both ends, leaving an opening in the center.

3 SEWING TOGETHER Machine sew the panels along the edges of the cushion next to the tacking stitches. Take care not to stitch into the ends of the opening by accident. Fasten off securely at the end, and remove the tacking stitches.

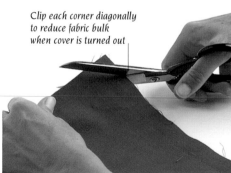

Clip each corner diagonally to reduce fabric bulk when cover is turned out

4 CLIPPING CORNERS Within the seam allowance, clip each corner to ensure that the cushion corners will be straight and pointed when turned out. Cut away the seam allowance to within ¼ in (6 mm) of the stitching. This will reduce the bulk and prevent tucking and wrinkling.

5 SLIPSTITCHING CLOSED Turn the cushion cover right side out. With your fingers, push out the corners of the cushion. Press the cover as flat as possible. Insert the inner pad through the cover opening, and push it well into the corners. Slipstitch together the sides of the opening *(see page 12)*.

Making cover slightly smaller than inner pad ensures a tight fit

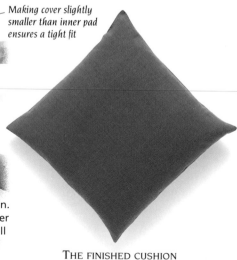

THE FINISHED CUSHION

SIDE OPENING WITH SNAPS

For a cushion without an edge trimming, such as piping or cording, a side zipper may prove too bulky at the seam, but snaps or a simple slipstitched seam will conceal the opening almost completely. Snaps along the edges of the opening will facilitate the removal of the cushion pad when the cover needs to be cleaned. To make up this cushion cover, you will need the cushion fabric and an inner pad, snaps, and the basic sewing kit.

1 CUTTING OUT PANELS Make up a paper pattern *(see opposite)*. When cutting out the pieces of fabric, add an extra 1¼ in (3 cm) seam allowance on one edge of both panels, for the side opening.

2 TURNING EDGES On each of the two fabric panels, turn the edge that has the extra seam allowance to the wrong side once by ⅝ in (1.5 cm) and press. Turn the edge under again by the same amount. Pin, tack, and slipstitch along the edge of the fold, then remove the tacking stitches.

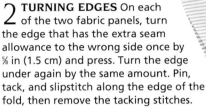

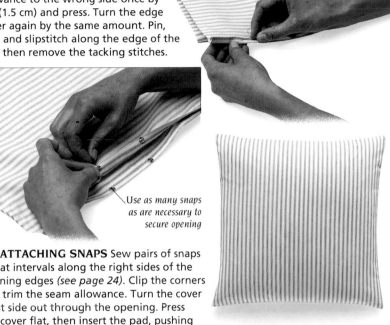

3 SEWING UP Place the panels right sides together, aligning the turned sides. Pin, tack, and sew 2 in (5 cm) at both ends of these sides, and remove the tacking stitches. Pin, tack, and sew the other sides, with a ⅝ in (1.5 cm) allowance. Remove the tacking stitches.

Use as many snaps as are necessary to secure opening

4 ATTACHING SNAPS Sew pairs of snaps at intervals along the right sides of the opening edges *(see page 24)*. Clip the corners and trim the seam allowance. Turn the cover right side out through the opening. Press the cover flat, then insert the pad, pushing it well into the corners.

THE FINISHED CUSHION

BUTTON FASTENING

A central fastening at the back of a cushion is one of the most secure means of closing an opening. A variety of fasteners can be used, including zippers, Velcro tabs or strips, and buttons. All types of fastener can be hidden behind a flange of fabric, but simple, elegant buttons can also be attractively displayed along the center back. To make up this cushion, you will need the cushion fabric and an inner pad, buttons, and the basic sewing kit.

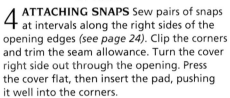

BUTTONS IN CENTER BACK

FRONT VIEW

1 CUTTING OUT Cut the cushion front using a pattern *(see opposite)*. Cut the paper in half. Pin it to a double layer of fabric. Adding 2 in (5 cm) for a center opening, cut two panels.

2 TURNING EDGES Turn the center edges of the backs under by ⅜ in (1 cm), then 1 in (2.5 cm). Pin, tack, and sew the edge. Make buttonholes *(see page 26)* on one turning.

3 SEWING UP Lay the panels right sides together. Overlap the backs by 1 in (2.5 cm), the holed one underneath. Pin, tack, and sew as opposite. Attach the buttons *(see page 26)*.

ROUND CUSHIONS

ROUND CUSHIONS are perhaps more of a decorative accessory than their square counterparts, and their circular shapes lend themselves to all manner of fanciful and creative edgings. Small round cushions, perhaps with frills or flanges around their edges, mix well among groups of other cushion shapes, especially on a large sofa or at the head of a bed. These round cushions and inner pads are easy to make and you can use a circular paper pattern as a guide to help you cut out the front and back panels of fabric; suitable commercially made inner pads of all diameters and thicknesses are also readily available.

SIMPLE ROUND CUSHION

To make a circular pattern for a round cushion, you will need either a plate of the appropriate size or a simple compass made from a length of string, a pencil, and a drawing pin, as used here. For the cushion, you will need fabric, an inner pad, and the basic sewing kit (see page 8). Because a side-mounted zipper is difficult to hide and can distort the cover fabric, either slipstitch an opening at the side of the cover or fix fastenings into the center of the back panel.

1 **MAKING PATTERN** Fold a piece of paper larger than the cushion size into quarters. Knot one end of a piece of string and cut it to half the cushion diameter in length. Hold or pin the knotted end at the inner corner of the folded paper and tie a pencil to the other end. Draw an arc. Carefully cut along this curve, then unfold the pattern.

Simple compass is useful for many soft furnishing techniques

2 **CUTTING FABRIC** Pin the paper on the fabric, and check that any patterns are correctly aligned. Cut out the front and the back panels of the cushion and place the pieces of fabric right sides together, being careful to match the weave and any pattern. Pin and tack the two panels together, ⅝ in (1.5 cm) from the edge. Leave a gap in the seam large enough to allow the inner pad to be inserted.

3 **JOINING PANELS** Machine sew along the tacking on the seam line. Take care not to sew across the opening. Remove the tacking stitches.

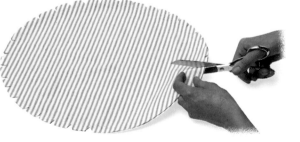

4 **NOTCHING** Cut notches around the seam allowance (see page 14). Pull the cover right side out and press it. Insert the inner pad through the gap, distributing its bulk around the rim.

Use slipstitches to close opening because they are easy to remove when it is necessary to clean cover

5 **STITCHING CLOSED** Slipstitch the opening closed (see page 12). When it becomes necessary to clean the cushion, carefully remove the slipstitches, using a seam ripper or a pair of small, sharp scissors, and take out the inner pad. After washing the cover, reinsert the pad and slipstitch the opening closed again.

THE FINISHED CUSHION

ZIPPER AT CENTER BACK

Zippers cannot be used in the side seams of round cushions, because they are too inflexible and would spoil the line. They can, however, be used in an opening running across the back of a round cushion, where they provide a strong and flat fastening. The zipper should be 5 in (13 cm) shorter than the diameter of the cushion and suited to the weight of the fabric.

1 MARKING UP Using a paper pattern *(see opposite)*, cut out the front cushion panel. Remove the pattern and cut it in half to make the back panel template. Pin this to a square piece of fabric, aligning the straight edge of the pattern with the straight grain of the fabric. Mark a cutting line ⅝ in (1.5 cm) from the edge of the pattern for the seam allowance.

2 CUTTING BACKS Cut out two back panels. Pin, tack, and sew the straight edges and the zipper to make a central seam with a zippered opening *(see page 27)*. Open the zipper, and lay the front and the completed back right sides together.

3 JOINING PANELS Pin, tack, and sew fabric pieces ⅝ in (1.5 cm) from the edge. Remove tacking stitches and cut notches around the seam allowance *(see opposite)*. Pull cover right side out through the zipper opening. Press, and insert the pad.

THE FINISHED CUSHION

FRONT VIEW

VELCRO TABS AT CENTER BACK

Velcro is ideal for center-back openings, although it should not be used on lightweight fabrics. Tabs will give a more flexible closure than a strip would. This technique can also be used for buttons and snaps.

1 MARKING UP Cut out the two back-panel halves *(see above)*, but allow 2 in (5 cm) for the turnings on the straight edges. Remove the paper pattern, and turn under the straight edges of both panels once by ⅜ in (1 cm), and then by 1 in (2.5 cm), pressing each time.

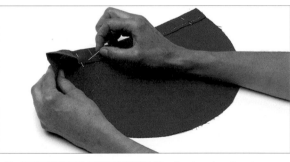

2 STITCHING TURNINGS Pin the turning in place. Secure it by machine sewing or slipstitching along the inner edge. If using buttons, make appropriately sized buttonholes in one of the turnings at this point *(see page 26)*. Lay the pieces right side up and overlap the turnings by 1 in (2.5 cm). If you have made buttonholes, place the edge with the holes in it on top.

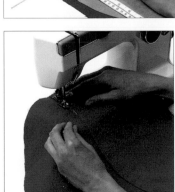

3 SEWING THE CENTER Pin, tack, and sew the back-panel pieces together along the overlapping straight edges. Sew inward from each end, leaving an opening for the pad.

4 SPOTS AND SEAMS Attach the spots, buttons, or snaps *(see page 24)*. Lay the front and back right sides together. Pin, tack, and sew ⅝ in (1.5 cm) from the edge: notch this allowance. Remove the tacking stitches. Pull right sides out and press.

THE FINISHED CUSHION

FRONT VIEW

BOLSTERS

LESS WIDELY USED THAN square and round scatter cushions, the bolster
cushion is a furnishing accessory that can add character as well as comfort to a
sofa, window seat, and, in, a chaise longue. Elsewhere in the home, a long and thin
bolster may be used in place of pillows on a bed. A bolster cushion of narrow diameter
can be laid against the foot of a door for keeping out drafts. Bolsters can be made to
match all manner of tastes by simply adding any one of a variety of decorations
– from formal piping and buttons to extravagant frills and tassels.

SIMPLE BOLSTER

Almost any type of fabric can be used for a bolster. However,
simple bolsters are ideally suited to plain or striped fabrics.
Frilled bolsters, on the other hand, look particularly attractive
when made up in a patterned fabric, such as a floral print.

Bolster inner pads are available ready made, but you might
choose to make your own *(see page 119)*. To make a simple
bolster, you will need cushion fabric, an inner pad, simple
compass *(see page 122),* and the basic sewing kit.

1 CUTTING OUT ENDS
Make a pattern for the ends *(see page 122)*. Mark the seam line on the paper pattern ⅝ in (1.5 cm) from the edge, and measure around it to find the circumference of the end panel. Cut out the circular fabric pieces for the end panels.

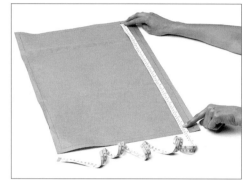

2 THE BODY
The main body width equals the circumference of end panel. Mark the width and length of bolster, plus a ⅝ in (1.5 cm) seam allowance, on paper. Use a drafting triangle to draw corners, then cut out the pattern piece.

3 SEWING THE BODY Pin the body pattern to the fabric, ensuring that any fabric motifs are correctly placed. Cut out the body. Fold it right sides facing, aligning the edges for the central seam. Pin, tack, and sew the seam, leaving an opening for the pad. Press the seam open.

4 ATTACHING ENDS
The end pieces need to be carefully aligned to the main body to avoid bunching. To do this, measure and mark quarters around both ends and the body with tailor's tacks *(see page 12)*. Align the tacks and pin the ends, right sides inward, to the body.

6 SLIPSTITCHING CLOSED Pull the fabric right side out through the central opening in the main body. Press the bolster and insert the inner pad. Slipstitch the opening closed.

Notch seam allowance around ends of cover to reduce fabric bulk

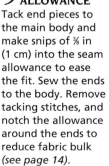

5 NOTCHING ALLOWANCE
Tack end pieces to the main body and make snips of ⅜ in (1 cm) into the seam allowance to ease the fit. Sew the ends to the body. Remove tacking stitches, and notch the allowance around the ends to reduce fabric bulk *(see page 14)*.

THE FINISHED BOLSTER

PIPED AND FRILLED BOLSTER

Simple frills, piping, gathered end panels, and contrasting or matching buttons or tassels are among the many decorative trimmings and treatments that can be used to transform a plain bolster into an unusual and attractive cushion. To make this bolster, you will need enough fabric for the panels and trimmings (the gathered ends will, of course, require more fabric than plain ends), an inner pad, simple compass *(see page 122)*, and the basic sewing kit.

1 MEASURING FOR WIDTH Make paper patterns for an end piece and the body *(see opposite)*. Measure the radius of the end pattern to find the width of fabric needed for gathered ends. Mark width on paper, adding 1¼ in (3 cm) for seam allowances. Check the measurements of this piece against the end-piece pattern.

2 MEASURING FOR LENGTH Measure around the pattern for the end panel as in step 1 opposite. Add 1¼ in (3 cm) for seam allowances, and mark this on the paper. Cut out this pattern piece, pin it to the cushion fabric, and cut out two end pieces around it.

3 SEWING END PIECE On one long edge of a piece for the gathered end, make a ⅝ in (1.5 cm) turning to the wrong side and press it. Bring the short edges of the panel together, the right sides facing. Pin, tack, and sew along these short edges, leaving a ⅝ in (1.5 cm) seam allowance. Remove the tacking stitches. Repeat for the other end panel.

Sew frill to seam allowance of main body piece

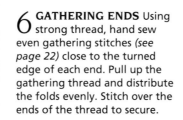

4 ATTACHING PIPED FRILL Make up the main body *(see opposite)*. The piping and frill *(see pages 20 and 22)* should be the same length as the fabric for the gathered end. Mark quarters on the frill and the body ends with tailor's tacks. Pin and tack the frills to each end of the main body, then pin and tack the piping to the frill seam line.

5 ATTACHING ENDS Pin, tack, and sew the unturned edges of the ends to piped and frilled body ends. Notch the allowances *(see opposite)*. Turn right side out through opening, then press.

6 GATHERING ENDS Using strong thread, hand sew even gathering stitches *(see page 22)* close to the turned edge of each end. Pull up the gathering thread and distribute the folds evenly. Stitch over the ends of the thread to secure.

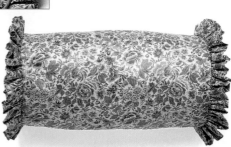

END VIEW

7 ATTACHING BUTTON The gathered ends should be tightly closed, so that buttons will cover the holes. Sew on the buttons *(see page 26)* at the centers of the gathered ends. Insert the pad through the opening in the body seam, then slipstitch it closed.

Sew button to gathered end of bolster

THE FINISHED BOLSTER

OPULENT SILKS
The low back and wide seat of this Asian-style sofa make a variety of pillows for reclining in comfort a necessity. Bolsters in an ivory-colored raw silk, rectangular pillows with gold and dusky-pink satin ends, and square pillows in gray flannel all feature a classic stripe that unifies the design and offers a modern contrast of texture.

EDGINGS

EDGINGS FRAME AND HIGHLIGHT CUSHIONS and add an informal elegance to your furniture. All sorts of cushion trimmings can easily be made or bought, and the techniques for applying them to any shape of plain cushion are straightforward. Cording, the easiest edging to apply, is simply sewn to the outside of the finished cushion cover. Other edgings, such as piping and frills, are machine sewn to the front panel of the cushion during assembly. Some trimmings, such as piping, not only look decorative but also strengthen the edges of a cushion, giving it a longer life.

SIMPLE PIPING WITH ZIPPER

A piped trim around the edge of a cushion, either of the same fabric or in a contrasting color, pattern, or texture, produces a more tailored effect than other trimmings. The following technique can be applied to both square and round cushions.

You will need the cushion panels cut to the size that you desire, an inner pad, piping cord and bias strip for the piping, a zipper 4 in (10 cm) shorter than the side of the cushion, and the basic sewing kit.

1 ATTACHING PIPING To find the length of piping needed, measure around the seam line of the cushion front panel and add 2 in (5 cm) for joining. Make piping to this length *(see page 20)*. Pin and tack the piping at the seam line along the four edges of the right side of the front panel.

2 JOINING PIPING ENDS Leave the overlapping ends of the piping free. Join the ends of the piping cord by thinning and binding them, and the ends of the bias strip either straight across or diagonally *(see page 21)*. Tack the piping to the cushion panel across the joined ends.

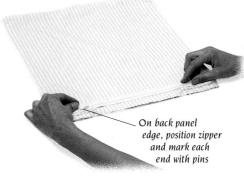

On back panel edge, position zipper and mark each end with pins

3 PLACING ZIPPER Place the front and back pieces of the cushion right sides together. Align the edges and any patterns on the fabric. On the back panel edge for the side opening, mark the length of the zipper with a pin at each end. Pin, tack, and sew in from the ends to these marks.

4 SEWING IN ZIPPER Press seam allowances open. Open the zipper and lay one side of it right side down on the piped seam allowance, on top of piping. Pin, tack, and sew zipper to seam allowance *(see page 27)*, using the zipper attachment on a sewing machine to get close to the piping.

5 SEWING SIDES Lay the panels flat, right sides up, and close the zipper. Pin, tack, and sew the free edge of the zipper to the second panel. Open the zipper. Fold the panels right sides together and pin, tack, and sew the other three sides. Trim the allowance at the corners, turn right side out, and press.

THE FINISHED CUSHION

THICK PIPING

Because thick piping is stuffed with wadding, it makes one of the most comfortable scatter-cushion edgings. A softer, more informal edging than simple piping, thick piping can be made in a fabric the same as, or complementary to, the cushion.

You will need cushion panels cut to the size you desire, medium-weight wadding, a bias strip 3½ in (9 cm) wide for the piping *(see page 20)*, the fasteners you are using, an inner pad, and the basic sewing kit.

1 CUTTING PIPING To find the piping length, measure around the seam line of a panel and add 2 in (5 cm) for joining. Cut the wadding into a strip 3⅛ in (8 cm) wide and the length of the bias strip, minus the allowance for joining. Roll the wadding tightly and lay it on the wrong side of the bias strip.

2 WRAPPING WADDING Fold the bias strip for the piping over the roll of wadding. Pin and tack along the length of the piping to form a filled tube, then stitch as close to the rolled-up wadding as possible without going through it.

Wadding should be length of bias strip minus diagonal ends

3 SEWING IN PLACE Lay the front panel of the cushion right side up. Pin and tack the piping around the edge of the panel, snipping into the seam allowance at corners to ease the fabric. Trim the seam allowance at the ends of the piping to within ¹⁄₁₆ in (2 mm) of the wadding. Join the piping ends *(see page 21)*. Sew the cushion as appropriate to the fastening.

THE FINISHED CUSHION

CORDED EDGING

Corded edging is simple to attach and, because of its stiffness, strengthens the edges of a cushion. The ends are secured inside the opening of a finished cushion, so this technique is eminently suitable for a cushion with a slipstitched fastening. With any other kind of fastening, use a seam ripper to make a seam opening ¾ in (2 cm) long on one side of the cushion. For this technique, you will need a completed cushion cover, cord or similar trimming, inner pad, and the basic sewing kit.

1 STITCHING IN CORD To find the length of cord needed, measure around the cushion, adding 2 in (5 cm) for securing and the length of the corner loops. Fill the cushion and leave a ¾ in (2 cm) gap in a seam. Tuck 1 in (2.5 cm) of one end of the cord into the gap and oversew to secure. Slipstitch the cord to the cushion edge.

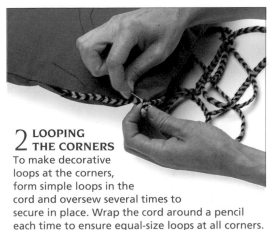

2 LOOPING THE CORNERS To make decorative loops at the corners, form simple loops in the cord and oversew several times to secure in place. Wrap the cord around a pencil each time to ensure equal-size loops at all corners.

3 FINISHING OFF When you have completed stitching the cording around the edge, tuck the end of the cord in the opening so that folded edges of the two ends meet. Overstitch them together, then slipstitch the opening closed.

THE FINISHED CUSHION

SIMPLE FRILL

Frills can be used to highlight a color or a pattern in a cushion fabric, or for their structural effect; of all the edgings for soft furnishings, they produce the softest appearance. To make this cushion, you will need two cushion panels cut to the size you desire, fabric for the frill, a zipper, if you are using one, an inner pad, and the basic sewing kit.

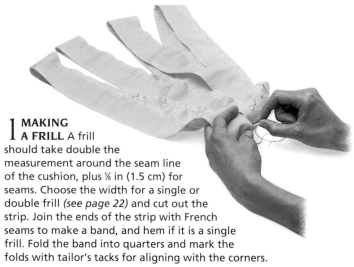

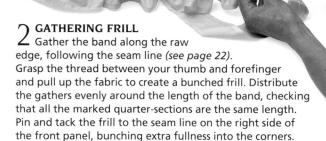

1 MAKING A FRILL A frill should take double the measurement around the seam line of the cushion, plus ⅝ in (1.5 cm) for seams. Choose the width for a single or double frill *(see page 22)* and cut out the strip. Join the ends of the strip with French seams to make a band, and hem if it is a single frill. Fold the band into quarters and mark the folds with tailor's tacks for aligning with the corners.

2 GATHERING FRILL Gather the band along the raw edge, following the seam line *(see page 22)*. Grasp the thread between your thumb and forefinger and pull up the fabric to create a bunched frill. Distribute the gathers evenly around the length of the band, checking that all the marked quarter-sections are the same length. Pin and tack the frill to the seam line on the right side of the front panel, bunching extra fullness into the corners.

3 ATTACHING FRILL Sew the frill to the front panel on the seam line, and remove the tacking stitches. Place the cushion panels right sides together, edges aligned. Pin, tack, and sew the panels together as appropriate for the chosen fastening. Trim the corners and remove the tacking stitches. Turn the cover right side out and press it.

THE FINISHED CUSHION

BOUND FRILL

For a smarter effect than a simple frill, a plain frill can be trimmed with a strip, or bias, of fabric in a contrasting or complementary color or pattern. If the frill contrasts with the cushion, it could be bound in the fabric used for the cushion.

To make up a cushion with a bound frill, you will need two cushion panels cut to the size you require, a strip of fabric for the frill *(see above)* and another for the trimming, the fastener you have chosen, an inner pad, and the basic sewing kit.

1 SEWING ON Cut frill and bias strip to the same length, adding ⅜ in (1 cm) seam allowance to the frill and ¼ in (6 mm) to the bias. Join the frill ends to make a band. Press the bias strip's long edges to the middle. Sew the bias to the frill *(see page 14)*.

2 BINDING FRILL Fold the bias strip over the edge of the frill. Pin and tack in place, then slipstitch to the frill band. Remove the tacking stitches. Gather the frill and make up the cushion as for a cushion with a simple frill *(see above)*.

THE FINISHED CUSHION

PIPED AND PLEATED FRILL

For a formal effect, piping works very well with a pleated frill, particularly on a round cushion. To make up this cushion, you will need cushion panels cut to size, the front one with piping sewn around the edge *(see page 128)*, fabric for the pleated frill, the fastener you have chosen to use, an inner pad, and the basic sewing kit.

Back panel will be positioned right side down on front panel and frill

Lay frill face down on right side of panel

ATTACHING THE FRILL

The frill band should be double the depth desired for the frill, plus 1¼ in (3 cm) for seams.

To find the length needed, measure around the seam line of the front panel and calculate as detailed on page 20, allowing for joins as necessary. Sew the ends to form a band, fold it lengthwise wrong sides together, press, and pleat. Mark the cushion front and fold and mark the band into quarters with tailor's tacks, to help align them. Pin and tack the frill to the front panel, and make up the cover as appropriate for the fastening.

Try to place any prominent motifs centrally on cushion

THE FINISHED CUSHION

GATHERED CORNERS AND TIES

This technique gently rounds the corners of a square cushion, providing a softer and more informal alternative to a plain square. A piped edge in contrasting fabric and matching decorative tie fastenings will both add to the appeal of this style of cover, although you could use almost any of the other edgings and fastenings shown in these pages, such as thick piping or even a frill. In order to make up this cushion, you will need cushion fabric for the front and back panels, cut to the size you desire as for a plain square cushion, bias strip for the rouleau ties, piping cord and bias strip for the piped edging, an inner pad, and the basic sewing kit.

1 **MARKING CURVES** On the wrong side of each panel, draw a quarter circle to round off the corners, using a round object or a compass. The bigger the curve, the rounder the corners will be. Trim the corners.

2 **GATHERING CORNERS** Hand sew gathering at the corners, ⅝ in (1.5 cm) out from the arc. Pull the threads to gather, then oversew the ends. Measure along the seam line to find the length of piping required, and add 2 in (5 cm) for joining. Pin, tack, and sew the piping to the panel *(see page 21)*.

3 **TURNING OPENING** Measure and mark the opening on the edge of the back panel. Turn the edge to the wrong side, press, and slipstitch. Lay the panels right sides together, edges aligned. Pin, tack, and sew the sides, leaving a gap.

4 **ATTACHING TIES** Make up fabric ties or rouleau strips *(see page 25)* and sew them along the edges of the opening opposite each other. Turn the cover right side out through the opening, and press it before inserting the inner pad.

THE FINISHED CUSHION

FLANGE EDGING

Flanges are often used as decorative edgings for pillowcases, but they are equally suitable for an elegant border on a cushion. In this technique, which is the simplest way of making a flanged edge, the flange is part of the same piece of fabric as that used for the cushion panels. This makes the assembly of the cushion very easy. Using a flange edging on a cushion rules out the possibility of having a fastening in one of the side seams, so the cushion cover has to fasten in the back panel, either with buttons *(see page 121)* or with a zipper or Velcro *(see pages 24 and 123)*. To make this cushion, you will need fabric for the cushion cover, the fastener you have chosen, an inner pad, and the basic sewing kit.

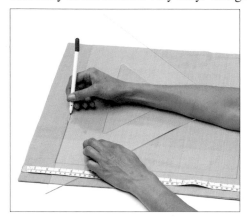

1 MARKING PANEL Cut the panels to size, with 2½ in (6 cm) extra for the flange edging and ⅝ in (1.5 cm) extra for the seam allowance all around. Join the panels as for a square cushion with a center-back fastening. Turn the cover right sides out. On the front, mark a line 2½ in (6 cm) from the edge all around in tailor's chalk, and tack along it.

2 JOINING PANELS Fit a double needle to the sewing machine and sew along the flange line. If your machine does not have a double needle, stitch around the cushion along each side of the tacking stitches; keep the lines parallel and ⅛–³⁄₁₆ in (3–5 mm) apart. Remove the tacking stitches. Press the cushion cover and insert the pad.

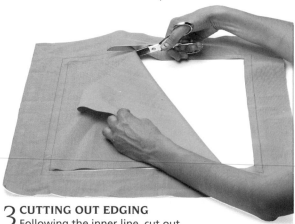

THE FINISHED CUSHION

SCALLOPED FLANGE EDGING

Rounded, serrated, or squared-off cutwork adds decoration to flanges. In this technique, the edging is made from separate pieces of fabric and attached to the cushion panels, so it could be made from fabric that contrasts with the cushion. To make this cushion, you will need fabric for the front and back cushion panels and the front and back edging pieces, an inner pad, fasteners, a simple compass *(see page 122)* or a glass for the scalloped edges, and the basic sewing kit.

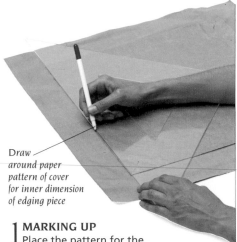

Draw around paper pattern of cover for inner dimension of edging piece

1 MARKING UP Place the pattern for the front panel on the wrong side of the fabric for the edging pieces. On the fabric, draw a line the depth of your frill, plus a ⅜ in (1 cm) seam allowance, from the pattern edge. Cut along this line. Draw a line around the pattern, remove it, and repeat for the second edging piece.

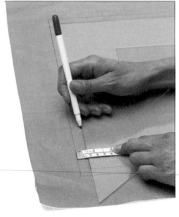

2 MARKING EDGING SEAM Using a tape measure and a drafting triangle as a guide, draw a second line on the edging pieces parallel to, and ⅝ in (1.5 cm) inside, the line you drew around the pattern. Draw the line right around the four sides of both pieces of fabric.

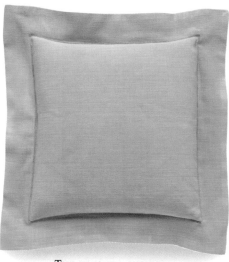

3 CUTTING OUT EDGING Following the inner line, cut out the fabric at the center of each edging piece, which can be used for a smaller cushion. When a center piece is laid on a cushion panel, it should be ⅝ in (1.5 cm) smaller all around than the seam line on the panel. If you are short of fabric and do not mind seams in the flange, you could use strips of fabric mitered at the corners *(see mitering lace, page 23)* for the edging.

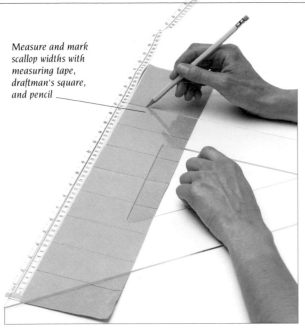

Measure and mark scallop widths with measuring tape, draftman's square, and pencil

4 MARKING EDGE Cut a strip of paper to the length and width of one side of an edging piece. Mark the paper strip into equal sections the width of a scallop. The edge should begin and end with a full scallop – adjust the width of the scallops if necessary.

Mark scallop curves on wrong side of edging piece

5 MARKING CURVES On one edge of the paper pattern, mark a series of curves between the dividing lines, using either the rim of a glass or a simple compass as a guide. The curves should not be too deep: draw around only about a third of the glass. Carefully cut out the pattern along the curves.

6 MARKING FABRIC Lay edging fabric wrong side up. Align straight edge of pattern with internal edge. Pin in place. Mark up curves with a vanishing-ink pen. Repeat around other three sides and other edging piece.

7 SEWING EDGE Place the two edging pieces right sides together with their edges aligning. Pin, tack, and sew the edging pieces together, stitching ³⁄₁₆ in (5 mm) from, and parallel to, the marked line of the curves on all four sides. Remove the tacking stitches.

8 CLIPPING ALLOWANCE Cut and trim around the curves, and clip into the edges. This will reduce the fabric bulk so the edging is not strained when turned right side out.

Trim into edges to reduce fabric bulk when scallop piece is turned right sides out

9 TOPSTITCHING EDGE Turn the edging piece right side out and press it. To flatten the edge, topstitch *(see page 15)* along the curved edge in three parallel rows, ¼ in (6 mm) apart, and starting ¼ in (6 mm) in from the curved edge.

10 ATTACHING EDGING Lay the edging on the right side of the cushion front, edges aligned, and pin, tack, and sew in place. Remove the tacking stitches and clip the corners. Make up the cushion.

THE FINISHED CUSHION

USING SPECIAL FABRICS

MAKING A CUSHION COVER provides the ideal opportunity to give new life to a small fragment of an old or unusual fabric. The choice of fabrics extends from the relatively well known, such as antique lace or European needlepoint, to the unfamiliar, like the panel of a Central African raffia skirt or part of a kilim. Many such fabrics are delicate, either intrinsically or through age, and they should be reinforced by being mounted on a strong backing cloth. It is also advisable to make up a cushion that can safely be dismantled later, leaving a precious textile intact for framing or further use.

RIBBON-AND-LACEWORK CUSHION

There are many examples of lacework, such as trimmings on garments, tablecloths, napkins, bedspreads, pillows, and sheets. When used as a decorative edging on cushions, lacework or fine linen can transform a simple cover into a fancy antique furnishing. The size of the cushion is determined by the amount of lace or linen available. The cushion below has been trimmed with ribbons and buttons. In addition to lace and adornments, to make this cushion you will need cushion fabric, an inner pad, and the basic sewing kit. Avoid using side zipper fastenings with lace edgings.

1 **MARKING PANEL** Lay the front panel for the cushion cover (*see page 120*) right-side up, tack the seam line ⅝ in (1.5 cm) from the panel edge, and mark the placement for the outer ribbon parallel to the seam line. Tack in place. Draw the positions for the inner ribbon, decorative bows, and the buttons, using a drafting triangle and a vanishing-ink pen or tailor's chalk.

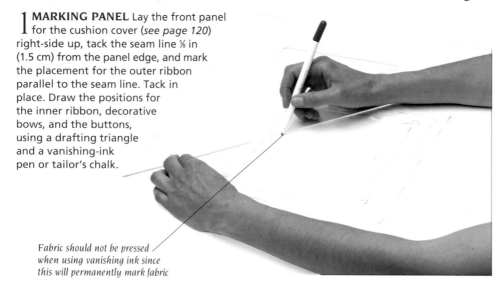

Fabric should not be pressed when using vanishing ink since this will permanently mark fabric

2 **ATTACHING RIBBON** Following the marked line, pin and tack the ribbon bordering the pattern in place on the face of the front panel. Attach the ribbon by slipstitching it along the edges, mitering at the corners and hiding the necessary joins (*see page 23*). Remove the tacking stitches.

3 **ATTACHING DECORATIONS** Stitch the buttons and bows in place and make up the cover (*see page 120*). Lay the lace along the edge and mark the position of the corners on it. Miter the lace at corners, and join the ends at one corner (*see page 23*).

4 **ATTACHING LACE EDGING** Stitch the lace to the cushion edge by hand. Use small, even slipstitches; bad stitching may be camouflaged by the lace, but it will be weak. Wash the cover if you used vanishing ink, then press it carefully and insert the pad.

THE FINISHED CUSHION

TAPESTRY CUSHION

Many densely woven and needleworked textiles – such as kilims and tapestries – make colorfully patterned cushion covers. However, such delicate textiles need backing for added strength. The backing also prevents the inner pad from showing through any gaps in the weave of the fragment. In addition to the chosen textile and the backing material, to make this cushion you will need an inner pad, the fastener you have chosen, and the basic sewing kit.

1 CUTTING OUT PANELS Needleworked textiles, such as this Swedish tapestry, are seldom square, so it is important to mimic the original by using it as a pattern. Lay the tapestry on the piece of backing fabric and secure it with pins. Working carefully, cut out the backing fabric, closely following the edge of the tapestry. Cut out the fabric for the back of the cushion using this same technique.

2 ATTACHING BACKING Lay the tapestry face up on the right side of the backing. Pin and tack together. Place the tapestry and back panel right sides facing. Pin and tack along the edge, leaving a ⅝ in (1.5 cm) allowance.

3 JOINING PANELS Following the tacking stitches, sew the front tapestry panel and the back panels together as appropriate for the fastening method you are using. Remove the tacking stitches and clip the seam allowance at the corners, taking care to avoid cutting through the old fabric. Turn the cover right side out, press, and insert the inner pad.

THE FINISHED CUSHION

FABRIC OPTIONS

Cushion covers can be made from a variety of fabrics, provided that the fabric is suited to the decorative or the functional use of the cushion. For color and delicacy, there are fine dress materials, such as muslin, which may have to be strengthened by backing with a stronger cloth. Because it is a light yet durable fabric, silk is ideal for use in making cushion covers, although the finest weaves need to be lined.

In a more exotic vein, the richly varied hand-woven and printed or embroidered tribal and folk textiles of Africa and India make ideal complements, and contrasts in pattern and texture, to ordinary furnishing fabrics. When seeking a more hard-wearing material, look out for densely woven rug fragments from well-worn oriental carpets or kilims, or a piece of closely worked old needlepoint.

COTTON
DRESS SILK

SHOT
SILK

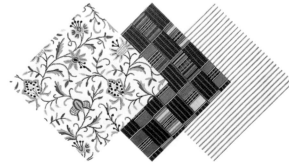

INDIAN
CREWEL WORK

COTTON AFRICAN
CHIEF'S ROBE

COTTON
TICKING

PERSIAN
KILIM PIECE

MODERN
NEEDLEPOINT

SIMPLE SEAT CUSHIONS

MOST HOMES CONTAIN A VARIETY of wooden seats – in the kitchen, dining room, study, or playroom – that are hard and uncomfortable. Making simple removable cushions for such chairs is easy. Seat cushions not only add comfort but also bring pattern and color to a room, and can make the furniture a part of the overall decorative scheme. You can choose from a variety of fastenings to anchor seat cushions to chairs. These range from simple fabric ties to elasticated tapes or Velcro strips, depending on the effect you want to achieve. Decorative embellishments include buttons and tufts.

SEAT CUSHION WITH TIES

When making up seat cushions, consider the location of the chair: for a busy area of the home, for example, choose a covering fabric that is easy to clean. Calculate the amount of material needed by measuring the base of the seat, and add an extra quantity for the ties as well as for the piping trim. To establish the length of piping required, measure around the edge of the seat. To make a pattern for cutting out the fabric for the cushion, you will need tracing paper and a felt-tip pen. You will also need 1½ in (4 cm) thick upholstery foam for the padding, and the basic sewing kit.

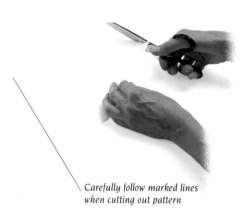

Tracing paper is easier to use than pattern paper for this technique

1 TRACING A PATTERN Make a pattern of the chair seat with a sheet of tracing paper. First, cut tracing paper slightly larger than the seat area. Lay the paper on the seat and crease it over the edge. On the paper, pencil around the perimeter of the seat. Where the seat meets the back, form the pattern around this obstruction by creasing, marking, and cutting out carefully.

Carefully follow marked lines when cutting out pattern

2 CUTTING PATTERN Remove the paper from the chair seat and fold it in half along the back to front axis of the seat. Make sure that the pattern is symmetrical from side to side, adjust if necessary, then cut it out. Check the fit on the seat, particularly around the uprights, and adjust if necessary.

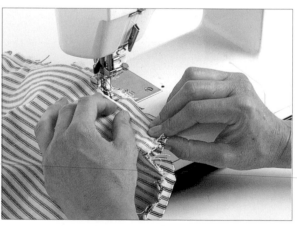

3 CUTTING FOAM Lay the pattern on the foam. Mark the shape with a felt-tip pen and cut it out of the foam using large shears. Pin the pattern to the fabric, and cut out two panels with a ⅝ in (1.5 cm) allowance all around. Measure the seam line of the cover to find the piping length, adding 2 in (5 cm) for the join.

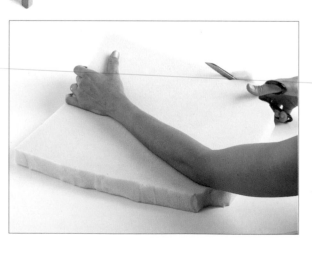

4 JOINING PANELS Make up the piping *(see page 20)*. Attach the piping to the right side of the cushion front. Lay the right sides of the front and back panels together, aligning the edges, and pin, tack, and sew, leaving a gap at the back for inserting the pad. Trim and clip the seams and corners. Pull the cushion cover right side out through the opening.

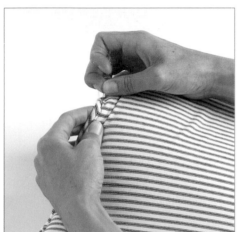

5 ATTACHING TIES Lay the cushion cover on the chair base and mark the positions for the ties. Cut two fabric pieces 24 x 1¼ in (60 x 3 cm) to make the ties *(see page 25)*. Fold the ties in half, pin in place, and oversew each to the inside of the piping on the lower cushion panel. For a more decorative effect, you could make wider ties, which would make larger bows.

6 CLOSING THE OPENING Press the seat-cushion cover and insert the foam pad through the opening. Ensure that the pad is pushed into the corners and curves of the cushion cover. Turn in the seam allowances of the opening, align the edges, and slipstitch closed. When the cushion cover needs to be cleaned, simply cut through the slipstitches to remove the pad.

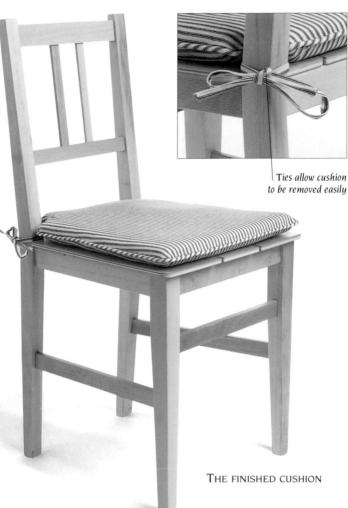

Ties allow cushion to be removed easily

THE FINISHED CUSHION

BUTTONED CUSHION

Buttoning is an upholstery technique that provides quick and easy decoration to furniture coverings, and it is particularly effective on a simple furnishing, such as a removable seat cushion or a box cushion *(see page 138)*. Fabric-covered buttons are used: they can be covered in a fabric with a contrasting color and pattern to the cushion, in which case you can use ready-made buttons, or you may want them covered in the fabric used for the cushion itself, in which case you will probably cover them yourself *(see page 26)*. In addition to the basic sewing kit, you will need a large upholstery needle and strong thread or twine.

THE FINISHED CUSHION

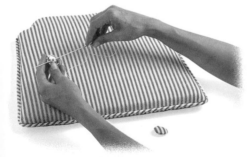

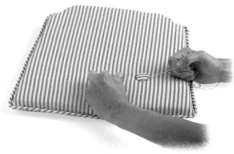

1 THREADING BUTTONS Mark button positions on the cover. Thread the needle with twine and push it into a mark, through the cushion, leaving 4–6 in (10–15 cm) of twine on the top side of cushion. Thread a button onto the needle. Return the needle, through the same hole, to the top side.

2 SECURING BUTTONS Thread onto the twine the second of the first pair of buttons, remove the needle, and fasten it to the cushion with a slipknot. Pull hard on both ends of twine until buttons sink well into the cushion. Securely tie off the ends around the shank of the button and snip off the surplus twine.

BOX SEAT CUSHIONS

BOX SEAT CUSHIONS padded with deep foam make comfortable and easy-to-clean accessories for wicker, metal, or wooden chairs, or for benches and garden seats that are used outside the home or in a greenhouse. Use a sturdy fabric, such as a heavy-duty cotton, for the cover. This will keep its shape and be simple to clean. To make it easy to remove the inner pad for cleaning, fit a full-length zipper in a welt along one side of the cushion.

SIMPLE BOX CUSHION

When making a box cushion, give added strength and a neat edging to the chosen furnishing fabric by piping the seams *(see page 20)*. Depending on the nature of the chair, it may also be a good idea to help secure the cushion in place with same-fabric ties *(see page 25)*. When measuring up, allow sufficient fabric for the top and bottom panels, the wide welt, and the piping, as well as any ties. You will also need piping cord, a zipper, tracing paper for pattern making, a felt-tip pen, a sharp, long-bladed kitchen knife for cutting out the foam pad, and the basic sewing kit.

1 TRACING PATTERN Trace the seat area for the box seat cushion *(see page 136)*. Transfer the traced pattern onto a sheet of white paper.

2 MEASURING SIDES Pin the pattern to the fabric and cut out the top and bottom panels of the cover with a ⅝ in (1.5 cm) seam allowance. Measure around the edge of the seat cushion pattern to find the length of piping and fabric needed for the welt. Make two lengths of piping *(see page 20)*, adding 2 in (5 cm) for joins.

3 CUTTING FOAM Lay the seat pattern on the foam and draw its outline on the pad with a felt-tip pen. Cut the foam to size with a sharp kitchen knife or an electric carving knife.

4 FITTING WELT Cut fabric to the length of three cushion sides plus 1¼ in (3 cm), and the depth plus 1¼ in (3 cm). For the fourth side, where the zipper will be, cut two pieces of fabric to the length of the side plus 1¼ in (3 cm), and half the depth plus 1¼ in (3 cm). Fix a zipper between these pieces in a seam *(see page 27)*. If you can get a long zipper, extending the zipped panel around the cushion corners makes it easy to insert and remove the pad. Pin together the welt sections. Check that the welt fits snugly around the pad.

5 SEWING WELT TO TOP PANEL Attach the piping to the top and bottom cushion panels *(see page 21)*. Place the welt and the top panel of the cover right sides together, edges aligning. Pin, tack, and sew the welt to the panel. Remove the tacking stitches.

6 ATTACHING BASE With the zipper open, pin, tack, and sew the welt and the bottom panel right sides together. Remove the tacking stitches and clip the corners. Turn the cover right side out and press it. Insert the pad, pushing it firmly into the corners.

THE FINISHED CUSHION

OTHER FILLINGS AND DECORATIONS

When they are made for use exclusively inside the home, for example on a sofa or a window seat, box seat cushions stuffed with a polyester or feather-filled padding prove more comfortable than if stuffed with foam. For feather fillings, an inner pad cover of a feather-proof fabric *(see page 6)* is necessary. Box cushions can be attractively finished with buttoning or tufting on the top and bottom panels, or by quilting the welt.

FEATHER-FILLED CUSHION

QUILTING THE WELT

You can give a deep-sided box seat cushion a decorative finish by quilting the welt when making up the cushion cover. To make up the quilted sides, you will need the fabric itself, plus wadding to pad the quilting, and muslin to back the welt. For this technique, you will also need the basic sewing kit. For the cushion filling, you can choose between foam, feathers, or polyester. To make a box seat cushion with a quilted welt, construct the cushion cover as opposite, but when you come to making up the welt, substitute the following technique.

1 PINNING WELT PIECES Cut out wadding and muslin to the same size as the fabric for the welt; if this will make the seams too bulky, cut wadding without a seam allowance, as here. Lay the fabric and the muslin right sides together with the wadding between them.

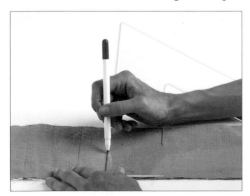

2 MARKING QUILTING LINES Pin and tack around the edges of the wadded welt and across it if necessary to prevent the fabric from slipping. Mark positioning lines for the quilting, using a drafting triangle and tailor's chalk or a vanishing-ink pen.

3 QUILTING Tack along the quilting marks, then machine sew along the tacking stitches. Remove the tacking stitches. Continue to assemble the cushion as detailed opposite and above, replacing the welt with the quilted side panel.

THE FINISHED CUSHION

SIMPLE UPHOLSTERY

JUST AS A DRAPERY, CURTAIN, OR SHADE CAN ENHANCE A WINDOW, SIMILARLY A FABRIC COVERING CAN TRANSFORM A CHAIR OR FOOTSTOOL. UNLIKE AN UPHOLSTERED COVER, WHICH IS SEWN SECURELY AND TACKED TO THE FRAME OF A CHAIR, A SLIPCOVER CAN BE REMOVED EASILY FOR CLEANING, OR CHANGED TO SUIT YOUR PREFERENCE. WHATEVER YOUR REQUIREMENTS — DECORATIVE OR PRACTICAL — YOU WILL FIND IN THIS CHAPTER ALL THE INFORMATION YOU NEED TO MAKE SLIPCOVERS. ALSO INCLUDED ARE SIMPLE INSTRUCTIONS FOR UPHOLSTERING A FOOTSTOOL OR OTTOMAN.

HARD-WEARING WEAVE
A footstool serves as a comfortable rest for tired legs and provides a surface on which to pile books or magazines. To withstand the rigors of everyday wear, it is best to cover footstools in a strong, durable fabric.

CHOOSING A STYLE

SIMPLE-TO-MAKE FABRIC COVERS can be used to give color, pattern, and texture to almost any form of seating, hard or soft, upright or reclining. The most popular and effective way of benefiting from covers, however, is to use them on living-room sofas and armchairs. A slipcover can give a new lease on life to a worn chair or sofa, while even the most ordinary piece of furniture can be transformed when covered with new fabric. Choose hard-wearing materials that offer protection and complement the scheme of decoration by working in combination with the other fabrics and furnishings in the room.

CENTERED DESIGN (above) *Toile* fabric is used to cover this straight-back dining room chair. The fabric's pattern is centered on the upright back and seat, while box pleats allow the skirt to lie smoothly over the contours of the chair legs.

FULL-LENGTH SKIRTS (left) To disguise mismatched dining chairs, try making full-length covers. Here, unbleached cotton slipover covers are finished with self-welting and generous box pleats for classic style.

CHAIR SLIPCOVERS (opposite) Slipcovers with self-covered buttons also provide an answer for well-worn armchairs. To prevent the covers from looking too busy, incorporate a plain fabric cover and pillows into the scheme.

City stripes

(opposite) Wool is naturally flame-retardant, durable, and anti-static, so a 100 percent wool pinstriped fabric adapts well for use in armchair upholstery. It is also easy to work with and can be fed through a sewing machine with relative ease. The snug-fitting material creates a well-groomed look, and because the beech legs have contemporary appeal, they are left on view to offer a contrast to the dark upholstery. Charcoal gray accessories, such as the checked rug and flannel gray footstool, help unify the look of this interior.

Cutaway detail

(above) These chair covers are cut away to expose the shape of the wrought-iron frame. On a practical level, the exposed frames make it easier to lift the chairs. The choice of hot pink, tangerine, and lime-striped silks teamed with ball fringe give a fun and flirty look to an otherwise formal setting.

Trunk table

(left) A trunk or chest is the ideal size and shape for a coffee table. To protect the surface finish, make a simple slipcover that can be removed easily for cleaning. Box pleats at each corner echo the trunk's straight lines, thereby enhancing the total look.

SIMPLE FITTED COVER

MAKING A SIMPLE FITTED COVER for an armchair is straightforward, as long as
you measure carefully. Before cutting out the fabric, make a plan on graph paper of the
dimensions of each section. Label each section as you cut it out. Pin, fit, and cut the sections
in place on the chair before sewing the cover together. Choose a durable fabric that is
suitable for upholstery, such as heavy cotton, damask, or cotton-linen blend, and check
that it is fire retardant – if it is not, you will need to use a flame-resistant interlining.
Make sure that the fabric can be either washed by hand or dry cleaned.

MEASURING

The piping for the simple fitted cover should be attached to
the seam lines around the outside back piece and to each front
arm piece, and along the skirt's top seam. Measure these seam
lines, and cut bias strips and piping cord, allowing for ⅝ in
(1.5 cm) joins where necessary *(see page 20)*. Remove the
seat cushion, and measure and make the cover *(see page 138)*.

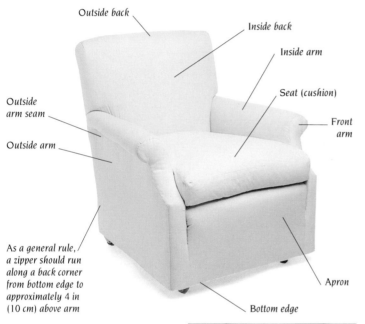

Outside back
Inside back
Inside arm
Outside arm seam
Seat (cushion)
Outside arm
Front arm
Apron
Bottom edge

*As a general rule,
a zipper should run
along a back corner
from bottom edge to
approximately 4 in
(10 cm) above arm*

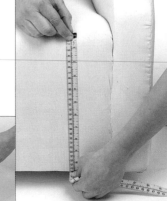

1 **OUTSIDE BACK** Measure
back width across widest
part. Add 1 in (2.5 cm) for
seams on each edge, plus
2½ in (6 cm) for opening at
lower edge of back piece and
an outside arm piece. Measure
bottom to top. Add 6 in
(15 cm) for bottom tuck-under,
and 1 in (2.5 cm) for top seam.

2 **INSIDE BACK** Measure from the
inside back top edge to the seat level.
Add 1 in (2.5 cm) for the top seam, and
6 in (15 cm) for the tuck-in at the back of
the seat. Measure across the inside back
from side to side at the widest point, going
around the corners to the back edges. Add
1 in (2.5 cm) for one side seam, and 2½ in
(6 cm) for zipper opening edge side.

3 **SEAT** Measure the seat of
the chair from the back to
the front edge. Add 1 in (2.5 cm)
for seam allowance at the front
and 6 in (15 cm) for the tuck-in
at the back. Measure the width
of the seat between the arms of
the chair, and add 12 in (30 cm)
to this measurement to allow
for the tuck-in at each side.

4 **APRON** Measure the apron
from the top to the bottom
edge. Add 1 in (2.5 cm) for the
seam at the seat front, plus 6 in
(15 cm) for the tuck-under along the
bottom edge. Measure width of the
apron between front arms, adding
1 in (2.5 cm) for each side seam.

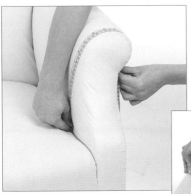

5 INSIDE ARM Measure the arm of the chair from the seat over the arm top, and down to the outer arm seam. Add 7 in (18 cm) for the tuck-in at the side of the seat and the outside arm-piece seam. Measure the length of the arm from front to back at the longest point. Add 2 in (5 cm) for the front arm piece and outside and inside back-piece seams.

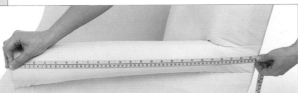

SKIRT

If you are adding a tailored skirt with corner pleats, remember that the skirt should be lined. When making the length of skirt, join widths of fabric to the total length required, and make the joins so that they are hidden either at corners or inside a pleat or fold.

1 SKIRT DEPTH Measure skirt depth, and add 1¼ in (3 cm) for seam allowances. Measure the lining to the same dimensions as the skirt fabric.

6 OUTSIDE ARM Measure the length of the arm from front to back at the longest point. Add 2 in (5 cm) for the front arm and outside back seams. Measure from the outside arm seam to the bottom edge. Add 1 in (2.5 cm) for the inside arm seam, and 6 in (15 cm) for bottom tuck-under.

7 FRONT ARM Measure the front arm at the widest and longest parts. Add 2 in (5 cm) to each of these measurements for the apron, outside arm, and inside arm seams. You will also need to add 6 in (15 cm) lengthwise for the bottom tuck-under.

2 SKIRT SEAM Measure each side, across skirt seam level, 7 in (18 cm) from floor. Add 5 in (12.5 cm) to each side length for three pleat folds, and 2½ in (6 cm) to ends for zipper opening.

MAKING A CUTTING PLAN

Plain fabrics and fabrics with small patterns are easy to use, while large patterns require more fabric for matching design motifs. Place any motif to the center of each fabric section. Make up a cutting plan. In the plan for the slipcover (*see technique, page 152*), arrows indicate the straight grain. Draw the dimensions of each fabric piece to scale on paper to enable you to estimate the amount of fabric and assist you in cutting it out. Cut the fabric into rectangles initially, and trim each piece to size as you fit it around the chair. Make a cutting list using the following guideline: outside back: 1; outside arms: 2; front arms: 2; inside back: 1; seat: 1; skirt: cut as required; apron: 1; cushion: cut as required; inside arms: 2; bias strip for piping: cut as required. When cutting out individual pieces, avoid confusion by pinning paper labels to each piece of fabric.

CUTTING PLAN FOR SIMPLE FITTED COVER

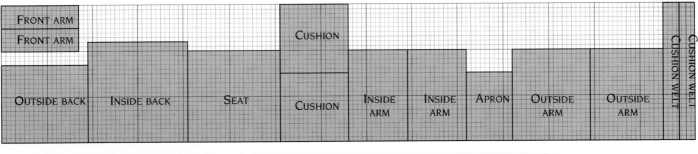

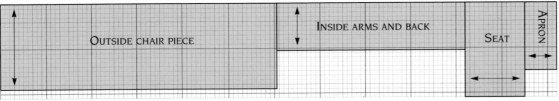

CUTTING PLAN FOR SLIPCOVER (*page 152*)

FITTING THE COVER

Before fitting the cover, decide whether to fit it right side or wrong side out. Here, the cover is fitted right side out, which facilitates the placement of pattern motifs. However, if it is fitted wrong side out, marking seams is easier. Fit each fabric piece to the chair according to its label *(see page 147)*, and trim to size. You will need the basic sewing kit.

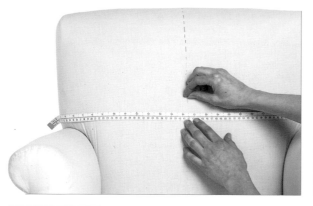

1 MARKING INSIDE BACK Measure the halfway point of the inside back. Using pins or tailor's chalk, mark a vertical line down the center line of the inside back panel on the chair.

2 PINNING FABRIC Place the fabric against the inside back, and center any pattern motif. Mark a line halfway down the fabric piece. Match this line with the line on the chair, and pin the fabric in place down the center.

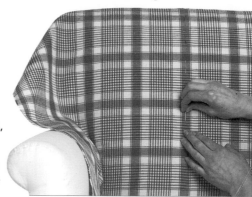

3 PINNING TOP AND SIDES Smooth the inside back fabric piece in place, and pin the top and sides of the fabric piece to the outside back of the chair. Cut away any surplus fabric at the corners.

4 WORKING AROUND ARMS Smooth and pin the fabric around the arms, then trim and clip the fabric to leave a 1 in (2.5 cm) seam allowance. Leave a 6 in (15 cm) allowance for tuck-in at the back of the seat, then trim away any excess fabric.

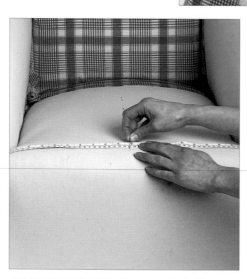

Pull and pin fabric around shape of chair to ensure a close fit

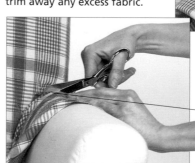

Cut away bulk of excess fabric at corners

Clip to fit when working around a curve, and always leave a 1 in (2.5 cm) seam allowance

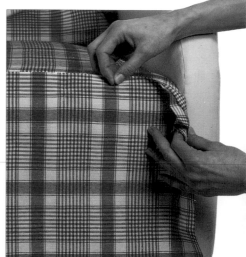

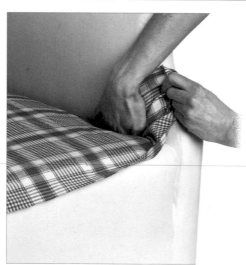

5 MARKING SEAT Measure the halfway point on the seat. Mark a vertical line down the center of the seat and along the center of the fabric seat piece. Place the fabric on the seat and match the two lines.

6 TUCKING IN FABRIC Center and pin the seat fabric along the front edge of the seat, and overlap the inside back piece. Smooth the 6 in (15 cm) tuck-ins in place at the back and sides. Pin the fabric at the sides.

7 PLACING APRON Center and pin the apron fabric piece near the top edge of the apron. Make sure the piece is positioned so that you have 1 in (2.5 cm) for the seams at the seat front, as well as at the arm fronts.

8 TRIMMING INSIDE ARMS Pin the inside arm pieces in place. Trim to shape, leaving 1 in (2.5 cm) for seams. Smooth the tuck-in allowance between the arm and seat.

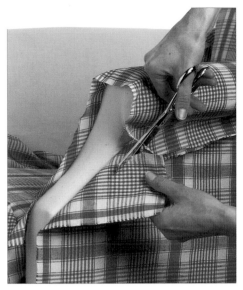

9 SHAPING OUTSIDE ARMS Pin the outside arm fabric in place. Trim to shape as necessary, allowing 1 in (2.5 cm) for front arm, inside arm, and outside back seams.

10 CUTTING FRONT ARMS Pin the pair of front-arm fabric pieces to the front arms. Cut the fabric to the shape of the front arms, then clip the seam allowances.

11 PINNING OUTSIDE BACK Mark the center line of the outside back of the chair. Place the outside back piece on the chair, then mark halfway. Allow an extra 2½ in (6 cm) for a zipper at the opening edge. Pin fabric near seam, then trim to shape. Allow 1 in (2.5 cm) for seams, and 2½ in (6 cm) at zipper opening edge.

12 PINNING SEAMS Work around the chair, and pin the fabric together at all the seams. Be sure to remember every seam line.

Pin close to all seam lines

MARKING ON WRONG SIDE

If the cover has been pinned to the chair with the wrong side out, you can use a vanishing-ink pen to mark the seam lines on the wrong side of the fabric as shown. You might also want to mark some matching points on adjoining pieces to help you align them when the cover has been removed from the chair.

13 DRAWING ACROSS SEAM ALLOWANCES Open the seam allowances in short lengths at a time, and run a vanishing-ink pen or tailor's chalk along the seam lines on the wrong side of the fabric. Mark the matching points for the seams by drawing across the seam allowances. On the straight seams these marks should be 6–8 in (15–20 cm) apart, and on the curved seams they should be every 2 in (5 cm) to ensure accuracy of fit.

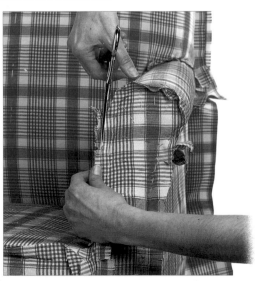

14 TRIMMING SEAMS Trim all seams to ⅝ in (1.5 cm), but leave the 2½ in (6 cm) allowance at the zipper opening edge. Remove all pins and fabric pieces from the chair, and relabel the pieces if necessary.

SEWING THE COVER

Before assembling the pieces right sides together by pinning, tacking, and sewing, make the piping *(see page 20)* with medium-weight piping cord to the length required *(see page 146)*. Also select cord for the drawstring that secures the corners of the cover underneath the chair, and choose the fastening, such as a zipper, for the opening at the bottom of the join of the outside back and an outside arm piece. To sew the fabric pieces together, you will need the basic sewing kit. Once you begin, check the fit of the cover and adjust it if necessary. Neaten raw seams as you go, and press them open.

1 SEWING CORNERS Pin, tack, and sew the corners on the top edge of the inside back piece to the outside back piece.

2 SEAT AND APRON Pin, tack, and sew the front edge of the seat piece to the top edge of the apron piece.

3 INSIDE ARMS TO BACK AND SEAT Sew one side of the seat to the inside arm. Continue around the seat seam, and attach the lower edge of the inside back piece to the back edge of the seat piece. Attach the other inside arm piece to the seat piece. Sew the inside arms to the inside back piece.

4 PINNING TUCK-INS Chairs are rarely perfectly square, so your fabric tuck-ins will often not match exactly. To square off the tuck-in, fold the excess fabric of the longer piece over the edge of the shorter piece near to an inside back corner. Next, pin, tack, and sew the outside arms to the inside arms.

Stitch piping to front arm piece along seam line

5 APPLYING PIPING TO FRONT ARM Pin, tack, and sew the piping to the seam line of the front arm pieces. Take care not to stretch the piping when applying it to the curve.

6 CHECKING FIT Pin and tack the outside and inside arm, and the apron, to the edge of the front arm piece, following the seam line. Place these pieces on the chair to check for fit before sewing. When sewing them together, use the zipper-foot attachment on the sewing machine. Repeat for other arm.

Check fit around front arm before sewing

Use a zipper-foot attachment to sew close to piping

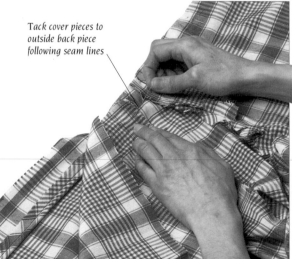

Tack cover pieces to outside back piece following seam lines

7 ATTACHING BACK PIECE Pin, tack, and sew the piping to the outside back piece at the seam line. Sew the rest of the cover to the back piece. Leave a 2½ in (6 cm) allowance for the opening at the lower edge of the back and outside arm pieces.

8 MARKING FASTENING
Put the cover on the chair, and mark the bottom edge of the chair on the fabric. This is the position for the bottom end of the fastening. Remove the cover and insert the zipper *(see page 27)* to the cover opening.

9 TRIMMING SURPLUS
Again, fit the cover onto the chair. Check that the surplus fabric at the bottom edge is the same dimension all around the chair, and trim if necessary.

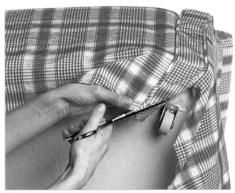

Trim cords to ease securing ends of piping to cover

Neaten turning allowance raw edge with bias strip

10 TRIMMING AROUND LEGS Lay the chair on its back, and unpick the corner seams to the level of the bottom edge of the chair. Trim the fabric to fit around the legs, leaving a ⅜ in (1 cm) allowance for the turnings.

11 SNIPPING CORD Because sewing through the ends of piping cord can be difficult, it is easiest to trim the piping cord at the ends by pulling it from the bias covering and snipping off ¾ in (2 cm).

12 ATTACHING BIAS STRIP Neaten the lower edge of the turning allowance around the leg by using a bias strip *(see page 20)* or by turning a ³⁄₁₆ in (5 mm) double hem. Repeat this step for the remaining legs of the chair.

13 SEWING DRAWSTRING CASING Make the drawstring casings by turning the raw edge of each bottom tuck-under section ⅜ in (1 cm) and then ¾ in (2 cm) to the wrong side, and pin, tack, and sew to secure.

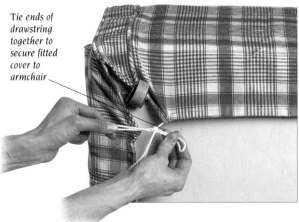

Tie ends of drawstring together to secure fitted cover to armchair

14 SECURING DRAWSTRING ENDS Place the cover on the chair, thread the drawstrings through the casings, and tie the ends with bows to secure. Smooth out any wrinkles in the chair cover, push down the tuck-ins, and check that the piping is lying straight.

THE COVERED ARMCHAIR

MAKING AND FITTING A SKIRT

Mark the position of the skirt's top edge with a line of pins around the cover. Here, the top edge of the skirt is 7 in (18 cm) from the floor. Check that the line is level, then remove the cover. Cut the fabric to the length and depth required *(see page 147)*. Join fabric to make length with plain flat seams *(see page 14)*. Cut the lining to the size of the skirt. Make any joins with plain flat seams. Press open seams. Place the skirt and lining pieces right sides together. Sew a plain flat seam ⅝ in (1.5 cm) from the lower edge. Turn the pieces right side out and press. The seam between lining and skirt should lie on lining side, ⅛–³⁄₁₆ in (3–5 mm) from edge.

1 ATTACHING PIPING
Pin and tack the piping to the cover along the pinned line, with the piped edge facing away from the bottom edge of the cover. At each edge of the cover opening, trim ¾ in (2 cm) from each end of the piping cord. Turn the ends of the bias strip ¾ in (2 cm) to the wrong side, and slipstitch the ends of the bias strip to neaten and close.

2 TRIMMING LINING Trim the top edge of the lining so that it is level with the skirt fabric. Tack the fabrics together ⅝ in (1.5 cm) along the top edge. Finish the raw side edges of the skirt piece with zigzag stitches.

3 SKIRT TO COVER Pin and tack skirt pieces to piped seam line of cover. Fold the three pleats so that the folded edges meet at the corners. Make 2½ in (6 cm) turnings at each side of the opening. Check that bottom edges of skirt match around chair. Sew in place on piped seam line.

THE FINISHED SKIRT

SLIPCOVER

A SLIPCOVER for a simply shaped chair or sofa is easy to make and requires only a limited number of fabric pieces. Although the fit of a slipcover will not be quite as snug as that of a simple fitted cover, it is much quicker to make. Use the cutting plan on page 147 to help you visualize the pieces required before you begin measuring the chair.

MAKING THE COVER

A slipcover can be made with ties secured to the underside of the chair, in which case the legs will be visible, or without ties, so that the fabric reaches the floor. To make a cover with ties, allow extra fabric for flaps at all the lower edges. These flaps are folded under the chair at the sides and tied around the legs at each corner. If ties are not required, add a hem allowance of 2 in (5 cm) instead of the extra fabric. You will need cover fabric and the basic sewing kit.

Outside back · Inside arm · Inside back · Outside arm · Front arm · Seat · Apron

MEASURING

Outside of chair: Measure around outside of the chair sides, and chair back at the longest point, from the center of one front arm to the other. Add 1 in (2.5 cm) for each outside arm-piece seam. Measure from the floor to the center of the top of an arm. Add 1 in (2.5 cm) for the top edge seam, and 5 in (12.5 cm) for the tie-under flap.

Inside arms and back: Measure from the seat level to the center of the top of the inside arms. Add 1 in (2.5 cm) for the top edge seam, and 6 in (15 cm) for the tuck-in. Make the inside back piece to this height by the same length as the outside back piece.

Seat: Measure the seat from the back edge to the front edge, adding 6 in (15 cm) for the back tuck-in, and 1 in (2.5 cm) for the apron seam. Measure the seat widthwise from the base of one inside arm to the other at the widest point, plus 6 in (15 cm) to each side for the tuck-ins.

Apron: Measure the apron piece as the width of the seat, plus 2 in (5 cm), by the drop from the seat edge to the floor. Add 1 in (2.5 cm) for the top seam and 2 in (5 cm) for the lower hem allowance. For tie-up flaps, add 1 in (2.5 cm) for seams and 5 in (12.5 cm) for the tie-under flap at the front. Decide on length and width of ties, and cut them out.

Cutting out: Make a cutting plan *(see page 147)*. When cutting out the fabric widths to make the inside and outside back pieces, consider the design motifs of the fabric, as well as the seam positions. Cut out the fabric along the straight grain.

1 MARKING CENTRAL POINTS Mark the central point on the back edge of the seat piece, and the central point on the inside back piece, using a vanishing-ink pen.

2 MATCHING CENTRAL PANELS Match the central points of the inside seat pieces. Lay the two panels of fabric right sides together.

Make all seams 1 in (2.5 cm) from raw edges

3 SEAT TO INSIDE BACK Sew seat piece to inside back piece. Trim the inside back allowance at corners, and neaten seam edges separately with zigzag stitch. Mark central point of front edge of the seat piece, and central point of the top edge of the apron piece.

4 SEAT TO APRON Match the central points of seat front edge and the apron top edge, then sew the seat piece to the apron piece right sides together. Stop at the edge of the seat seam, and snip into the seat seam allowance to turn the corners at the top of the apron.

5 OUTSIDE TO INSIDE CHAIR Pin, tack, and sew the outside back piece to the inside back piece, with the right sides together. The seams should be 1 in (2.5 cm) from the edges. Do not sew front edges of the arms.

6 SEWING ARM EDGES At the front edges of the arms, pin, tack, and sew the outside back piece to the inside back piece, with the right sides together. Stop at the edge of the seat seam.

7 OUTSIDE CHAIR TO APRON Pin, tack, and sew the outside back piece to the apron piece, with the right sides together. Make sure that the seat piece seam is turned back out of the way.

Keep seat-piece seam allowance away from apron and back-piece seam line

8 MARKING LENGTH Put the cover on the chair and check the length. Trim the cover to reduce the bulk if necessary, but leave a 2 in (5 cm) seam allowance. Mark the required length with tailor's chalk or pins. Remove the cover, and turn and sew a double 1 in (2.5 cm) hem. Press and refit the cover.

THE COVERED ARMCHAIR

TIE-ON COVER

Lay the chair on its back, and trim excess fabric at corners to fit around the legs. Leave a 1 in (2.5 cm) hem allowance for the edges. Turn ⅜ in (1 cm) double hems at side edges of the flaps, and ⅜ in (1 cm) double hems on the longer edges. Make four pairs of fabric ties *(see page 25)*. Sew ties to the flap corners. Fit the cover. Secure ties around the chair legs.

NEW LEASE ON LIFE
If the covers are slightly worn
but the furniture is otherwise
in good condition, it is worth
recovering favorite pieces
of furniture in slipcovers.
Introduce new colors or two
coordinating fabrics to avoid
repetition, and use remnants
to make pillows or throws.

TABLE LINENS

MORE THAN SIMPLY PROTECTING A TABLETOP, TABLE LINENS ALSO

PROVIDE A SIMPLE WAY OF INTRODUCING AN ELEMENT OF COLOR,

PATTERN, AND TEXTURE TO A ROOM. PIECES OF FABRIC HAVE

LONG BEEN USED NOT ONLY AS PRACTICAL COVERINGS FOR

PROTECTING THE TOPS OF FINE TABLES, BUT ALSO AS A MEANS OF

DRESSING UP EVERYDAY FURNITURE. TABLECLOTHS AND NAPKINS

ARE EASY TO MAKE AND REQUIRE ONLY THE SIMPLEST OF

STITCHES. ALMOST ANY FABRIC, FROM DELICATE NETTING AND

SILKS TO HEAVYWEIGHT VELVET, CAN BE USED. THIS CHAPTER

DEMONSTRATES HOW TO MAKE PLAIN AND DECORATIVE

TABLECLOTHS AND NAPKINS IN A VARIETY OF STYLES AND SHAPES.

PLAIN BORDER
A deep border in coordinated plain cotton
gives substance to this check tablecloth. For
a professional finish, the corners have been
mitered so they fall into crisp, neat points.

CHOOSING A STYLE

TABLE LINENS do not need to be restricted to the dining room: they can be used to set a style for all types of tables. Plain linen or cotton tablecloths are practical and elegant, and can be enhanced with trimmings, while patterned fabrics can be chosen to coordinate with other materials in the room. The shape of the tablecloth generally follows the shapes of the tables and such cloths are a comfortable length when they rest on the knees of diners. Dressing tables or vanities look good covered with a long drape of fabric, while round tables can be covered with two or more layers of contrasting materials in different lengths.

TEXTURE AND CONTRAST
(above) Appliqué circles placed strategically over this purple tablecloth draw attention to the individual place settings. The larger circle defines the table center, and the best spot for placing flowers or food.

COTTAGE-STYLE NAPKINS
(right) Traditionally, hand-embroidered napkins and table linens were used at teatime. These sturdy, printed cotton napkins in vivid pink and green combine a cottage-style gingham and 1950's rose motif. Made from fabric remnants, the napkins are hemmed and the corners mitered.

TIED WITH RIBBON
(above) Napkin folding can be time consuming and unnecessary for informal meals. To add style to everyday napkins, tie ribbons into loose bows around each one. Sheer ribbons in pale blue combined with fresh flowers provide a delicate finish to plain white linen.

ENGLISH EMBROIDERY
(opposite) A white cloth with an English embroidery heart motif has been designed to conceal the table legs. Folded pleats at the top of the fabric help the cloth fit the contours of the circular table, while cotton tabs tied in bows give a decorative finish.

WHITE TABLE LINEN
(opposite) Regardless of the style of the room or its color scheme, white table linen has a timeless appeal that makes it suitable for any occasion. For formal dinners, use white linen napkins rolled up in silver napkin rings, or for more informal family gatherings, simply fold the napkins into squares. Here, a white tablecloth with a knotted fringed edge makes a change from plain hems and reflects the relaxed style of the garden flowers that form the table centerpiece. For fringed tablecloth edges, choose a cotton fabric with a loose weave, since this will make it easier to tease out and separate the individual threads with a needle.

SCALLOPED EDGE
(above) Gingham is a suitable fabric for table linen as it is widely available, inexpensive, and easy to wash. For added interest, try a castellated, zigzag or scalloped edge. For a finished look, use the gingham squares as a guide to make sure that the cut shapes are the same height and width. Here, a mother-of-pearl button is sewn to the center of each scallop for decoration.

LAYERED TABLECLOTHS
(left) Rectangular and square tablecloths often do not cover the base of circular tables. But placed diagonally, one on top of the other, they can create an attractive layered look. This classic white damask tablecloth sits on top of an ethnic fabric in gray and cream, creating a highlight in a room dominated by dark walls. Generously proportioned, both cloths flow onto the floor to give a luxurious finish to the dining room.

TABLECLOTHS

THE FABRIC USED FOR TABLECLOTHS should be durable and easy to clean. Your choice of the shape and style of a tablecloth should depend on its use. Full-length tablecloths function well as coverings for display tables, while kitchen or dining tables should have coverings that drop no farther than the seat level of surrounding chairs. Calculate the amount of fabric required, based on accurate measurements of the table. For large tables, avoid making fabric joins that will be visible on the top of the tablecloth by placing a full width of fabric at the center, and adding extra widths at the sides. Join widths with flat fell seams *(see page 15).*

MEASURING

For all shapes of tablecloth, you will need to know the dimension of the tabletop and the required drop before cutting out the fabric. To determine the required drop for a tablecloth that will cover a kitchen or dining table, measure from the edge of the tabletop to the seat level of a surrounding chair. Find the dimensions for a full-length, decorative tablecloth that will be used on a small display table by measuring from the edge of the tabletop to the floor. To measure and cut out a circular tablecloth for a round tabletop, follow the instructions in steps 1–3 below.

ROUND AND OVAL TABLES

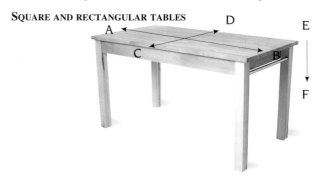

For a square cloth for a round table, measure table's diameter (A–B), and add twice the drop (E–F), plus a 1 in (2.5 cm) hem allowance. This will be the measurement for both sides of the cloth. For a rectangular cloth for an oval table, measure the table's length, and add twice the drop, plus a 1 in (2.5 cm) hem allowance. Measure up in the same way along the width. For an oval cloth for an oval table, pin a paper template of the tabletop to fabric, and add drop (E–F), plus a 1 in (2.5 cm) hem allowance.

SQUARE AND RECTANGULAR TABLES

For a square tablecloth for a square table, or a rectangular tablecloth for a rectangular table, measure the tabletop width (C–D), and add twice the required drop (E–F), plus a 1 in (2.5 cm) hem allowance. Measure the tabletop length (A–B), and add twice the required drop (E–F), plus a 1 in (2.5 cm) hem allowance.

CUTTING OUT A CIRCULAR TABLECLOTH

A circular tablecloth will need to have an equal drop all around. Make an arc-shaped template and use this as a guide to cutting out the fabric to the correct shape. For this technique, you will need a marker, a length of string, and the basic sewing kit. Make a compass by knotting one end of the string around a thumbtack and tying the other end to the marker. You will need to adjust the distance of the string depending on the radius of the tablecloth.

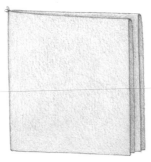

1 FOLDING FABRIC Cut out a fabric square so that each side is equal to the diameter of the tablecloth. This length is twice the drop, plus the table's diameter. Fold the fabric right side together into quarters.

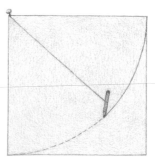

2 MARKING PATTERN Cut a square pattern to the size of the folded fabric. Pin the simple compass at one corner of the pattern. Draw an arc across the paper. Cut out the pattern along the marked line.

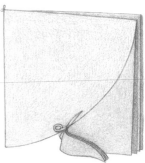

3 CUTTING FABRIC Pin the pattern corner to the top of folded fabric corner. Trace arc across folded fabric. Cut fabric along arc. If a hem is required, add necesssary allowance to arc before cutting out the fabric.

OILCLOTH TABLECLOTH WITH BOUND EDGE

When you wish to make a tablecloth for everyday use, you will need to select a fabric that is not only durable, but also easy to keep clean. Cotton fabric is simple to wash but can become stained. A plastic-coated fabric or an oilcloth wipes down easily and is stain resistant. For this technique, you will need the oilcloth fabric and the basic sewing kit.

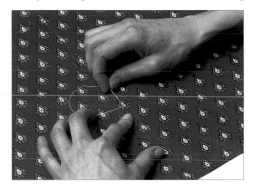

1 JOINING WIDTHS Measure the table and calculate the dimension of the fabric you will need *(see opposite)*. Join fabric widths with flat fell seams *(see page 15)*. First, match the pattern and temporarily secure joins with ladder stitch *(see page 13)*.

2 SEWING WIDTHS Fold the fabric widths right sides together. Pin, tack, and sew along the join ⅝ in (1.5 cm) from the raw edge of each fabric width. Trim one seam allowance to ¼ in (6 mm). Repeat this, if necessary, for any other joins.

3 FINISHING SEAM Fold the wider seam allowance over the shorter one. Press the fold flat. Pin and tack near the raw edge of the wider seam. Turn the fabric right side up and machine sew along the tacked line. Press the seam flat.

5 ATTACHING BINDING STRIP Open out the binding strip. Place the right side of the binding strip and the right side of the tablecloth fabric together, matching the raw edges. Pin, tack, and sew along the fold line of the binding strip.

Fold long edges of bias strip to right side

4 MAKING BINDING Make a bias strip to the length of the tablecloth's perimeter by twice the desired edging width, plus ¾ in (2 cm) for folds *(see page 20)*. Fold and press the long edges ⅜ in (1 cm) to the right side.

6 FOLDING CORNERS At the corners, pinch the binding strip and continue sewing up to, but not over, the fold. Turn the fabric and continue stitching the binding strip to the fabric.

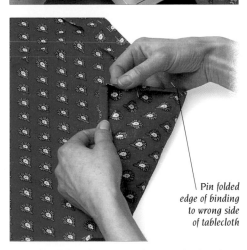

Pin folded edge of binding to wrong side of tablecloth

7 MITERING BINDING Miter the binding at the corners *(see page 19)*. Turn the binding over the raw edge of the fabric, and pin, tack, and sew its folded edge to secure it to the wrong side of the fabric *(see page 14)*. Wrinkles will disappear with use.

THE FINISHED TABLECLOTH

TABLECLOTH WITH KNOTTED FRINGE EDGING

To make up this square tablecloth, you will need a loosely woven fabric that matches the overall design scheme of the room, plus the basic sewing kit. Bear in mind that if you are using a fabric with a woven pattern rather than a printed one, the warp and weft threads may be of different colors, resulting in edging that is not the same color on all sides.

1 SEPARATING THREADS Measure the round table and cut out a square of fabric *(see page 162)*. Lay the fabric on a flat surface. Use a long needle to tease away threads from one of the raw edges. Carefully separate and remove one thread at a time.

Separate cross-threads with a long needle

2 REMOVING THREADS Remove the threads by pulling each strand away from the fabric. Continue separating and removing threads all around until you reach the desired fringe depth. The fringe should be long enough for knotting. Here, it is 3 in (7.5 cm) long.

Pull away cross-threads from fabric to leave fringe edging

3 GROUPING FRINGE Working along one edge at a time, divide the fringe into small groups of an equal size. Separate each group into two.

4 KNOTTING FRINGE Make a knot with each of the smaller groups of fringe. Push it toward the edge of the cloth to prevent the fabric from unraveling. Repeat knotting all around the cloth.

THE FINISHED TABLECLOTH

LINEN TABLECLOTH WITH LACE EDGING

A linen tablecloth with a lace edging creates a traditional effect. If you have an old tablecloth with a lace edging, consider removing the edging and attaching it to new fabric. For this technique, you will need linen fabric, lace from an old tablecloth, and the basic sewing kit. Wash the old lace, cover it with a damp cloth, and press. Cut the fabric so that it fits within the lace edging, adding 4 in (10 cm) all around for hems. Join widths with flat fell seams *(see page 15)*.

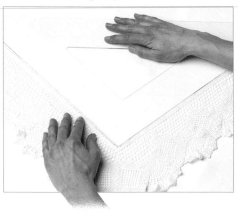

1 ALIGNING CORNER Lay the linen fabric on a flat surface and place the edging around it, aligning the corners. Use a try square to make sure that the corners of the edging are as square as possible. Measure the edges to ensure they are of equal length.

2 POSITIONING EDGING Use a vanishing-ink pen, tailor's chalk, or pushpins to mark the inner edge of the lace on the linen fabric. Remove the edging.

For a professional finish, always use a try square when marking fabric

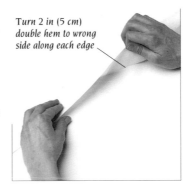

Turn 2 in (5 cm) double hem to wrong side along each edge

3 **MARKING FABRIC** You will need a large, double hem for antique lace to give it extra support. Here, a 2 in (5 cm) double hem is required. Mark a line 4 in (10 cm) – twice the double hem – from the first line. Cut fabric around this outer line.

4 **TURNING HEM** Working along each of the four edges at a time, fold a 2 in (5 cm) double hem, and press.

Trim along mitered corner fold to remove excess fabric

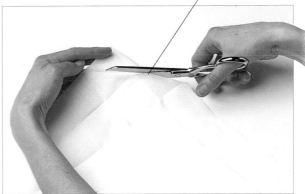

5 **TRIMMING CORNER** To form corners, unfold the two layers of fabric at each corner, then fold the first turning into a miter (see page 19), and press. Unfold the mitered corner and trim along the fold. Refold the double hem and miter each corner.

6 **TACKING HEM** Pin and tack ⅜ in (1 cm) from the inner edge of the hem. Use slipstitch or topstitch to secure the hem.

Tack along inner edge of hem

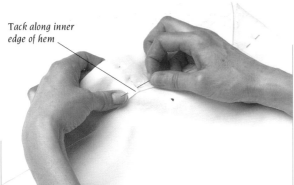

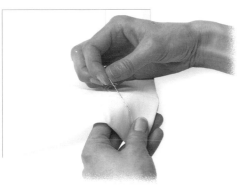

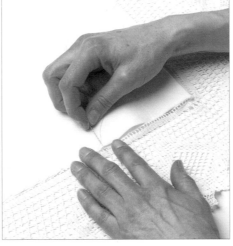

7 **STITCHING CORNER** At the four mitered corners, neaten the miters by slipstitching the folded edges together.

8 **ATTACHING EDGING** Lay the fabric on a flat surface and carefully position the edging around it. Tack the edging to the fabric, using large slipstitches – do not use pins, which could damage the fragile lace.

9 **SECURING LACE** Secure the lace edging carefully to the fabric, using slipstitch or shallow zigzag stitch (see page 14). Press the finished tablecloth.

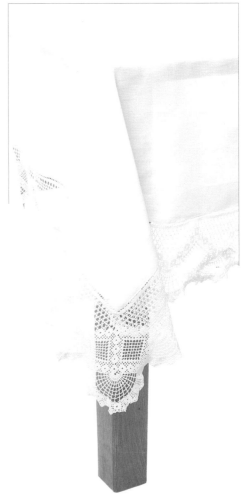

THE FINISHED TABLECLOTH

FRINGED TABLECLOTH

When choosing the material for this tablecloth, bear in mind that loosely woven, medium-weight fabric lends itself best to a fringed edging. For this technique, you will need the fabric and the basic sewing kit. Measure your table *(see page 162)*, then cut out the fabric to the required size, adding extra for the fringe allowance and for any seams.

1 FRAYING EDGE Lay out the fabric on a flat surface. Using a long needle, separate and remove a thread at a time from one edge of the fabric. Continue fraying the edge until the fringe reaches the depth you desire. Fray the remaining edges until you have created the same depth of fringe on all four sides.

2 SECURING EDGE To prevent the fabric from unraveling further, secure the unfrayed edge of the fabric with zigzag stitch *(see page 14)*. Press the tablecloth before use.

THE FINISHED TABLECLOTH

FRINGED TABLECLOTH WITH SCALLOPED EDGE

Ready-made trimmings can be used to decorate the edges of tablecloths, adding character to these furnishings. The fabric you choose for a tablecloth should depend on the nature of its use; a plastic-coated fabric is ideal for a kitchen table. You can create scallops along the edges of the fabric – this is a simple task, since this fabric does not fray and therefore does not require hemming. For this technique, you will need a plastic-coated fabric, fringe, saucer, and the basic sewing kit.

1 MARKING FABRIC Measure your table and add the desired drop of the tablecloth *(see page 162)*. Mark this dimension on the wrong side of the fabric, using a try square, tape measure, and vanishing-ink pen.

2 POSITIONING SCALLOP On the wrong side of the fabric, mark the scallop positions along the line. Try to fit an equal number of scallops on each side, and one complete scallop around each corner. This might take a few attempts.

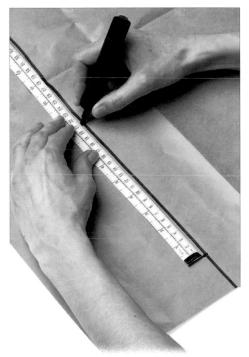

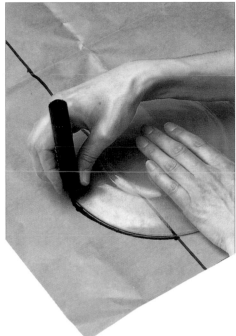

Use vanishing-ink pen to trace around scallop template

3 **MARKING PATTERN** On a piece of paper, mark a line longer than the length of one scallop. Measure and mark the exact length of one scallop on this line.

4 **DRAWING SCALLOP** Use a saucer or other circular object as a guide for drawing a suitable curve between the scallop marks on the paper.

5 **TRACING PATTERN** Cut out the pattern, and place the straight edge against the marked line on the wrong side of the fabric. Trace around the template.

6 **CUTTING OUT SCALLOP**
Following the marked scallop positions along the line, carefully cut out the scallops around the fabric.

Plastic-coated material is self-neatening and does not require hemming

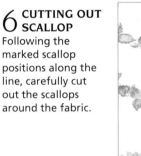

7 **ATTACHING FRINGE**
Plastic-coated material is self-neatening and therefore does not require a hem. Tack the ready-made fringe to the scalloped edge of the fabric. When you have attached the fringe along all four sides, machine sew it in place.

Fringed edging softens effect of stiff, plastic-coated material

THE FINISHED TABLECLOTH

FULL-LENGTH TABLECLOTH WITH TASSELED EDGING

A full-length tablecloth is ideal for dressing a small table or stand. It can also be used as an undercloth when dressing a table with layers of contrasting fabric, acting as a skirt under smaller fabrics. To make this full-length tablecloth with edging, you will need heavyweight fabric for the tablecloth, edging, a length of string, marker, and the basic sewing kit.

1 JOINING FABRIC Measure the table and drop, minus the depth of the edging *(see page 162)*. Join sections of fabric, if necessary, with flat fell seams *(see page 15)* to make a large square of cloth that is equal to the dimensions of the table and drop. Fold the fabric right sides together into quarters.

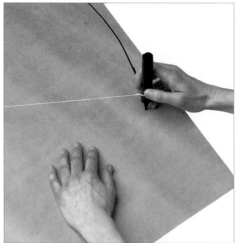

2 MAKING PATTERN Make a square template to the size of the fabric when folded. Using a simple compass pinned to a corner of the template, draw an arc across the paper from one corner to the other *(see page 162)*.

3 MARKING FABRIC Cut out the paper pattern along the arc. Pin the pattern to the folded fabric, aligning the arc with the open edges of the folded fabric. On the wrong side of the fabric, trace around the pattern, adding ¾ in (2 cm) for a single turned hem. Cut out the fabric along the marked line.

4 STITCHING HEM Open out the fabric. Neaten the raw edge of the fabric by turning a ¾ in (2 cm) hem all around. Pin, tack, and sew the hem, then remove the tacking stitches.

Pin edging along hem to temporarily hold it in place before tacking and sewing

5 PINNING EDGING Measure the circumference of the tablecloth. Cut the edging to the same length as the tablecloth's circumference. Pin the edging along the hem, keeping a straight line.

6 JOINING ENDS Tack and sew the edging to the tablecloth. Where the ends of the edging meet, oversew to make a neat join. Press the fabric carefully before fitting it on the table.

THE FINISHED TABLECLOTH

TABLECLOTH WITH GATHERED SKIRT

To make this two-piece tablecloth, you will need fabric for the tablecloth and piping, piping cord, a length of strong twine, and the basic sewing kit. Measure the tabletop (see *page 162*). Make a square of fabric to this dimension, joining fabric widths as necessary with flat fell seams (see *page 15*). Fold the fabric right sides together into quarters.

1 MARKING FABRIC Make pattern to size of folded fabric. Cut out a quarter circle *(see page 162)*. Pin pattern to wrong side of fabric. Trace around it, adding ¾ in (2 cm) for seams. Cut fabric along marked line. Make piping to length of table's circumference. Add 4 in (10 cm) for joining *(see page 20)*. Cut out fabric widths for skirt to depth required, plus 2 in (5 cm) for seams and hems by one-and-a-half times piping length.

2 ATTACHING PIPING Pin, tack, and sew the piping to the right side of the top panel, with the piping seam allowance to the outside edge. Join the ends of the piping together.

Attach piping to right side of top panel

3 MAKING SKIRT To make one length of fabric, pin the widths of the skirt together, matching any motifs *(see page 16)*. Make joins with plain flat seams *(see page 14)*.

4 HEMMING SKIRT Neaten the lower edge of the skirt with a row of zigzag stitches *(see page 14)*. Turn a ¾ in (2 cm) hem to the wrong side along the lower edge, and herringbone stitch or machine sew to secure.

5 ATTACHING TWINE Cut twine to the table's circumference. Place it ¾ in (2 cm) from skirt's top edge. Sew zigzag stitches over twine to secure *(see page 22)*. Mark quarter intervals around edge of top panel. Make matching marks on skirt's top edge.

Lay fabric pieces together, aligning quarter-circle marks

6 ALIGNING FABRICS Place top panel and skirt right sides together. Align the quarter-circle marks. At the marks, pin the skirt to the top panel along the piped edge.

7 SECURING SKIRT Pull the twine to gather skirt, working first from one end and then the other, so that half of the skirt is gathered at a time. Once the gathers are evenly distributed, pin, tack, and sew the skirt to the top panel ⅝ in (1.5 cm) from the raw edges. Press the tablecloth on the right side.

THE FINISHED TABLECLOTH

NAPKINS

NAPKINS ARE THE MOST FREQUENTLY used table linen, and should therefore be made from durable and easy-to-clean fabric. Although there are no hard-and-fast rules, you should try to match the size of the napkin with its intended use – a small napkin is adequate for informal occasions and light meals, while a large napkin is more suitable for dinner parties and formal events. There are plenty of sturdy, colorful fabrics to choose from, and you can make napkins to either match or contrast with your other table linen. Napkins can also be edged with decorative trimmings such as binding or scallops.

PLAIN NAPKIN

When choosing fabric for small napkins, consider using scraps from other soft furnishings. Napkins can be made to any size, but should be no smaller than 12 in (30 cm) square.

When cutting out, make sure to match the grain of the fabric and cut the corners perfectly square. To make this simple napkin, use suitable fabric and the basic sewing kit.

Use draftsman's square and vanishing-ink pen to mark fabric

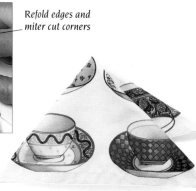

Refold edges and miter cut corners

1 MARKING FABRIC Mark the fabric to the required size, adding an extra 1¼ in (3 cm) to each side for turning double hems. Make sure that you achieve a perfect square.

2 TRIMMING CORNER Fold a ⅝ in (1.5 cm) double hem on all sides, and press. Unfold edges. Miter corners *(see page 19)* along first fold line, and press. Unfold corners. Cut across each corner.

3 FOLDING MITER Refold edges and finish mitering corners. Slipstitch hems and miters, or topstitch using a sewing machine *(see page 15)*. Press the napkin before use.

THE FINISHED NAPKIN

NAPKIN WITH BOUND EDGE

For this technique, you will need napkin fabric, edging fabric, and the basic sewing kit. Cut a square piece of fabric to the size required. Cut two binding strips to the length of the napkin, adding ¾ in (2 cm) for turnings, by double the depth

of the edging required. Cut two more binding strips to the length of the napkin, plus 1½ in (4 cm), by double the edging depth required. Fold and press ⅜ in (1 cm) turnings to the wrong side along the long edges of the binding strips.

Trim inner ends of binding to reduce fabric bulk

1 ATTACHING BINDING Open out the binding strips. Place the shorter binding strips on two opposing napkin edges, right sides together. Match the raw edges. Pin, tack, and sew along fold line of binding seam allowance. Press seams open.

2 TRIMMING BINDING ENDS To reduce the binding fabric bulk, trim the ¾ in (2 cm) overhangs at the ends of the longer strips to blunt points.

3 PINNING BINDING Place the longer binding strips on the remaining opposing sides of the napkin, right sides together. Sew them along the binding fold line. Fold the corners inward and trim the seam allowances. Fold all strips over the raw edges of the napkin. Pin and tack in place. Slipstitch the binding to the fabric along the binding's folded edge.

THE FINISHED NAPKIN

SHEER NAPKIN WITH SCALLOPS

This type of scalloped edging is produced using a simple hand-sewn technique. It works best with lightweight and sheer fabrics. For this technique, you will need lightweight or sheer fabric and the basic sewing kit. Cut out the fabric to the size required, adding ⅝ in (1.5 cm) all around for the scalloped hems.

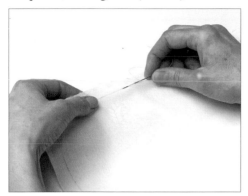

1 TACKING HEM LINE On the wrong side of the fabric, use a vanishing-ink pen to mark the hem line ⅝ in (1.5 cm) from the edges. Tack along the line. Fold each edge twice to meet the tacking line, and press.

2 SECURING CORNER Starting at one corner, oversew across the corner, securing it to the wrong side of the fabric with four or five stitches *(see page 14)*.

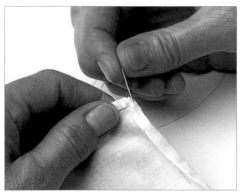

3 BEGINNING SCALLOP Insert the needle at the outer edge of the hem near the corner. Push the needle diagonally to the inside of the hem – the wider the diagonal, the larger the scallops will be.

4 STITCHING HEM Oversew the hem and insert the needle perpendicularly to the edge. Push the needle through to the inside of the hem so that it emerges at the same exit point as in step 3.

5 FINISHING SCALLOP Oversew the hem again, exiting from the same inside point, to form a scallop. Make one blanket stitch to lock in thread *(see page 13)*. Continue the handsewing process along the edge of the napkin and the remaining sides. Oversew each corner with four or five stitches.

THE FINISHED NAPKIN

CUT SCALLOPS

You will need medium-weight fabric and the basic sewing kit. Cut the fabric to size, allowing ¾ in (2 cm) extra for the edging. Make a paper strip 2 in (5 cm) wide by the napkin length. Fold the paper into sections equal to each scallop length *(see page 166)*. Draw a curve on the paper perpendicular to the folded edge. Cut along the curve and unfold pattern. Pin the pattern to one edge of the fabric. Draw the outlines of the scallops. Mark the outlines on the remaining three sides of the fabric.

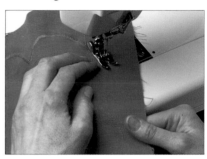

1 STITCHING SCALLOPS Topstitch along the scallop lines to prevent the fabric from stretching *(see page 15)*. Machine sew a close zigzag *(see page 14)* along the marked lines to border the edges of the scallops.

2 TRIMMING EXCESS Carefully cut away the excess fabric close to the zigzag stitching line. Press the napkin before use.

THE FINISHED NAPKIN

MIRROR SEQUINS
An off-white embroidered
cotton tablecloth is dotted with
mirror sequins that glint in the
candlelight. Seat cushions in
the same fabric bring pattern
and texture to the plain calico
slipcovers. For this special
occasion, crepe paper napkins
in pearl and oyster, gleaming
glassware, and tea lights add
sparkle to each place setting.

LAMPSHADES

IMPORTANT FURNISHING ACCESSORIES, LAMPSHADES NOT ONLY

REDUCE THE GLOW FROM ARTIFICIAL LIGHT SOURCES, BUT ALSO

DIRECT AND COLOR THE LIGHT IN A ROOM. MAKING YOUR OWN

LAMPSHADES IS A REWARDING TASK, BECAUSE YOU CAN DESIGN

SHADES SPECIFICALLY TO COMPLEMENT THE DECOR IN EACH

ROOM. FABRIC LAMPSHADES CAN BE MADE FROM A VARIETY OF

MATERIALS, INCLUDING REMNANTS FROM THE MATERIALS USED TO

DECORATE A ROOM. PAPER OR CARD LAMPSHADES WILL GIVE A

MODERN DIMENSION TO YOUR DECORATIVE SCHEME. PLEATED

PAPER SHADES CAN BE ASSEMBLED FROM REMNANTS OF

WALLPAPER, AND PLAIN CARD SHADES HAVE THE ADVANTAGE OF

BEING SUITABLE FOR MANY TYPES OF LIGHTING FIXTURES.

PAPER AND WOOD
Alternative materials, including handmade
paper and thin wood veneers, make effective
lampshades. They can be attached to the frame
with tape or stitched with leather, rope, or cord.

CHOOSING A STYLE

ALTHOUGH THEY ARE OFTEN considered to be peripheral accessories, lampshades can play a key role in a decorative scheme. The size and shape of a lampshade are important design considerations; a shade will look best when it is in proportion to the lamp base and in style with the room. The color and texture of the material used for the shade will directly affect the appearance of the lampshade and the quality of the light. A translucent cover of silk, lightweight cotton, or paper casts a soft glow of light, whereas dark or completely opaque materials are impenetrable and simply direct the light above and below the lampshade.

CONICAL SLANT
(above) A slender conical shade in gray brown directs the light both upward and downward. This has the effect of casting direct light onto the table and chair making it a good spot for reading. The tall, pencil-thin stand has been chosen to balance the style of the shade and the stand's dark matte finish complements the color scheme.

BLACK LACQUER
(above) The architectural shape of the lamp's white base and black lacquer shade provide interest in an otherwise empty corner of the room. In addition, the base stands out against the russet paneling and the black shade echoes the iron hinges on the shutters.

STRIP WEAVE
(right) Lampshades woven out of strips of plastic are easiest to produce when built on a straight-sided or cylindrical frame. The flexible strips of plastic, used here, allow light to filter through for a more textural look when in use.

DRUM SHADE
(opposite) Cylindrical shades allow a wide beam of light to be cast both above and below making them a good choice for hanging fixtures and table lamps. The parchment sides of this drum shade allow light to filter through, throwing the leaf pattern into silhouette. The black ash base balances the wide drum-shape proportions of the shade.

TRIMMING DETAIL

(opposite) With such a diversity of trimmings available, it is possible to find a perfect match for your lampshade. The box shade echoes the square base of the ornate silver candlestick. Fan-edge trimming and a fine braid give an elegant but understated finish.

GRAND SCALE

(right) A large pendant shade such as this will work only in spacious rooms where it will not obstruct the movement of those passing by. Centered above the table, the lamp directs the beam of light onto the tabletop but not into the eyes of those seated around it. The shade's pale color blends with the furnishings, preventing it from clashing with its surroundings.

INDIAN INFLUENCE

(below) The pleated cream silk lampshades have a cool and simple effect in this room dominated by rich decorative details from the Indian sub-continent. When the lights are on, they cast a soft ambient light, illuminating the corners of the room as well as casting a gentle light over the sofa and chair.

LAMPSHADE FRAMES

RIGID LAMPSHADE frames, which are made of lightweight metal, are needed to provide support, structure, and shape for many types of lampshades. The frames are available from specialist suppliers in a wide variety of shapes and sizes. Lampshades made from self-supporting stiff paper or lightweight cardboard or a stiff, single-sided adhesive plastic to which wallpaper or fabric is stuck, can be supported by specially made lower and upper rings, which are obtainable in different diameters. When choosing a frame, you will need to decide on the size and shape of the lampshade, and take into account the material for the cover.

CHOOSING A FRAME

The exact shape of a lampshade is determined by the size and style of the frame, or – in the case of a ring-mounted lampshade – by the diameter of the upper and lower support rings and the distance between them. Fabric lampshades always need the support of a rigid frame; cardboard and paper are best suited to being supported on specially made rings.

FRAMES
Lampshade frames are available in an extraordinary variety of shapes and sizes to suit every decorative style. They are designed to fit lamp bases, pendant light fixtures, and even candles. Lightbulb clips are used for supporting very small lampshades. The metallic frames are sold either unfinished or coated in white enamel paint.

DUPLEX FRAME

SINGLE-SIDED
LAMP-BASE FRAME

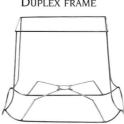

SQUARE LAMP-
BASE FRAME

LIGHTBULB CLIPS

FRAMES WITH GIMBAL FITTINGS
For versatility, choose a frame that has a swiveling gimbal, since this will allow you to fit the lampshade either to a lamp base or to a pendant light.

BOWED OVAL FRAME

BOX FRAME

DRUM-SHAPED FRAME

CONICAL FRAME

LAMPSHADE RINGS
Pleated and small shades made from stiff paper or cardboard need only an upper ring fitted with a mounting ring, or gimbal. Shades made from light paper require a lower ring for extra support. Ensure that rings form a circle and that the struts are aligned before you assemble the lampshade.

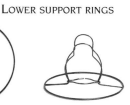

LOWER SUPPORT RINGS

GIMBAL RING
FITTING

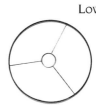

PENDANT
RING FITTING

BULB-CLIP
RING FITTING

PAINTING LAMPSHADE FRAMES

Paint bare metal frames and support rings to prevent the covering material from being stained by rust and to stop the binding tape from slipping when you bind the uprights and rings. You will need medium-grade sandpaper, a small paintbrush, enamel paint, and a paint solvent for diluting it.

1 PREPPING SURFACE
Prep the surface of the frame or support ring by rubbing it down evenly and smoothly with a piece of medium-grade sandpaper.

2 APPLYING PAINT
Carefully paint the frame or support ring, using a small paintbrush. Avoid the surfaces that will be in direct contact with a light bulb.

TOOLS AND EQUIPMENT

Making a shade does not require special tools; since accuracy in cutting out and assembly is important, however, ensure that the equipment is in excellent working order. The tools required for making fabric and paper shades are basically the same, with the few exceptions noted below. Additionally, you will need some equipment from the household tool kit, the basic sewing kit, and a specific lampshade frame or support ring.

FABRIC AND PAPER LAMPSHADES

You will need medium-grade sandpaper, enamel paint, solvent, and a small brush for painting the frame. To bind the frame, you will need lampshade binding tape and clear glue that will not stain fabric or paper. Use clean clothespins to hold the shade material in position on the frame while the glue is drying.

LAMPSHADE BINDING TAPE

CLEAR GLUE

CLOTHESPINS

SANDPAPER

ENAMEL PAINT

SMALL PAINTBRUSH

PAPER LAMPSHADES

Use paper scissors for cutting. Place a weight on glued paper joins until dry. For measuring, use a strip of card as a compass; pivot it with a drawing pin secured to a cutting board. Attach the cover to the rings using masking tape. Use adhesive-coated pvc for smooth-sided wallpaper or fabric shades. Score creases with a knife edge. Use a hole punch for pleated shades.

KNIFE

THUMB TACKS

MASKING TAPE

PAPER SCISSORS

ADHESIVE-COATED PVC

CUTTING BOARD

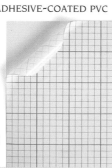
HOLE PUNCH

TAPING A LAMPSHADE FRAME

After painting the frame or rings, apply the binding tape. Loosely woven tape designed for the purpose is bound to the frame or rings, presenting a surface to which you can either sew a fabric or glue a paper shade cover. Estimate how much tape you will need by measuring the circumference of the rings and the lengths of the vertical struts, and double this measurement. Do not bind the internal wires that hold the shade to the light fixture. You will also need the basic sewing kit.

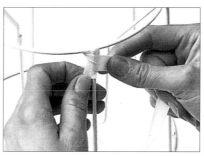

1 **SECURING TAPE** Tape the vertical struts, starting and finishing in each case at a top or bottom support ring. Secure the binding tape in place by folding one end under the top ring and down the outside of the strut to a length of approximately 1 in (2.5 cm).

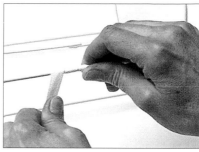

2 **TAPING STRUT** Wind the tape in a spiral along each strut, covering over the initial fold and making ⅛ in (3 mm) overlaps. Wind the tape as smoothly and as tightly as possible to avoid unsightly ridges and to prevent the possibility of the tape slipping.

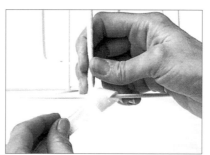

3 **KNOTTING END** At the other end of the strut, wind the tape over the outside of the lower ring to the back, and pass the end through the loop to form a half-knot. Pull the knot tight and cut the tape. Tape all but one of the remaining struts in this way.

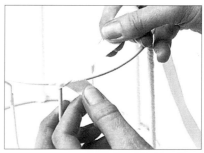

4 **TAPING TOP RING** Start at the upper end of the untaped strut. Place the tape end on the outside of the ring. Wrap the tape around it and the strut to hold the end in place. Tape around the ring, making figure eights at the tops of the struts.

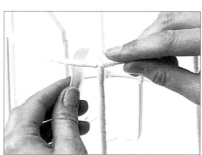

5 **TAPING STRUT** Wind the binding tape down the untaped strut and around the lower support ring, again securing it in place at each strut with a figure eight.

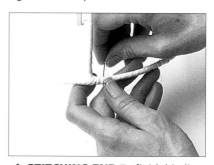

6 **STITCHING END** To finish binding the frame, fold under about ¼ in (6 mm) of the tape end and stitch it neatly to the outside of a bound ring. Check the fit of the tape on the wire. If it twists over the wire, it will need to be unwound and reapplied.

FABRIC LAMPSHADES

MADE FROM FABRIC THAT IS GATHERED, stretched, or pleated over a frame, fabric lampshades provide the opportunity to create original, personal accessories to add to your furnishings. For the external fabric, use furnishing or dress material that is reasonably pliable. This is an essential quality, since the fabric needs to be stretched over the lampshade frame to ensure a tight fit. If a fabric is suitable, you can use scraps to coordinate with larger soft furnishings in a room. You will also need an inner fabric lining to conceal the frame; this should be pale in color to reflect the light outward from the shade.

GATHERED LAMPSHADE

Choose a lampshade frame and paint it, if necessary. Bind the upper and lower rings, where the fabric will be attached, using specially made tape *(see page 181)*. Allow enough outer fabric for binding strips and a gathered frill. You will also need lining fabric, clear fabric glue, and the basic sewing kit. Cut out the fabric and lining on the straight grain to twice the circumference of the lower ring, by the height of the frame, and add 2 in (5 cm) all around for seams.

1 **SEWING EDGES** With the right sides together, tack and sew the two short edges of the outer fabric, ⅝ in (1.5 cm) from the edges, to form a circular shape. Turn right side out.

2 **SEWING GATHERING STITCHES** To enable you to make folds in the fabric, sew a line of gathering stitches *(see page 22)* ⅝ in (1.5 cm) from the top and bottom edges.

Sew gathering stitches ⅝ in (1.5 cm) from edge

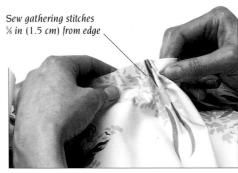

3 **GATHERING FABRIC** Place the fabric over the frame, and fit it to the shape of the frame by pulling up the gathering stitches around the top edge. Arrange the gathers so that they are neat, plus spaced and sized equally, and pin the fabric to the tape binding the upper ring.

4 **PINNING FABRIC** Pull up the gathers around the lower ring. Pin the fabric to the tape binding the lower ring. The gathers should be tighter around the upper ring than around the lower ring. Unpin to adjust the gathered fabric. Stretch the fabric between the rings, form the gathers into folds, and repin the fabric to the tape binding the rings. Trim the surplus fabric from the rings.

Pin lining to tape binding frame's rings, adjusting gathers as you go

5 **PINNING LINING** Slipstitch the gathered fabric to the tape binding the rings. Prepare the lining with gathering stitches ⅝ in (1.5 cm) from top and bottom edges. Pin the lining to the bound rings, adjusting the gathers, as above.

6 **SEWING LINING** Slipstitch the gathered lining to the tape binding the upper ring.

7 **FITTING LINING** As you work around the upper ring, you will encounter the frame's inner supporting struts. Cut the lining to fit it around these, using a pair of scissors.

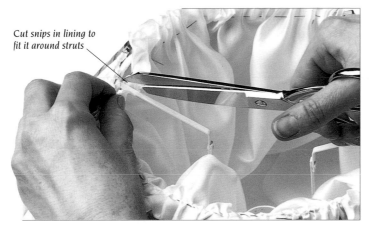

Cut snips in lining to fit it around struts

8 **TRIMMING LINING** Trim the surplus lining fabric around the top ring, cutting as close as possible to the stitching so that there is a minimum of fabric bulk.

Attach binding to upper ring using fabric glue

9 **ATTACHING BINDING** Make a bias strip from the outer fabric *(see page 20)* to use as a trim for top edge of shade to hide raw edges and stitching. Attach binding with fabric glue. Slipstitch lining to tape binding lower ring. Trim surplus fabric.

SECURING BINDING

To make a neat join in the binding, press the turned ends of the bias strip, overlap them, then use fabric glue to attach the binding to the ring. Clean clothespins are very useful for holding the bias strip firmly in place around the ring while the fabric glue is drying.

10 **ATTACHING FRILL** Cut out a length of outer fabric to twice the circumference of the lower ring, by two and a half times the required depth of the finished frill. Fold the strip lengthwise, right sides together. Press, then sew gathering stitches 3/16 in (5 mm) from the raw edges. Pull up the gathering stitches so that the frill fits the lower ring. Pin and slipstitch the frill through the edge of the main fabric to the lower ring.

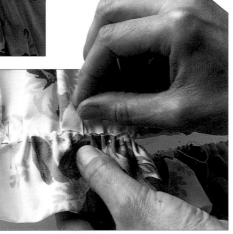

Glue binding in place once frill has been attached

11 **ATTACHING LOWER BINDING** Complete the lampshade by making a second bias strip that is equal to the circumference of the lower ring. Glue the binding to the top of the frill so that it conceals the raw edges and stitching.

THE FINISHED LAMPSHADE

TAILORED LAMPSHADE

A tailored, fabric-covered lampshade can be made to fit most frame shapes. Choose a frame, paint it if necessary, and bind the top and base rings, as well as an opposite pair of uprights, with binding tape *(see page 181)*. Select the outer and lining fabrics. A white silk lining will reflect the light outward from the interior of the shade. Measure the circumference of the lampshade at its widest point, and add 6 in (15 cm). Measure the shade height, and add 3 in (7.5 cm). Cut out the outer fabric along the bias to these dimensions. You will also need the basic sewing kit and clear fabric glue.

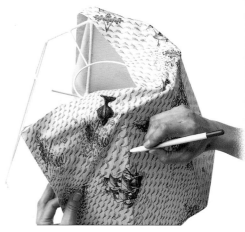

1 **PINNING FABRIC TO UPRIGHTS**
Cut the outer panel of fabric in half. Pin one piece of the fabric to the frame. First, pin the fabric to the taped uprights, stretching the fullness around the frame, then pin it to the taped rings.

2 **PINNING FABRIC TO RING** Work around frame, pinning fabric to top and base rings between the pair of taped uprights. Pull fabric taut to remove any creases, and apply the pins inward.

3 **MARKING FABRIC** As long as the fabric is stretched taut, you will have a clear outline of one half of the frame. Draw the shape of this outline on the fabric, using a vanishing-ink pen or tailor's chalk. Draw between the pins, following the lines of the rings and the two uprights.

4 **CUTTING OUT FABRIC** Unpin fabric from frame. Cut out, following drawn line, adding ¾ in (2 cm) all around. Cut out an identical panel on the bias. Cut out two panels of lining, using a panel of outer fabric as a pattern.

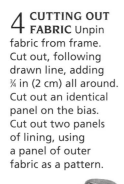

5 **SEWING OUTER PANELS** Lay the two outer fabric panels right sides together, and pin, tack, and sew them along the two short sides to form a tube of fabric. Do the same with the lining fabric. Press the fabrics, and turn the outer fabric to the right side.

6 **POSITIONING OUTER FABRIC** Remove the tape from the two upright struts, and slide the outer tube of fabric over the lampshade frame. As you do this, make sure that the two seams run along a pair of opposing upright struts.

Match fabric seam to strut when pulling lampshade over frame

7 **PINNING FABRIC** Pin the fabric to the top and base rings. As you pin it, pull and snip the fabric allowance to avoid any creasing. Make sure that the side seams do not move out of line with the two upright struts.

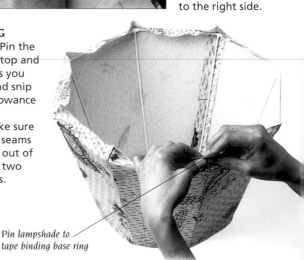

Pin lampshade to tape binding base ring

8 SEWING FABRIC
Oversew the fabric to the binding tape on the rings, using doubled cotton thread. Work around the rings, making small stitches through the fabric to the outer edge of the binding tape.

9 TRIMMING FABRIC
Use a sharp pair of scissors to trim the excess fabric around the ring by cutting as close as possible to the stitching.

10 PINNING LINING
Place the lining fabric inside the frame, right sides to the inside of the frame. Match the seams with those of the outer fabric before stretching and pinning the lining to the top and base rings.

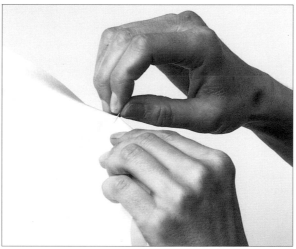

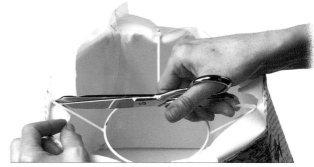

11 CUTTING INCISIONS
Make short incisions in the lining, so that it fits neatly in place around the gimbal supports. Adjust and pin the lining fabric, keeping it taut. Oversew the lining all around, making sure that the stitches are on the outer edge of the shade, so that the edging will conceal them.

12 TRIMMING FABRIC
Trim the excess lining fabric around the top and base rings. Neaten the points where the gimbal supports meet the top ring by covering each join with a piece of lining fabric. Cut out strips of lining on the bias – each should measure 1¼ x 2 in (3 x 5 cm). Fold under the long edges of each strip by 6 mm (¼ in), and press.

13 ATTACHING STRIPS
Wrap the lining strips around and over the tops of the gimbal supports and top ring, and glue them in place. When dry, trim them to match the outer edge of the shade. Make up edging by cutting two bias strips of fabric to the same lengths as the circumferences of the rings, by 1¾ in (4.5 cm) wide. Turn the long edges under by ⅜ in (1 cm) , and press. Glue edging to top and base rings. Work in 6 in (15 cm) lengths at a time. Fold the ends under by ¼ in (6 mm), and overlap the turnings by ¾ in (2 cm). Use clothespins to secure the strips while they are drying.

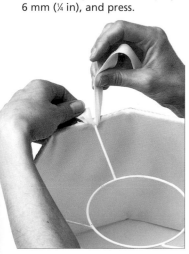

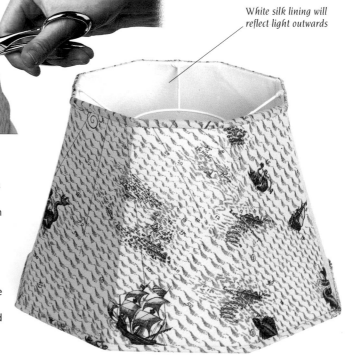

White silk lining will reflect light outwards

THE FINISHED LAMPSHADE

PAPER LAMPSHADES

MAKING YOUR OWN PAPER or cardboard lampshades can be one of the most satisfying and rewarding home decorating projects. You can construct a variety of lampshades for lamp bases or pendant fittings, using plain or patterned paper. The sides, which are supported by a standard lampshade ring with a gimbal, can be either pleated or flat. Self-reinforced by its own folds, a pleated paper lampshade can be made from a variety of weights of paper, ranging from cartridge to light cardboard. A flat-sided shade must, however, be made with substantial cardboard, or paper reinforced with a commercial lampshade lamination.

PLEATED PAPER LAMPSHADE

Choose the paper or cardboard, and decide on the height of the finished shade. Select an appropriately sized painted wire ring to support the lampshade at the top, and a length of ribbon. You will also need a hole puncher, ruler, try square, craft knife, pencil, scissors, table knife, and glue. Calculate the circumference of the completed lower edge of the lampshade. Decide how deep you wish the pleats to be – here they are ¾ in (2 cm) from the point to the trough. Depending on how deep the pleats are, multiply the circumference by approximately two to give the total length of paper required.

Calculate dimension of lampshade and mark length and width on thick paper or cardboard

1 MEASURING Divide the circumference by size of one pleat – in this case, 1½ in (4 cm) – and round up to an even number for the total of pleats needed. Using a ruler, try square, and sharp craft knife, cut the paper into one or more strips to the total length calculated above, by the height of the finished shade.

Mark pleat depths at even intervals along top and bottom long edges

2 MARKING PLEATS Mark intervals to correspond with the pleat depth along the top and bottom long edges on the wrong side of the paper. If you are using more than one length of paper, allow extra paper for the glued joins, continue the sequence of pleat marks across the joins, and keep the marks on the inside.

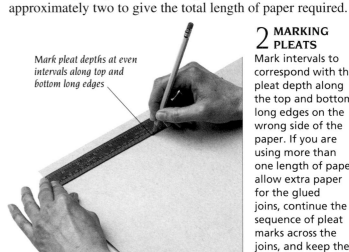

3 FOLDING PLEATS To make crisp pleats, press down and draw a crease line between the marks, using the blunt edge of a table knife or dressmaker's scissors; guide the blade with a metal ruler. Fold the creases into alternate pleats over the edge of a table. If joining strips to make up a complete length, glue the strips within a pleat.

4 MAKING TEMPLATE Cut out a piece of cardboard measuring ¾ x 2 in (2 x 5 cm). Draw a central line down the length of this template, and make two holes with a hole puncher, one for the gathering ribbon, 1 in (2.5 cm) from the top edge, and the second a little over 1 in (2.5 cm) below this, for the supporting ring. Place the template on one side of each fold, and accurately mark the punch holes with a pencil.

5 PUNCHING HOLES Grip each double pleat between the jaws of the punch at the marks, and punch through the paper. In this way, punch pairs of holes in the pleats. At each end of the paper, leave the final pleat unpunched ready for gluing.

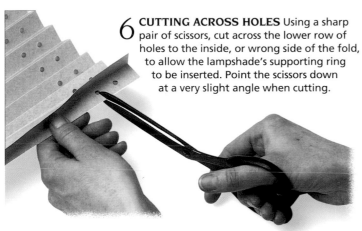

6 **CUTTING ACROSS HOLES** Using a sharp pair of scissors, cut across the lower row of holes to the inside, or wrong side of the fold, to allow the lampshade's supporting ring to be inserted. Point the scissors down at a very slight angle when cutting.

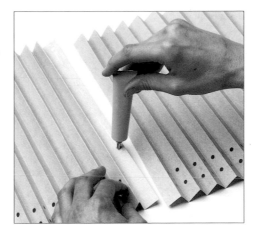

7 **GLUING ENDS** Secure the ends of the paper by applying glue to the surface of each end fold. Join the two ends to make a complete pleat. Allow the glue to dry thoroughly.

8 **SECURING ENDS** Hold the ends together until the glue has dried. Using the template, mark a pair of holes through the overlap. Punch the holes. Using the scissors, cut through the lower holes to the inside.

Punch two holes in glued pleat

9 **THREADING RIBBON** Cut a piece of ribbon to fit through the top set of holes – here, approximately 1 yd (1 m) has been cut. Wind tape around the leading end, and thread the ribbon through the holes.

SEALING ENDS OF RIBBON

To prevent the ribbon from fraying when it is threaded through the holes, seal the leading end with tape after you have cut the ribbon. Knot the other end of the ribbon to prevent it from slipping out of place.

10 **INSERTING RING** Ease open the top of the shade, and insert the ring. Carefully fit half of the ring through the lower set of punched, cut holes. Fit the other half of the ring.

Fit frame ring through lower row of punched holes

Ribbon secures shape of pleated lampshade

11 **TYING RIBBON** Form the shade into its final shape by drawing together the ends of the ribbon. At the same time, spread the lower edge of the shade to the required circumference. Tie the ribbon, and trim it to size, if necessary. Once you have mounted the shade on the lamp, you can turn it to hide the knotted ribbon.

THE FINISHED LAMPSHADE

PLAIN-SIDED CONICAL LAMPSHADE

You can construct a paper lampshade using either paper stiffened with a commercial laminate, or heavy cardboard supported by two rings, one with a lamp-fitting gimbal. Decide on the proportions of the lampshade, and select and paint the rings. You will also need a tape measure, try square, ruler, pencil, glue, hole puncher, scissors, craft knife, clothespins, masking tape, and a weight. In order to glue the cardboard to the rings, prepare the rings by taping them.

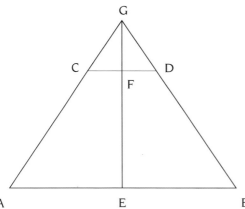

1 MEASURING Use a try square, ruler, and pencil to draw a diagram of the cross section of the lampshade. Measure the rings' diameter (A to B and C to D), and the shade height from the center of the bottom ring to the center of the top ring (E to F). The measuring, drawing, and cutting out must be accurate in order for the lampshade to fit well.

2 MAKING COMPASS Construct a simple compass, using a strip of cardboard about ¾ in (2 cm) wide, and slightly longer than the line G to B. Draw a central line down the compass, lay it on the diagram, and mark on the line the points G, D, and B.

Mark points corresponding with ring positions on card compass

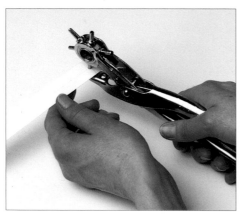

3 PUNCHING HOLES Using the smallest setting on the punch, make two holes in the cardboard compass along the line, slightly above points B and D. Align the bottom edges of the holes you punch – the position of the pencil point – with points B and D.

4 DRAWING ARCS Tape the lampshade cardboard, right side down, to a piece of board. Affix the compass firmly to the board with a pin at point G. Draw an arc with the pencil in hole D, followed by another with the pencil in hole B. These arcs give the shape of the cardboard needed to cut it out.

5 MEASURING LOWER RING Measure the circumference of the lower lampshade ring with a tape measure. Add 2 in (5 cm) for the seam overlap to the circumference. Mark this dimension on the longer arc, using a tape measure set on its edge. Work in 4 in (10 cm) stages for accuracy.

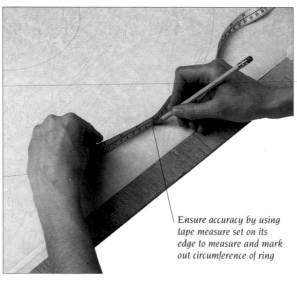

Ensure accuracy by using tape measure set on its edge to measure and mark out circumference of ring

6 DRAWING END MARKS Remove the compass, and rule two lines from point G, across the shorter arc, to the end points of the measured circumference of the lower ring that are marked on the longer arc.

Use clothespins to hold cardboard in place

7 CUTTING OUT Cut out the cardboard, using a craft knife and ruler for straight edges, and a pair of scissors for the curves of the two arcs.

8 POSITIONING RINGS Bend the cardboard around the top gimbal and ring, using clothespins to hold the cardboard in place. Insert the lower ring, and pin it to hold it temporarily in position. Take time to position the cardboard tautly over the rings, all the while adjusting it and the clothespins, so that the rings lie flush with the edge of the cardboard, and the overlap is even all around.

9 MARKING OVERLAP When you are certain that you have a snug fit, mark the overlap made by the extra cardboard at the top and bottom on the inside of the cardboard, using a sharp, soft pencil.

10 TRIMMING OVERLAP Detach the lampshade cardboard from the rings, and add a ½ in (12 mm) seam overlap parallel to your marks, using a pencil and ruler. Cut off the excess overlap with the scissors.

11 WEIGHTING CARDBOARD Apply glue to the tongue of the overlap, align it with the marks, and join cardboard. Avoid smearing glue on the surface. Press the join flat with a ruler and weight. Let stand for at least 30 minutes for the glue to set.

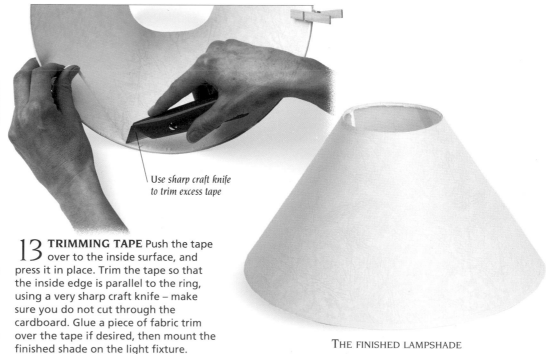

12 TAPING RINGS Once the glue is dry, fit the rings again, using the clothespins to hold them in place. Make sure that the support wire of the gimbal is perpendicular to the seam. Use masking tape to secure rings. Apply tape to the outside surface in 4 in (10 cm) sections, with a ¼ in (6 mm) overlap. Reposition tape as you work around shade, and smooth it into place on the cardboard's surface.

Use sharp craft knife to trim excess tape

13 TRIMMING TAPE Push the tape over to the inside surface, and press it in place. Trim the tape so that the inside edge is parallel to the ring, using a very sharp craft knife – make sure you do not cut through the cardboard. Glue a piece of fabric trim over the tape if desired, then mount the finished shade on the light fixture.

THE FINISHED LAMPSHADE

INDEX

ACKNOWLEDGMENTS

Author's acknowledgments

I dedicate this book to my parents.
   For the research, making up, and assembly of all the soft furnishings, I would like to thank Alison Kingsbury.
   To the following I extend my thanks for assistance throughout the project: Louise Greenwood, Ali Edney, and Tracey Turner of Liberty; Karen Buswell of Mulberry at Home; Annabel Lewis of V. V. Rouleaux; Martin Long at The Carpet Library; Beattie and Trish at Rossiters; Lyn Sherwood and Ian Mankin of Ian Mankin Ltd.; Caroline Brandenberger; Liz Crouch; Harrington Evans; and Diana Ekins.

The following have kindly supplied props:
Gloria Birkett tapestry cushion cover 135; Designers Guild 53, edging 74, check fabric 79 and 80–81; Diana Lampshades, Hampshire supplies and advice 180–189; Frome Feather Company, Somerset filled cushions; Habitat UK chair 136–137, chair 138–139, round and rectangular tables 162–169; Liberty, London patterned fabric 40–41, 45, 46–47, patterned fabric 48–49, 50, 53, all patterned fabric 48–49, 51, 52–53, patterned fabric 60–61, 62–63, 105, 125, 131, floral fabric 170; Litvinoff & Fawcett, London bed and mattress; Magenta, London curtain headings 40; Malmic, Nottingham lace edging on curtain 42 and pillow 94; Mulberry at Home patterned fabric 16–17, 64–65, patterned fabric 79, fabric 82–83, 106, 164, 168–169, printed voile 171, 182–183, 184–185; Papyrus, Bath & London 186–187; Rossiters, Bath brass fittings 36; V.

V. Rouleaux, London all ribbons and edging; Rufflette® tab-top curtain gliders 34, heading tapes 40; Swish curtain hooks, hanging and track systems 35.

Publisher's acknowledgments

Dorling Kindersley would like to thank: Mark Ronan, Candida Ross-MacDonald, and Sharon Lucas for editorial assistance; Tim Scott and Colette Ho for design assistance; Emily Hedges and Jess Walton for picture research; Noel Barnes and Doug Miller for page make-up and computer assistance; Pat Coward and Hilary Bird for the index; Andrew MacDonald for artwork; Simon Moore, Ben Pulsford, and Charlie Cork for set building.